"If American women jointly drafted a list of their burning questions on the subject of modern women and the Catholic Church, it would mirror this book's table of contents. This book takes on both the thorniest dilemmas and the best-kept secrets of the Catholic Church's teachings concerning women, with thoroughness, intelligence, and honesty."

— Helen Alvaré, J.D.
Associate Professor of Law
George Mason University School of Law

"In *Women, Sex, and the Church*, a group of faith-filled women ... expertly take on critics of the Church's teaching on sex. As a highly readable, provocative exposition of the case for the Church's vision of sex, marriage, and sexual difference, it could not be more timely."

— Mary Shivanandan
Professor of Theology
John Paul II Institute for Studies on Marriage and Family
at The Catholic University of America

"This is an important work, addressing a critical area of confusion in our time. With balance, clarity, and keenness, the contributors to this volume expose key fallacies behind many of the cultural assumptions taken for granted today regarding women, marriage, careers, fertility, sexuality, vocation, male-female complementarity, women priests, and being Catholic. A remarkable work, and a great read."

— Rev. Tadeusz Pacholczyk, Ph.D.
Director of Education,
The National Catholic Bioethics Center

"*Women, Sex, and the Church* is a clear and concise treatment of the critical issues facing women in the light of the Catholic Church's teaching and our American culture. Each selection is well-written and well-documented. This presentation is a *tour de force*—highly recommended."

— Kimberly Hahn
Author of *Life-Giving Love: Embracing
God's Beautiful Design for Marriage*

"A clear, accessible, and faithful account of the Catholic Church's teaching on some of today's most controverted issues. It should be required reading for every son, brother, fiancée, husband, father, seminarian, and priest. These women know something about life, and in listening to them you come away wanting to become a better man."

— Rev. Paul McNellis, S.J.
Boston College

"Attracted to the Catholic Church but find your feminist spirit getting in the way? These women offer convincing evidence that respect for women and Catholicism are quite reconcilable—and that perhaps it's the world's view of women rather than the Church's that ought to be put into question."

— Fr. Frank Pavone
National Director, Priests for Life

"Think the Catholic Church is sexist? Or tired of hearing the media say it is? Written with wisdom, common-sense, and humanity, *Women, Sex, and the Church* is a compelling and empowering invitation for contemporary women to embrace Jesus Christ and his Church with grace and confidence."

— Mary Cunningham Agee
CEO and Founder, The Nurturing Network

Women, Sex, and the Church

Women, Sex, and the Church

A Case for Catholic Teaching

Edited by Erika Bachiochi

Pauline
BOOKS & MEDIA
Boston

Library of Congress Cataloging-in-Publication Data

Women, sex & the church : a case for Catholic teaching / edited by Erika Bachiochi.
   p. cm.
 Includes bibliographical references.
 ISBN 0-8198-8320-4 (pbk.)
 1. Women--Religious aspects--Catholic Church. 2. Sex--Religious aspects--Catholic Church.
3. Catholic Church--Doctrines. I. Bachiochi, Erika. II. Title: Women, sex, and the church.
 BX2347.8.W6W655 2010
 282.082'09051--dc22

             2010004630

The Scripture quotations contained herein are from the *New Revised Standard Version Bible: Catholic Edition*, copyright © 1989, 1993, Division of Christian Education of the National Council of the Churches of Christ in the United States of America. Used by permission. All rights reserved.

Quotations from any Pope or Papal document used with the permission of the Libreria Editrice Vaticana, 00120, Città del Vaticana.

Excerpts from the English translation of the *Catechism of the Catholic Church* for use in the United States of America, copyright © 1994, United States Catholic Conference, Inc. — Libreria Editrice Vaticana. Used with permission.

Cover design by Rosana Usselmann

Cover photo by Yuri Arcurs / istockphoto.com

Published by Pauline Books & Media, 50 Saint Pauls Avenue, Boston, MA 02130-3491.

Printed in the U.S.A.

www.pauline.org

Pauline Books & Media is the publishing house of the Daughters of St. Paul, an international congregation of women religious serving the Church with the communications media.

2 3 4 5 6 7 8 9   17 16 15 14 13 12

For the late Professor Elizabeth Fox-Genovese:
Though none of us was your student,
you were a teacher to us all.

Contents

Part III

WOMEN IN THE CHURCH, THE HOME, AND THE WORLD

Acknowledgments

A collaborative effort such as this can never come to be without the insight, diligence, and generosity of many people. First, of course, I must mention the book's talented and committed contributors, whose expertise, humility, and good cheer made the project a real pleasure from the outset. I thank them for honoring the time constraint put on the project by the imminent arrival of my baby, Joseph Jeffery Bachiochi. My deep gratitude also goes to their families and communities who sacrificed coveted time with them so they could offer much of themselves to this work.

I also wish to thank those who generously gave of their time and talents to the book by serving as readers: Dr. Mariette Murphy; Michael Marcucci, Esq.; Jennifer Clark, PhD; Elizabeth Kirk, Esq.; Kevin Elrod; Clarke Forsythe, Esq.; Katie Dardis; Lori Kelly; Paige Cunningham, Esq.; and Marcia Barlow. This book would not be the book it is without your expertise. Thanks, too, to my enthusiastic research assistants, Helen and Molly Keefe, who contributed to this project with good humor despite my requests for yet another reference.

Sister Grace Dateno and Sister Lorraine Trouvé of the Daughters of St. Paul were instrumental to this project, both in its beginnings and its endings. Sister Grace shared my enthusiasm for the idea from the start, and graciously walked me through the publication process. Sister Lorraine served as a sophisticated reader and careful editor. I am immensely impressed by, and grateful for, their patience, encouragement, and expertise.

I am also deeply indebted to my own parish community, namely, the women of Saint Catherine of Siena parish in Norwood, Massachusetts, who prayed for the project, cared for my children while I worked, and always offered encouragement and support. If every woman knew generous and holy women like you, a book like this would never have to be written.

I especially wish to thank my family. First, my parents and in-laws: your support and encouragement of my work—both professional and at home—is humbling. Second, my children: Anna, Gabriella, Lucy, Peter, and J.J. The love you have given me—and required of me—has been transformative. I thank God for the magnificent gift that is each of you. A special word of thanks to you, J.J., for waiting to come until the manuscript was complete.

Lastly, I am unable to articulate the love and support my husband, Dan, has offered me on this project—and in all of life. Among husbands, there is simply no comparison.

— EAB

Introduction

I grew up in a broken, non-churchgoing, nominally Catholic home. As a young child and a teen, I both witnessed and then lived a life diametrically opposed to Catholic Church teaching on sex and marriage. Concentrating on Women's Studies early in college, I identified with a radical feminist contingent and was adamantly anti-Catholic. For these reasons and more, I am an unlikely candidate to bring together the women who contributed to this book.

Yet, by the grace of God, it is precisely because of these reasons that I have felt compelled to do so. A long and painful road led me back to the doors of my baptismal faith. It was a road on which I can recall falling to my knees repeatedly. First, asking the God who had already pulled me from the clutches of anxiety and despair whether he had a Son who had come in flesh, as my Christian acquaintances were claiming. Then, begging him to show me a church in which to reverence him that was *not* the "antifeminist" Catholic Church. And then finally, resigned to the movements of my soul toward the Church, bringing to God each qualm I had about Rome, asking him to grant me clarity.

Along the way, I discovered that a high percentage of girls whose parents had divorced shared my unease about life, love, and relationships, and that many of us acted out in ways that served only to perpetuate our fragile self-esteem. Patiently reserving my heart for one man required constant prayer and vigilance, but it allowed God time to heal my wounds and to teach me the virtues of friendship.

I also came to see that the doubts that had surfaced interiorly about abortion, just before my flirtation with Christianity, were quite reconcilable with my feminist spirit. Though I can speak for no other feminist of radical leanings, it became obvious to me that my particular drive to eradicate gender differences spoke more of my low self-worth than it did of any rational claim to merit. Once I came to understand the irresistible love God has for each one of us—a love whose healing power I had personally experienced—the nature of my feminism changed. My desire to work for the benefit of women (and children) did not lessen; I simply recognized original and personal sin, not the patriarchy, as my adversary, and self-sacrificing, redemptive love, rather than legal commands, as the primary vehicle for cultural transformation.

My "reversion" to the Catholic faith was borne of experiences and insights like these, and then confirmed by intense intellectual study. The teachings of the Church on sex and marriage are not easy to live. Through them the Church asks us to do much that is against our (fallen) nature, much that is against our culture. But by prayerfully living according to Church teachings on sex and marriage, we are not only protected from much emotional, physical, and spiritual harm, but these teachings also have the power to transform us into persons capable of both giving and receiving the selfless love for which we were designed. It is a love that works wonders, that delights, that restores. It is a love that delivers a peace that I, personally, never imagined possible.

———

Despite boasting one-fifth of the world's population, the Catholic Church is by no means a "popular" institution. Classical teachings on abortion, premarital sex, divorce, and especially contraception, are thought by many—both outside the Church and within—to reek of, at best, old-fashioned ideas of sex and, at worst, patriarchal views of women. The reservation of the priesthood to men, for its part, is often simply regarded as male chauvinism. These Church teachings lead many to wonder how any self-respecting woman or woman-loving man can stay and pray within the Catholic Church.

Yet, it hasn't always been so. Historically, it was precisely the early Church's teachings on polygamy, divorce, birth control, abortion, and infanticide that most attracted pagan women into the Christian fold.[1] Moreover, Rome hasn't always stood alone on these controversial matters. Every Christian church, and therefore most Christians, agreed with Rome on each of these practices up through the beginning of the last century.

The modern advent of the birth control pill, liberalized views of women, and the sexual revolution inaugurated a cultural reordering throughout the Western world wherein principles and institutions that had traditionally guided decision-making on even the most "private" of matters were trumped within the span of a generation by the preferences of the apparently autonomous individual.

Indeed, a 2005 study published in *American Catholics Today* indicated that the majority of Catholics now look to themselves rather than to the Church as the "proper locus of moral authority" on issues of abortion, divorce, birth control, and "nonmarital" sex—despite their continued allegiance to the Church on matters of social justice and concern for the poor.[2] Catholic voters differ little with their nonreligious counterparts on their views of abortion, and Catholics seek civil divorce in similar numbers. But perhaps most strikingly, few believe that ignoring the Church's teachings on sex and marriage makes them any less Catholic. For many, and for perhaps many more since the sex abuse scandal that erupted in 2002, sex has simply become an aspect of life on which the Church no longer has authority to teach.

One could assume that many ordinary Catholics dispensed with the teachings on sex and marriage during the turbulent 1960s for the simple reason that these teachings are difficult to live, that they require, for some of us, a degree of self-control and selflessness that is beyond ordinary means.

But history reveals another force at work as well. For just as the world was coming to believe that there was more intrinsic value to sex than procreation, and that there is more to being a woman than birthing and nurturing children, the Church, too, was articulating a more nuanced understanding of human sexuality and the nature of women. A substantial number of vocal theologians believed that such development of doctrine was a sure sign that, at long last, the Church would "modernize" its teachings on abortion, sex, and marriage—and on the priesthood as well. This hoped-for view prevailed among progressive-minded academics and activists to such an extent that the Church was ill-prepared to handle their immediate protest of *Humanae Vitae*, the 1968 encyclical reaffirming the Church's prohibition of contraception. Almost overnight, Catholics, whether in the pews or in the seminaries, received the strong impression from dissident theologians (through the mouthpiece of the media and the lecterns of the Catholic colleges at which they taught) that the Church was wrong about its teaching on contraception—and perhaps about much else when it came to human sexuality. The only responsible thing for a thoughtful Catholic to do, according to these academics, was to ignore Church teachings and "follow one's conscience."

To be fair, the Church did give these theologians a foothold for their views in the Vatican's modern reconsideration of sex and women. While the Church had always prioritized the procreative, or baby-making, aspect of conjugal sex, buttressed by theological treatises that derided sexual pleasure even within marriage, she began to draw much more attention to the unitive, or love-making, aspect of marriage in the modern period. Similarly, the Church's views on the nature of women also shifted. Increased papal attention to the dignity and equality of women, just prior to the Second Vatican Council, was ratified in the Council's denunciation of sexual discrimination and support for greater recognition of the rights of women. In the wake of these changes, many waited with bated breath for the Church to dismantle restrictions on abortion, contraception, divorce, and sex outside of marriage, and to clear the way for a married priesthood open to women.

But no change came—or has come, in the decades since. Indeed, Pope John Paul II and Pope Benedict XVI have taken every opportunity to reaffirm the Church's constant teaching on abortion, sex outside of marriage, divorce, contraception, and the priesthood. They have done this even as they continue to articulate, and rearticulate in new ways, the Church's modern recognition of the dual purposes of sexuality and of women's fundamental equality with men.

Many Catholic feminists, such as Rosemary Radford Ruether and Lisa Sowle Cahill, among others, take this "staunch" reaffirmation of old doctrines within new theoretical frameworks to reveal that whatever the *rhetorical* elevation of interpersonal unity in the sexual union and the declaration of the equal dignity of the sexes, the Church's adherence to these traditional sexual taboos *itself* indicates that sexism is still alive and well in the Catholic Church. Regarding the Church's views on sex and women, Ruether writes:

> Feminist Catholics believe that the root of this defect [in the Church's worldview on sexuality and women] is the view that sexuality is sinful in itself and opposed to the higher spiritual life, allowable only within heterosexual marriage for the purpose of procreation, and the concomitant view of women as a lesser form of humanity, linked with the inferiority of the body and sexuality, whose primary destiny is motherhood. Only by remedying these views of sexuality and women can progress be made on developing more adequate teachings that will liberalize Church policies on celibacy, divorce, homosexuality, contraception, and abortion.[3]

And while Cahill in her book *Women and Sexuality* applauds the new "personalist" themes in John Paul II's writing on sexuality in what has since become known as the theology of the body, she writes:

> In the end, the personalist shift has been incomplete. Current teaching attaches [to this personalist account] conclusions once derived within the old biologistic, procreative, and hierarchical model of sexuality, and especially women's sexuality (as defined primarily in terms of motherhood, domesticity, and submission to the husband/father instead of equal partnership).[4]

But even more than the teachings on sex and marriage, what is most problematic for these older Catholic feminist theologians and ordinary feminist-minded Catholics alike is the Church's insistence that the priesthood is an exclusively male institution. For surely it is possible to simply—and quietly—attempt to live as one wishes, ignoring much of the Church's teachings on sex (though not so much on marriage) in hope that the Church will come around some day. But for the all-male priesthood, feminist Catholics share an unequaled antipathy; for them, their "institutional second-class status" is evident at each Mass when men alone serve at the altar.[5]

For centuries, theologians linked restrictions on abortion, sex, divorce, and the priesthood with the assumed inferiority of women. It is simply inconceivable to these older Catholic feminists that once women's inferiority was rejected, such teachings would continue to be regarded as worthy of assent. But that is exactly what the Catholic Church has claimed to be true.

In her illuminating book *The Catholic Priesthood and Women*, Sister Sara Butler, professor of dogmatic theology at Saint Joseph's Seminary in New York and a contributor to this volume, explains how the Church simultaneously affirms traditional doctrine while rejecting traditional rationales for such doctrine. Writing solely about the issue of the exclusivity of the priesthood, she details the misunderstood difference between the "deposit of the faith"—those teachings (or doctrines) handed down by the apostles orally (i.e., tradition) or through the written word (i.e., Scripture)—and how theologians have understood such doctrines. Whereas the deposit of the faith remains the same for all time, the way in which theologians understand and then explain such Church doctrine can and does change over the course of history. This happens as new questions are raised and prior explanations challenged by new insights, discoveries, or ideas about the world. Thus, Butler argues, while many theologians once based their argument for the male priesthood on the assumed inferiority of women, this doctrine has actually always been grounded in the *facts* of sacred history. Such facts concern Jesus' example in choosing the Twelve and the unbroken tradition of the Church since then—though it wasn't until 1977 that the Church found it necessary to say so.

Similarly, though individual theologians had sometimes relied on false ideas of women's subordinate status to *explain* Church teachings on sexuality (that both sex and women were made solely for procreation), they do not *depend* on such ideas for their validity.

Rather, the Church's teachings on abortion, sex, marriage, and the priesthood depend on that which all other Church doctrines depend: the words and deeds of Jesus Christ and his apostles recorded in Sacred Scripture, guided by the Holy Spirit and the light of reason, preserved in the tradition of the Church.

Contrary to the old Catholic feminist view, it's not that these controversial Church teachings are wrong *in themselves*; it's just that the modern world is in desperate need of a pro-woman *explanation*.

Pope John Paul II has been called *John Paul the Great* in part because he began the difficult task of reexamining and rearticulating biblical truths and Church teaching in light of modern philosophical insights into the human person and human experience, foremost among them freedom and equality. John Paul II's theology of the body, and the "new feminism" he championed, have afforded many intellectually curious Catholics a strong theoretical explanation for many truths of the faith that have been challenged in recent decades, especially those concerning sexuality and the role of women in the Church and in the world.

His writings have provided a unique philosophical critique of the secular humanist and feminist ideas that abound in Western culture. Catholic new feminist writers, inspired by *On the Dignity of Women* (1988) and his *Letter to Women* (1995), have expounded on John Paul's vision of the equality and complementarity of the sexes. These writers have challenged secular feminists who either blindly deny gender differences or refuse to admit that such difference should amount to anything in the public (or private) sphere. John Paul's consistent refrain and lived witness that true freedom is found in total self-gift has allowed his followers to confront a Western society based, in part, on claims of individual autonomy and false notions of liberty as license. He taught that the self-donation for which the human person is made is ultimately realized in the sexual union of the spouses. This teaching has elevated the meaning of sex at a time when our consumerist culture has debased sex, treating it as simply another form of entertainment.

And yet, despite the rich theological explanation of these controversial topics in recent years, as well as a vibrant orthodox faith practiced by many John Paul II-inspired young Catholics, the Church continues to be perceived as anti-woman and anti-sex, sometimes virulently so. It's as though some inside (and outside) the Church cannot fathom how the Catholic Church can so appreciate the dignity of women and the beauty of sex, and yet still stand firm in her views on abortion, sex, marriage, and the priesthood. For many, a deep disconnect remains between the Church's new, modern emphasis on equality and freedom, and her continued adherence to traditional teachings.

A *practical, pro-woman* defense of these controversial teachings is required to bridge the gap. As the late Elizabeth Fox-Genovese, a social historian and convert to Catholicism, whose elegant writings always evinced a deep concern for the welfare of women, wrote: "[A] viable new feminism must directly confront the realm of practice ... the real terrain of struggle ... [f]or most women understand their lives within [that] context."[6] Ordinary Catholics (and non-Catholics alike) need to understand, in non-theological terms, why self-respecting women and women-loving men can faithfully live these controversial Church teachings in the modern world. This book intends to help them do just that.

Marshaling sociological, biological, and medical evidence; anecdotal accounts; and personal experience, the women who write in this volume challenge the common misconception that the Church's teachings are anti-women and anti-sex. Rather, these women believe that it is precisely the Church's controversial teachings on abortion, sex, marriage, and contraception that bespeak the Church's love of women—and reverence for sex. Recent empirical evidence reveals just how harmful breaking from these teachings has been for women, their children, and our culture over the past few decades. Moreover, this harm has disproportionately affected those for whom the Church holds a special concern: the poor. Indeed, the women who write these chapters argue that, contrary to popular belief (and old-guard Catholic feminism), following Church teachings on sex and marriage, in spite of the sometimes arduous difficulty of doing so, actually helps women to flourish—physically, emotionally, relationally, and socially.

⸺◆⸺

Before launching into a pro-woman account of each of the Church's controversial teachings *in practice*, it is necessary to elucidate the Church's *theoretical* understanding of equality and freedom. For in many of the cases examined in the chapters that follow, the harm that has come to women as a result of straying from these teachings is due to a fundamental cultural misunderstanding of these two key concepts. In chapter 1, then, philosopher Laura Garcia will look first at the Church's modern view of the complementarity of the sexes, or equality in difference, and corroborate this theory with recent biological and sociological data on the differences between men and women. Garcia will then explain the Church's account of human freedom, its difference from the secular view of freedom as license or autonomy, and its perfection in the self-giving acts of interdependent persons.

Reflecting upon my work as editor of *The Cost of "Choice": Women Evaluate the Impact of Abortion*, I will take up the issue of abortion in chapter 2. I will show how Church teaching not only reverences every human life as unique and sacred, but in so doing, dignifies every mother, whether rich or poor, healthy or infirm, in her call to nurture new life in her womb. Abortion (alongside contraception) has been regarded as the sine qua non of the modern-day secular feminist movement. Yet, abortion has harmed women, physically and emotionally, in our relationships with men, and in our very social status as women. Societal structures will not change for the benefit of women and their families when women are willing to sacrifice their own offspring to further their educational and career aspirations. Moreover, abortion advocates often argue that poor and desperate women are the prime beneficiaries of liberalized abortion laws. On the contrary, I will show how the Church's life-affirming message is actually the true champion of the poor.

In chapter 3, Cassandra Hough, founder of both the Anscombe Society at Princeton University and the Love and Fidelity Network, discusses the emotional and physical pitfalls for young women who engage in sex devoid of love and marital commitment. Recent studies and ample anecdotal evidence reveal that premarital, and especially casual sex, is inherently anti-woman. Regardless of whether young women want to be emotionally unaffected by sex—in the way it *seems* young men often are—the truth is that sex binds those who engage in it. This bonding makes women's attempts to enjoy casual sex along the lines of the promiscuous male almost impossible. Early sexual activity focuses young women's energies on young men, rather than on their own studies and goals, thus increasing the likelihood of depression and poor academic performance, among other setbacks. Perhaps most devastating of all is that, unbeknown to most women, sexually transmitted diseases are not gender-neutral: STDs are far more harmful to women than to men—especially to their future fertility and the health of their future offspring. Hough makes the case that the woman who waits for a man to commit is better prepared to find him in the first place—and to enjoy lasting love, free from the emotional (and sexual) baggage that often results from loveless sexual encounters.

In chapter 4, economist Jennifer Roback Morse, author of *Smart Sex: Finding Life-Long Love in a Hook-Up World* and *Love and Economics: It Takes a Family to Raise a Village,* and founder of the Ruth Institute, points to dozens of studies that show that, on the whole, married individuals are happier, healthier, more sexually satisfied, and more prosperous than single, cohabiting, or divorced individuals. Married women especially benefit when they share a lifelong commitment with their spouses. Though secular feminists criticize the institution of marriage for its lack of freedom and autonomy, indissoluble marriage actually increases a woman's freedom to choose a path in life that a great many women wish for themselves: a life in which they are free to devote much of their time to their children. Moreover, Church teachings that promote monogamous, permanent marriage are especially crucial for poor women whose lives are greatly improved by it, and for whom divorce strikes an especially brutal financial blow. In chapter 5, Angela Franks, author of *Margaret Sanger's Eugenic Legacy*, tackles by far the most controversial of the Church's sexual teachings: contraception. She discusses the historically eugenic and anti-woman rationales for contraception, and the ways that contraception has hurt women in their relationships with men. Then, explaining the Church's teaching on the crucial distinction between contraception and natural family planning, Franks shows how the latter is far more respectful of women's bodies, the different sexual appetites of women and men, and the sacred relationship between spouses.

It has been said that natural family planning is one of the best kept secrets of the Catholic Church; this is especially so for those women and men who desire children but have been unable to have them. Just as the couple using NFP respect—rather than suppress—the natural fertility of the woman when the couple elect to postpone pregnancy, NFP-inspired reproductive medicine (i.e., NaProTECHNOLOGY) also has had tremendous success in assisting women to conceive. In chapter 6, educator Katie Elrod, writing with obstetrician Paul Carpentier, describes this holistic and cutting-edge approach to women's reproductive health and illuminates the reasons for its success. The writers contrast such an approach with assisted reproductive technologies (ART). Such technologies are fraught with risk for both women and the children conceived through them. In ignoring the natural signs and symptoms of women experiencing infertility or miscarriage, these writers argue that the ART industry places profit motives ahead of respect for and attention to women's bodies.

Once a proponent of ordaining women, dogmatic theology professor Sister Sara Butler takes up the subject of the priesthood in chapter 7. She explains the Church's rationale for reserving the ministerial priesthood to men, and shows how these reasons in no way contradict the inherent dignity and equality of women. Looking first at the fundamental reasons for the Church's teaching, she then describes the Church's theological explanation for this much-maligned teaching.

In chapters 2 through 7, contributors defend the Church's positions on what are understood to be definitive teachings, teachings that have been understood in different ways throughout history as our knowledge changes, but are not themselves up for debate. Chapter 8 turns to a subject upon which there is no definitive Church teaching, and about which many modern-day women struggle: balancing the need (or desire) to work with care of one's family. Relying on the social teachings of the Church, St. Thomas Law School professor Elizabeth Schiltz seeks to bring an authentically Catholic perspective to this timely question, introducing secular feminists to Catholic thought, and Catholics to some like-minded secular feminists.

I conclude the volume with an examination of the relationship between the Church's celebrated concern for the poor and her more controversial sexual teachings. As it turns out, the data reveal that authentic social justice cannot be separated from Catholic teaching on sex and marriage, as much as some in the Church would like to try. This truth is evinced by the disproportionate harm that straying from these Church teachings has had on the poor, especially poor women and children. Today, as in all times, the Church stands as a prophetic witness to the inherent worth of the human person regardless of his or her social status. The Church also courageously maintains the unpopular conviction that in promoting the intrinsic value of life, the dignity of the sexual union, and the indissolubility of the marital bond, she is protecting the poorest of the poor. Inasmuch as women of all walks of life have suffered at the hands of a culture that has denigrated sex, marriage, and life itself, *all* women of faith possess a distinctively *feminine* mission of cultural renewal: to reveal to the world the way of attentive, humanizing, self-giving love.

Erika Bachiochi
East Walpole, Massachusetts
December 12, 2009
The Feast of Our Lady of Guadalupe

Part I

FOUNDATIONS

1

Authentic Freedom and Equality in Difference

Laura L. Garcia

Many of my academic friends take issue with the Catholic Church's teachings on women. Some disagree with moral principles regarding sex, marriage, and abortion, or with the Church's practice of reserving priestly orders to men. But others react more to a rather vague gestalt, to a kind of cloud that hangs over the Church and manifests itself in the media and in popular culture. It's almost axiomatic in the media these days that the Church fails to appreciate women's full humanity (equality) and to promote opportunities for women in the public square (freedom). Given this situation, some find it shocking to learn that there are highly educated, seemingly sensible, reasonably well-adjusted women in and outside of academia who embrace Catholic teaching with enthusiasm and gratitude, including Catholic teaching on so-called women's issues. Perhaps we can take a closer look here at what motivates their positive reaction to the Church.

It may be helpful to divide this rather large topic into three more specific questions. First, and most fundamental, what is current Catholic teaching, as expressed in official documents and declarations over the past three decades, about the nature of human beings and the meaning of masculinity and femininity? Second, what has been the practice of members of the Church hierarchy in their dealings with women? Finally, do the Church's moral teachings and sacramental practices undermine the freedom and equality of women? I will have much to say about the first question, and others in this volume will address the third. As to the second question, while the historical details are outside my expertise, I suspect that some women's experiences of the Church, through the actions of some of her priests and bishops, have been harmful and demeaning. Such experiences might lead a person to assume that, in some way or other, Catholic teaching must support or justify bad behavior toward women. That assumption is a faulty one. But until recently the Church offered little by way of official teaching on the significance of gender and its place in the Christian worldview.

All of that changed in the 1980s when, on the occasion of the United Nation's Year of the Woman, Pope John Paul II published two ground-breaking documents: *On the Dignity and Vocation of Women* (*Mulieris Dignitatem*) and *On the Role of the Christian Family in the Modern World* (*Familiaris Consortio*). These laid out the philosophical and theological grounds for the consistent teaching of the Church on the equal dignity of women and men. They offered an expansive, almost cosmic, account of the vocation of women that insisted on a place for women in every corner of the public square. In fact, John Paul II suggested that the mission of the Church's laity is more likely to be motivated and spearheaded by women than men.[1] While acknowledging the wrongs done to women in the past, including those inflicted by members of the Body of Christ, John Paul II also emphasized the important contributions of women to salvation history, to the Church and its mission, and to the lives of countless men, women, and children. Finally, he offered an interpretation of key biblical passages on the relationships between women and men that honored the text without tipping the power balance in favor of men.

Previous attempts to honor women's equality, including most strains of secular feminism, have employed a strategy of homogenization, downplaying differences between the sexes in order to justify a moral policy of equal treatment. John Paul II's approach is just the opposite—he acknowledges, even glories in, the differences between the sexes, finding in this very fact the basis for the equal dignity of each and their equal need for each other. This view is captured by the term "complementarity," a word that speaks of differences to be sure, but of differences that enrich each partner in the relationship, so that the resulting combination is greater than the sum of its parts.

In what follows, I will take a closer look at this complementarian view, offering support for both of its central claims: first, that women and men share equally in the dignity proper to human persons, and second, that gender-specific differences between women and men are the basis for natural gifts or aptitudes that together contribute to human flourishing (for individuals as well as for families and larger communities).

Male/Female Equality

For most of the twentieth century, promoting the cause of women meant fighting against a prevailing historical and cultural assumption that women are inferior to men by their very nature—insufficiently rational or objective. Combating this perception meant focusing on that which is common to women and men, a shared human nature that does not admit of degrees. As women have challenged these stereotypes over the past few decades, they have proved by their achievements—scholastic, professional, even athletic—that they could perform on a par with men. While these achievements helped to change the public perception of women, they are not in themselves the foundation of equality between women and men. The crucial equality that must be recognized here is a moral one, that women have the same personal dignity and rights as men. They are, therefore, equally entitled to others' respect and goodwill, as well as to the legal and political privileges that flow from this deeper respect for persons.

The moral point is fundamental, not just for society in general, but also for the collaboration of women and men in the family and in the Church. As the United Nations officially declared in 1950:

> All human beings are born free and equal in dignity and rights. They are endowed with reason and conscience and should act towards one another in a spirit of brotherhood. Everyone is entitled to all the rights and freedoms set forth in this Declaration, without distinction of any kind, such as race, color, sex, language, religion,

political or other opinion, national or social origin, property, birth
or other status.[2]

The realization of this fundamental moral truth in legal and social
institutions is an ongoing process. But the early American feminist movement of the suffragists appealed to such principled reasoning long and
often in order to pursue societal progress.

On the other hand, the feminist movement as it continued into the
1960s and 1970s began to make some proposals for advancing the cause
of women that, it must now be admitted, were seriously flawed. Some
actively undermined relationships between women and men (relationships that are important to many women). Other proposals foundered on
unwarranted assumptions about the malleability of men's and women's
personalities. In a sense, the very success of women's achievements in the
professions contributed to a shift in the strategy for achieving equality.
Rather than invoking a moral principle as their predecessors had, these
feminists set out to prove that women could do whatever men did as well
or better than men could do it, in an effort to force men to accept women
as their equals.

Sadly, this project was doomed from the start, and for many reasons.
Some women worked themselves to exhaustion trying to do justice to
their home and family life while climbing the corporate ladder, working
toward tenure, or maximizing billable hours. Feeling the tension between
work and family life, some "outsourced" domestic work and child care to
housekeepers, landscapers, nurseries, au pairs, after-school programs, and
the like. Others, instead, simply abandoned any thought of marriage or
children in order to better compete with men. In her provocatively entitled essay "Motherhood: The Annihilation of Women," Jeffner Allen calls
for a twenty-year moratorium on having children, warning: "Until patriarchy no longer exists, all females, as historical beings, must resist, rebel
against, and avoid producing for the sake of men."[3]

While Allen represents an extreme position, many women would sympathize with her point that motherhood makes it harder to compete with
men in the pursuit of power and prestige. Yet, by the time her essay
appeared in 1983, women were beginning to reassess whether power and
prestige were what they had most wanted in the first place. Western societies do tend to define personal success in these terms, but such default
cultural assumptions have been shaped largely by men. These assump-

tions emphasize the individual over the group, and work that produces monetary gain over work that simply serves others' needs. Women, on the other hand, tend to place a high value on relationships and give great importance to the kind of care for others that is largely unremunerated. Such care is motivated by love and concern rather than by monetary gain (let alone public prestige).[4]

Why did "second-wave feminism" (in contrast to the feminism of the suffragists) abandon human rights, grounded in a shared human nature, as the primary foundation for women's equality? One obvious reason is that to ground human rights in human nature would entail acknowledging that abortion is gravely immoral. A human being at the very first stages of life is as fully human as any other member of the species; he or she is already part of the human family—one of us. Anyone who has read a book about pregnancy or seen an ultrasound image of an unborn child knows that abortion takes the life of a woman's son or daughter. It does not simply eliminate a "product of conception" or a mere "clump of cells," as pro-choice feminists are wont to argue. The unborn child already has his or her own genetic pattern, separate from that of the parents, and needs only nourishment and time to develop into an infant, toddler, teenager, and adult. For many women, these are indeed inconvenient facts. Hence, leaders in the National Organization for Women and lobbyists from Planned Parenthood and NARAL (a league of abortion providers) have spent millions to propagate the message that equality for women depends on the availability of abortion. Pro-choice has become the central dogma of mainline feminism.

What increasingly troubles younger women about this article of faith is that treating access to abortion as a necessity for career-minded women simply capitulates to the prevailing (largely male) attitude that productive work is incompatible with pregnancy, childbirth, and attentive nurturing of children. Why accept such an absurd view? It is true that most mothers of newborns or small children express a desire either to stay at home for a few years or to work part-time.[5] But a truly pro-woman policy would be to make these options real possibilities for women so they can integrate their public and private lives without being penalized.

Women are already an essential part of the workforce in Western economies. It is foolish to effectively coerce them to choose between exercising their talents in the public sphere (and resorting to abortion when

pregnancy might inconvenience their employers), and living as permanent exiles from public life. John Paul II calls for a more enlightened set of
social goals in this regard:

> There is no doubt that the equal dignity and responsibility of men
> and women fully justifies women's access to public functions. On
> the other hand the true advancement of women requires that clear
> recognition be given to the value of their maternal and family role,
> by comparison with all other public roles and all other professions.
> Furthermore, these roles and professions should be harmoniously
> combined, if we wish the evolution of society and culture to be
> truly and fully human.[6]

A truly egalitarian society is not a society in which men's and women's
roles are indistinguishable. Rather, it is a society that gives equal importance, respect, and financial support to the work and contributions of all
of its members.

Does the persistence of gender-based differences mean we must
despair of achieving meaningful equality between the sexes? Not at all.
But it might be that equality cannot be grounded in the now-discredited
assumption that gender is irrelevant. Rather, it must be based on the truth
that men and women share equally in a common human nature. It is in
virtue of being human that we are owed the respect and goodwill of our
fellow human beings. Many have attempted to find a different basis for
human rights, appealing to attributes like intelligence, consciousness, or
the capacity to make moral choices. But such theories fail to extend basic
rights to the very ones most in need of protection—children, the elderly,
the ill, or the disabled.

Further, human capacities admit of degrees—a person can be more or
less rational, more or less aware, and so on—but human nature is an all-or-
nothing affair. No human being is "more human" than any other.[7]
Grounding human dignity in human nature has the advantage, then, of
placing the struggle for women's rights within the same moral category as
the struggle for the rights of racial or religious minorities. Recognizing the
equal dignity of women and men, grounded in their shared nature as
human beings, does not require that women and men be treated as interchangeable in all of their social roles. It does require that women be treated
with the dignity proper to persons, who are by nature able to consider alternative means to an end and to choose freely which of these to pursue. A

human is a moral agent, responsible for his or her attitudes and choices. A human is a subject, not merely an object; that is, humans have an inner life of thoughts, emotions, desires, plans, and choices. A human person is a self, unique and irreplaceable. Though some are less capable of exercising their reason and will (e.g., infants, the elderly, the developmentally disabled), strictly speaking, no one human can act for another, love for another, or choose for another. These facts about human persons are the basis for the fundamental moral law that it is wrong, at any time and in any place, to treat a person merely as a means to an end (that is, as an object).[8]

Taking human nature as the ontological basis for the equal dignity of all human beings provides a basis for male/female equality that is compatible with acknowledging differences between women and men. Many feminists have feared that acknowledging such differences will reinforce patriarchal arrangements in the family and in the wider society. But anthropological research on women's roles in what anthropologists describe as "egalitarian societies" reveals that divisions of labor and other gender-specific features do not necessarily lead to patriarchy.

Social scientist Margaret Andersen describes an interesting anthropological study of several societies described as egalitarian vis-à-vis gender roles. The study lists three conditions that seem to make equality possible: (1) The economic well-being of each individual depends on the well-being of the whole group; (2) There is no sharp dichotomy between the public and private spheres; and (3) Those making decisions will also be carrying them out.[9] With respect to this last point, it is true that when economic and political institutions are dominated by men, women will find themselves living with decisions in which they did not participate; but in any society of significant size, so will most men. One advantage of a complementarian theory in this respect is if there are important differences between women and men, there is strong reason to include both women and men in decision-making institutions.

The first two aspects of egalitarian societies are closely related—recognizing that the common good is crucial to the good of individuals highlights the importance of each person's contribution to the common good, be it inside or outside the home. Andersen and her colleagues might be surprised to learn that John Paul II's complementarian vision encourages policies that would promote both of these outcomes. Part of the power of his view is that it makes men and women aware of the unique contributions of the opposite sex. Again, equality is presupposed here; it is to be neither a one-sided dependence nor a hierarchy of power, but two (or more) people working side by side on shared goals that are deeply important to them all.

With respect to the second aspect of egalitarian societies, it must be admitted that in today's economies, some split between public and private life is inevitable. Still, this need not be a wall of separation. Even if we assume that women will be more involved than men in the private sphere of home and family, which they seem more inclined to, this promotes patriarchy only if one forgets the first feature of egalitarian societies, that the good of each individual is intertwined with the good of the whole. Since the common good requires skilled, dedicated attention to both private and public life, it is false and foolish to underestimate or undervalue the importance of women's contributions to both spheres. Strong families are as necessary to a healthy society as are capable workers—in fact, they are far more important.

Mars and Venus: Male/Female Differences

Current research in biology and in the social sciences overwhelmingly supports the claim that there are deep-seated biological and chemical-based differences between girls and boys, women and men.[10] Since the 1960s, this claim has been vigorously denied by many feminists, in spite of its correspondence with common sense and ordinary experience. The concern is that acknowledging gender-specific differences of any kind beyond the obvious physical ones will justify the kind of restrictive and condescending attitudes toward women that were characteristic of earlier times, prior to the advent of feminism as a movement in the academy and in the media. This concern is partially justified, since some thinkers *have* condoned and even defended the oppression of women based on real or imagined differences between the sexes. Still, it makes little sense to ignore differences that are overwhelmingly supported by the empirical evidence. Nor is this necessary, since equality does not require sameness, whether of gender, race, ethnicity, age, ability, or beliefs. Further, feminists' ideological commitment to gender sameness has resulted in proposals for family and social life that are wildly unrealistic. While some of our attitudes and expectations about the opposite sex and ourselves are heavily influenced by culture, it is simply false to assume that (even in principle) these can be adjusted so as to become completely gender-neutral.

In an exhaustive review of the literature on sex differences (the bibliography alone runs nearly seventy pages), Steven Rhoads, a professor of government and foreign affairs at the University of Virginia, concludes that the empirical evidence for deep-seated and important differences between males and females is overwhelming.[11] He also makes the important point that ignoring these differences is more damaging for women than it is for men, because the goal of a gender-blind society tends to transform itself into the goal of making women more like men. Even if the end is to "empower" women, the path to power is usually defined by those who already have most of it—i.e., men. As a result, male interests, values, and priorities set the agenda for women aspiring to break into the ranks of the powerful. As it happens, women have largely succeeded in this quest, arriving at positions of influence undreamed of by their grandmothers. But among these successful women, many have been surprised to find that they are not appreciably happier or more fulfilled by their public accomplishments.[12] No doubt some berate themselves for a lack of proper ambition, but others begin to wonder whether economic power and public prestige have primary value for them. I will explore this theme at greater length in the section below on freedom.

Past generations have accepted as a matter of common sense and experience that there are clear differences between boys and girls. Anecdotal evidence abounds, and many a devotee of gender neutrality has become a reluctant convert when the first child arrived. But now scientific evidence from fields as diverse as anthropology and neurology is also producing a steady stream of data in support of received wisdom on this subject. It turns out, in fact, that differences between males and females are inscribed in our very brains.[13] For example, females have more neurons connecting the right and left hemispheres of the brain, and women's brains are more "networked." Women use both sides of the brain regardless of the task in which they are engaged. Men, instead, are able to focus on some tasks with one side of the brain alone, oblivious to (for instance) emotional cues in the environment. *Scientific American* reports on a recent study pinpointing the brain difference that gives girls an advantage in verbal ability:

Girls completing a linguistic abilities task showed greater activity in brain areas implicated specifically in language encoding, which decipher information abstractly. Boys, on the other hand, showed a lot of activity in regions tied to visual and auditory functions, depending on the way the words were presented during the exercise.[14]

Further examples of this kind abound in the current scientific literature, as noninvasive research on the brains of living subjects has been made possible by MRIs and PET scans. It turns out, for example, that women hear better than men, detecting a wider variety of sounds and variations in tone than men. Men and women also react differently to stress, and the difference in testosterone levels means that males are naturally more aggressive than females. In fact, differences between the sexes are so great that neurobiologist Larry Cahill reports:

In a comprehensive 2001 report on sex differences in human health, the prestigious National Academy of Sciences asserted that "sex matters. Sex, that is, being male or female, is an important basic human variable that should be considered when designing and analyzing studies in all areas and at all levels of biomedical and health-related research."[15]

It turns out that some medications effective for men with certain mental disorders are much less effective for women with the very same mental illness.[16]

Gender differences alone tell us little about the prospects for male-female relationships. Will these tend to be fruitful and productive or hostile and alienating? Difference makes either of these possible, and it is safe to say that both are realized in some male-female relationships, or even in the same relationship at different times. Complementarity theory claims that the differences between men and women are such that the strengths of each combine in positive and productive ways to achieve common goals.[17]

The most basic, long-term collaborative project a man and woman undertake is marriage and the care and formation of their children. In this project, nothing succeeds like a mother and father who both work hard at preserving their marital friendship and meeting the needs of their children. Sociological evidence is overwhelming on this point, in spite of the protests of some feminists who claim that fathers are irrelevant to the family (except, perhaps, for their income).[18]

Although isolated exceptions exist, fathers and mothers bring different skills to the table when it comes to preparing children for adult life. Women, sensitive as they are to persons and their needs, provide children with encouragement, understanding, and support. The mother/child relationship is often held up as our closest paradigm of unconditional love. While most men are less sensitive to emotional cues, they have advantages of their own, including greater physical strength and stronger reactions to perceived threats to the family. Since males are oriented more toward the world of action and objects, they help prepare children for their role in the world outside the family. Measuring themselves against one another and against objective (public) criteria, they measure their children in the same way and encourage them to develop the skills that make for success.[19] Often in family life, women strengthen relationships while men focus on making the family secure, both physically and financially.

To note these tendencies is not to restrict men and women to determinate social roles. Rather, it simply acknowledges the reality that, by and large, women and men pursue the goals they see as important and feel capable of addressing. It is true that most women today contribute in some way to family finances and that most men provide significant emotional support to children. But the existence of gender-based differences may also be seen as a positive good. These differences can make men and women grateful for each other's particular strengths, encourage them to seek each other out, and provide a model for human relationships within the give-and-take of family life. Prospective employees in colleges and corporations are often told that they will join a family, not just an impersonal group or a well-oiled machine. Whatever the truth behind these claims, the fact that they are made shows a residual cultural awareness that the family (at its best) represents a kind of model for satisfying human relationships.

Turning to the public sphere, it may at first appear that women's sensitivity to the needs of persons and greater interest in the health of their relationships is, at best, a handicap in the competitive world of work. On this subject, as on many others, much depends on the relative value of economic goals and what might be called human goals, or the common good. A culture dominated solely by a utilitarian quest for power, pleasure, and profits tends naturally to become inhuman. It weighs everything, including human persons, on a cost/benefit scale of utility, and readily discards those who are deemed a net burden on society's resources. While both men and women can appreciate the danger of this consumer mentality, women's appreciation of the value of persons gives them a heightened sensitivity to the poisonous potential in a culture of use. Recent Catholic teaching on the vocation of women, far from restricting women to a narrow domestic role, calls on them to exercise a global, even cosmic role in promoting a culture of life and civilization of love. John Paul II spoke often of the "genius" of women, referring especially to women's insight into the value of each human life and the primacy of persons over things:

> "[Woman's] unique contact with the new human being developing within her gives rise to an attitude toward human beings, not only toward her own child, but every human being, which profoundly marks the woman's personality." ... Women first learn and then teach others that human relations are authentic if they are open to accepting the other person: a person who is recognized and loved because of the dignity which comes from being a person and not from other considerations, such as usefulness, strength, intelligence, beauty, or health.[20]

This passage captures the heart of the Church's moral vision, and calls on women to defend that moral vision in the wider culture. "This is the fundamental contribution which the Church and humanity expect from women. And it is the indispensable prerequisite for an authentic cultural change."[21] At this point, some may wonder whether there is anything left for men to do. Certainly; but the vocation of men is no doubt a topic for another book.

Authentic Freedom

Does the very notion of a vocation unique to women restrict women's freedom in such a way as to undermine their personal happiness and fulfillment? The answer to this question depends on the definition of the two key terms "freedom" and "happiness." While there are many kinds of freedom and many uses of the word, I wish to focus on the way freedom has been understood in standard feminist theories on one hand and in Catholic moral philosophy on the other. Oversimplifying a bit, I may characterize the two contenders as *freedom as autonomy* versus *freedom as the power to love.* These definitions of freedom correspond to two quite different conceptions of happiness. One view considers happiness as the fulfillment of one's desires, especially desires for wealth, comfort, and influence. The other view regards it as the fulfillment of one's need to receive and give love.

The standard feminist view is also the prevailing cultural view: freedom means autonomy—literally, being "a law unto oneself." Such freedom tolerates no constraints or obstacles to fulfilling one's own wishes, whatever they may be. Happiness is thought to consist in satisfying desires, or as many as can be satisfied without coming into conflict with other (more intense) desires. In its current form, this view rejects attempts to objectively assess these desires—any such critique is dismissed as inherently unjustifiable or, at best, judgmental.[22]

Abandoning in this way what we might call "the philosophical project," or the idea that we can make truth claims about anything, has produced a good deal of social confusion and chaos. It has led to the sanguine but misguided hope that we can govern our communities without committing to any particular view of human nature. This view has sadly captured the imagination of many people in public service, producing legislators and judges who see their roles as benign referees. They strive to adjudicate among competing interests without taking as their guide a normative set of principles. This posture finds classic expression in the majority opinion of the U.S. Supreme Court in the 1992 case of *Planned Parenthood v. Casey*: "At the heart of liberty is the right to define one's own concept of existence, of meaning, of the universe, and of the mystery of human life. Beliefs about these matters could not define the attributes of personhood were they formed under compulsion of the State."[23]

Unfortunately, this is a clear case of liberty as autonomy run amok. Liberty is said to include not just freedom to pursue one's desires, but also the freedom to decide what it means to be human, and even to decide what kind of universe one lives in. But no one (with the exception of God) is free to decide what kind of universe humans inhabit, what human nature is, or what purpose human life has. Those conditions precede the existence of particular human beings, and "definitions," opinions, or beliefs about them are true or false independent of any person's wishes or choices. Still less can having mere opinions about these topics be the defining mark of personhood.

Reading the court's statement as sympathetically as we can, however, let us assume that the liberty it intends to preserve is the freedom to *choose one's own beliefs* about the big questions. Of course the Bill of Rights also protects the *freedom to express these beliefs* and, in the case of religious beliefs, the *freedom to worship* in accordance with them. Still, none of these freedoms bears on the question that was before the court in *Casey*, namely, whether a pregnant woman should be free to obtain an abortion, and if so, whether that freedom should be subject to any constraints whatever. The answer to that question naturally requires an answer to a prior question: Does an abortion take the life of an innocent human being or, put more philosophically, what is the moral status of a human fetus? While there is still some public disagreement about the answer to that question, it is monstrous to claim that each pregnant woman should be allowed to answer it according to her own preferences. One can only imagine the reaction of earlier feminists had they been told that, in view of the persisting disagreement about the moral status of women, it would be left up to each father or husband to decide the issue. When basic human rights are at stake, freedom as autonomy easily becomes freedom for tyranny, where the powerful prey upon the powerless.

Beyond this, viewing freedom simply as a means to pursue our own agenda implicitly assumes that fulfillment of our desires is the key to happiness. While young children may hold some such view, adults generally recognize that many of the things we desire are bad for us or harmful to others. Even perfectly legitimate desires, such as for food or drink, can be satisfied in such a way as to undermine our health and happiness. Further, the desire-satisfaction model of happiness is overly individualistic. A desire is always a private mental state of a particular person, even when others share the object of the desire, while happiness crucially involves positive relationships with others. Of course we might try to simply add loving relationships to the list of things desired, but a desire for love requires a significant change of focus. It means turning one's attention away from purely self-directed desires toward the needs and welfare of the other. And genuine concern for the good of another person is not the same as wanting to satisfy as many of that person's desires as possible— another reason to be suspicious of the view that happiness consists in maximal desire-satisfaction. If it does, we would seek it for our children and our friends as well as for ourselves; but we don't.

A very different understanding of freedom, articulated by ancient Greek philosophy as well as by Catholic moral teaching, conceives of freedom as the *power to choose the good*. This conception presupposes that there is an objective good for human beings and that we know what it is (at least to a large extent). While many of today's academics and public intellectuals dispute both presuppositions, one often finds these same thinkers regularly recommending social and economic policies based on what they think is good for human beings. As Aristotle pointed out many centuries ago, rational beings seek their ultimate end—happiness—by using their reason to judge what will further that end and what will undermine it. Even the most unreflective among us has to make a judgment about the right road to happiness. Fortunately, no one starts from scratch in that quest, since our parents and grandparents (and their parents and grandparents) have acquired a great deal of wisdom about what is good for us.

Essentialism, or the view that there exist some universal truths about human beings, has a bad name these days. But in practice it seems we all count on there being enough common ground among members of the human race to make some universal normative claims possible. These are universal not in the sense of being endorsed by every human being, but rather in the sense that the vast majority of people in every time and in every culture accept them. For example, giving free rein to one's appetites is bad for humans, but so is attempting to suppress one's appetites altogether. Hence the Aristotelian doctrine of the golden mean, which defines the virtue of temperance as the middle ground between excess (gluttony) and deficiency (self-starvation). Naturally there will be some disagreement on such matters as how to characterize human nature (what is common to all human beings qua human) and what genuinely helps or hinders human flourishing. But we can hardly avoid addressing them, since we necessarily seek our own happiness and are so designed as to govern our actions by reason. Instinct alone will not guide us to our end.

Parents especially do not have the luxury of agnosticism about the human good. Fortunately, one does not need a full-blown moral theory to know that it is good to share toys and bad to bite one's friends. We might look to the goals of parenting, in fact, for clues to the meaning of happiness, since all parents want their children to be happy. In pursuit of this goal, mothers and fathers work to instill such virtues in their children as kindness, honesty, self-discipline, perseverance, courage, loyalty, and the like. They insist that their children eat breakfast, go to school, and do their chores, not because the children want to but because it's good for them. In the short term these measures might seem to limit freedom. But parents know that they are really conditions for developing a more important freedom—the freedom of self-mastery. A person who is driven by passions and appetites is enslaved by them, and tends to treat others as a means for fulfilling those passions and desires. But a person who is self-possessed is able to give freely of him or herself to others, treating them as ends in themselves—an essential ingredient of love.

Looking at freedom in this light shifts our perspective from the individual to the group—the family, parish, neighborhood, school, and so on. In order to make these personal relationships work, individuals must come to value the good of others as their own good. They must be willing to sacrifice some of their own personal interests for the sake of the common good. While many desires can remain unfulfilled without harm to our happiness, no one can survive without love. And genuine love is always a gift; it is not based on merit and it cannot be coerced. As we have seen, the kind of freedom parents want most for their children is the freedom to form loving relationships with others, and family life is a school of love. In these early relationships, children (ideally) first receive the unconditional love of their parents and other relatives, and then grow to love the other family members in this same unconditional way.

Recognizing the inherent dignity and value of each human person and responding appropriately to that value is at the heart of the moral life. Further, since humans are naturally social and oriented toward communion with others, love is the key to human happiness. Our relationships with others come with a wide variety of expectations and different levels of investment of time and talents, but each can and should include an attitude of genuine concern for the good of the other. On this view then, human beings are made for love; giving and receiving love is the key to our happiness. Hence, the most important freedom for persons is *the power to love*.

At this point, we have described two competing conceptions of freedom, and their respective conceptions of happiness. With these in mind, let us return to the question raised at the beginning of this section: Does the existence of a "vocation" for women, as explored by Pope John Paul

II in his apostolic letter *On the Dignity and Vocation of Women*, restrict women's freedom in such a way as to undermine their personal happiness and fulfillment?

Since to have a vocation is to be in some way called to a particular task, a vocation generally does restrict a person's freedom to pursue other personal desires and interests. The extent of that restriction, however, depends on the nature of the vocation. John Paul II claims that women have a greater sensitivity to persons and to the value of each human life, and that this gives them a moral obligation to preserve and promote those values in both private and public life. Notice two important features of that vocational claim: (1) it allows for the possibility that men are also obliged to promote these values, in whatever ways they can best do so; and (2) it does not specify what women should do in order to exercise their vocation. It is a fairly sweeping goal that can no doubt be furthered in a myriad of ways. It excludes only the effort to "masculinize" women, to reshape them according to the characteristics of men.[24] Talk of "women's roles" or "a woman's place" can raise alarms, as it appears likely to confine women to the home as the place where this role is exercised. But John Paul II's language of a vocation for women implies no such thing. While he seeks both protection and respect for women who are focusing on the home front, he also expects women to exercise their influence in every aspect of culture—business, politics, the arts, journalism, education, and athletics.

Some will object that while a vocation for women may allow for women's involvement in public life, women with children are still likely to expend more energy than men when it comes to caring for the home and the children. Promoting the value of the person naturally includes placing a high value on new human life. It means taking a positive and generous attitude toward having children, seeing them as a gift to the family and to the community. Contrary to what some have thought, Catholic teaching does not ask couples to have as many children as they possibly can. Rather, couples are to be "open" to new life, both in spirit and in fact—willing to welcome the children they conceive, and leaving their conjugal acts open to the possibility of conception. (Such openness may, of course, include abstinence during fertile periods should a couple prayerfully determine it would not be responsible to conceive at a particular time.) As feminists have been quick to point out, bearing new life with generosity asks more of the wife than it does of the husband, since she will carry the baby for nine months and will likely continue to be the primary source of the baby's nutrition for several months more.

Welcoming children, then, requires a greater sacrifice from the mother, in that it places greater restrictions on her freedom to pursue her other interests. If happiness consists in the maximal satisfaction of one's self-directed desires, then clearly motherhood is a blow to happiness. On the other hand, if happiness consists in loving and being loved, then mothers have the inside track. This is not to deny that mothers make many difficult sacrifices and that they feel the pinch—they are only human, after all—nor does it justify a condemnation of mothers who enter (or return to) the paid workforce. Every girl and woman should be encouraged to develop her talents, exercise her gifts, and follow her dreams (as should every boy and man). But women should also be allowed to have dreams that don't coincide with those of men. It may be that the kind of competition for power and prestige that appeals to many men holds little appeal for many women. In fact, it might even be that power and prestige ought to hold less appeal for men, and that they will learn this by hearing more of what women value.

While much of secular feminism vehemently rejects anything resembling a vocation for women (as opposed to a generic human vocation), the 1990s introduced some new voices into the feminist conversation. Several of these were willing to entertain the possibility that women are overwhelmingly more likely than men to want to be the primary caregivers for their children. Rhoads' book is replete with studies and anecdotal evidence that support this very claim. "In the United States, feminists studying marriage often acknowledge that most wives are content with the division of labor in their marriage even though they do substantially more child care and housework."[25]

Lest the task of raising children be underestimated, philosopher Sara Ruddick argues persuasively in her 1989 book *Maternal Thinking* that mothering requires intellectual and emotional skills at least as demanding as those required in highly paid public professions. Ruddick speaks of the attentive love that mothers exercise toward their children and of the importance of focusing on the distinctive gifts and abilities of each child. Ruddick also suggests that a woman's experience of pregnancy and birth makes her especially sensitive to the value of each human body. She writes, "Every body counts, every body is a testament to hope. The hope of the world—of birthing women, mothers, friends, and kin—rests in the newborn infant. The infant's hope resides in the world's welcome."[26] While many feminists continue to measure success in terms of professional achievement, others have begun to develop a more woman-centered ethics of care. They take as morally central the things women tend to value (personal relationships) and the qualities necessary to preserve those things (compassion, empathy, attentiveness, and the like).[27]

The new feminism envisaged by John Paul II and emerging in the work of scholars energized by his vision is one of the most exciting intellectual developments in recent history. This is a feminism that promotes the equality and dignity of men and women as partners in a shared humanity and encourages them to collaborate in shaping a culture worthy of the human person. It replaces a failed model of freedom as license with a positive conception of freedom as the precondition for genuine love. And it encourages women to use their talents, insights, and influence to help transform a lost and disillusioned culture into a civilization of love.

Part II

LOVE, SEX,
AND REPRODUCTION

2

The Uniqueness of Woman:
Church Teaching on Abortion

Erika Bachiochi

bortion is one of the most contentious issues dividing our society today. The issue has created a cultural rift even within the Catholic Church herself. Though the institutional Church remains the most vocal pro-life advocate on earth, those who identify themselves as Catholic favor abortion rights in the same proportions as the rest of the American population.[1]

In the view of pro-choice Catholics, the sanctity of an individual's conscience, and especially a woman's right to "self-determination," are foundational for what they claim is their *Catholic* belief in the dignity of the human person. According to their most vocal representative, Catholics for a Free Choice, to deny a woman the ability to make her own decision about abortion would be to deny her the freedom and moral agency given her by God. These Catholics believe their support for abortion rights is entirely consistent with fundamental Church teaching on social justice and concern for the needy. The more radical among them accuse the Church's all-male hierarchy of fearing—and seeking to control—women's sexuality and reproduction.[2]

Meanwhile, confusion about Catholic teaching on abortion abounds, especially among Catholic lawmakers.[3] During the 2004 and 2008 American presidential campaigns, several Catholic politicians found themselves at odds with their local bishops. These bishops had to reiterate the Church's teaching that individual conscience does not supersede the constant moral teaching of the Church on abortion (indeed, that proper formation of conscience requires an understanding of those teachings).[4] More, the bishops had to correct an even more pernicious, yet widespread, societal misunderstanding perpetuated by these lawmakers: that religious belief alone grounds opposition to abortion and therefore precludes its debate in the public square. These recent politicians were restating that which so many pro-choice Catholic politicians have claimed over this decades-long dispute: "As a Catholic, I believe that life begins at conception, but as an American, I cannot impose my religion on others."

The trouble for these politicians, and the media who continually misstate the Church's view, is that opposition to abortion does not rest on a *religious belief* that human life begins at conception. While it is undeniable that those who are pro-life are disproportionately religious, that human life begins at conception is not a *religious* tenet; it is a *scientific* fact.[5]

Every modern embryology textbook states that once fertilization has occurred, a new human life exists, a separate and distinct individual, with its own unique DNA. So long as nothing deprives this nascent human being of a suitable environment or nourishment, it possesses all the organizational information it needs to *direct itself* to maturation. The tiny blastocyst certainly appears to the naked eye just like any other clump of cells. But unlike skin cells, muscle cells, or even the ova and sperm from which it was formed, it is an individual human organism, capable of developing into a mature human being. Despite its utter dependence on its mother at this early stage of life, this tiny human being is doing exactly what new human beings do at this stage of life—developing, and by his own internal self-direction.[6]

The philosophical, and potentially religious, question arises when we ask: Does this nascent human life at its vulnerable beginning equal the dignity and worth of other human beings? Or does its smaller size, incomplete development, or dependence, make it unworthy of the human rights extended to fully mature human beings? This is where the debate over human life has morphed, of late, into a debate over personhood, at least in academia. It is conceded that human beings exist at fertilization. But it is argued that legal protection should extend only to "persons" who have attributes or functions far more developed than that of the embryonic human being.[7]

The human embryo clearly cannot exercise the rational mental functions that pro-abortion philosophers claim endow a human being with the status of personhood (and so, in their view, human rights). But then neither does an infant or a comatose patient, both of whom enjoy full human rights. Still, precisely because the human embryo, infant, and comatose patient share a *human* nature, as opposed to an animal, vegetative, or inanimate nature, they each possess the radical, or fundamental, capacity for such rational mental acts.[8] In other words, our rational functions do not make us human; rather, our human nature gives us the capacity to be rational. It is thus by nature of our humanity that human beings are endowed with pre-political, inalienable human rights. It is by nature of our status as *human beings* that we should be given every protection due to human *persons* under the law.[i]

The embryo, fetus, infant, and adolescent are all human beings at different stages of human life.[9] Their human capacities for reason and emotion, love and honor, develop through time. Any attempt to nonarbitrarily determine an alternative moment when a human being, present at fertilization, becomes a human person, worthy of protection under the law, is rationally impossible. Indeed, upholding the rational functions of an adult as the philosophical basis of human rights denies any but the strong and powerful the right to equal treatment under the law. Where else have we seen human beings denied the human rights accorded to persons? Slavery comes to mind—our historical refusal to recognize human beings with black skin as persons worthy of legal protection.[10]

---

i. The U.S. Supreme Court in *Roe v. Wade* held that the Fourteenth Amendment to the U.S. Constitution does not include the unborn in its reference to "person" 410 U.S. 113, 157 (1973). Nevertheless, the states can protect the unborn as "persons" under statutory law, as long as the law does not apply to abortion. The majority of states (37 at this writing) currently have actively enforceable fetal homicide laws that address unborn children killed by violent acts committed against pregnant women. Of these, 25 states have legal protection from conception. That is, states can, and in fact do, protect fetal life despite academia's preoccupation with the requirements of philosophical "personhood." See *Defending Life: Proven Strategies for a Pro-Life America*, Americans United for Life, 2009.

The debate over personhood still rages as a distraction in the halls of academia, with pro-abortion philosophers seeking ways to deny the legal equality of the unborn child on various spurious grounds.[11] But there is simply no debate over the issue that really matters: the presence of human life at fertilization. Some abortion advocates understand the science and have publicly conceded the humanity of the unborn for some time now. For instance, in 1995, Naomi Wolf stated in the *New Republic*: "The pro-life slogan, 'Abortion stops a beating heart,' is incontrovertibly true."[12] Camille Paglia recently wrote on Salon.com, "I have always frankly admitted that abortion is murder, the extermination of the powerless by the powerful."[13] And in *Conscience*, the magazine of Catholics for a Free Choice, former president Frances Kissling declared, "[W]hatever category of human life the fetus is, it nonetheless has value ..."[14]

So if the abortion debate is not really about whether human life begins at conception, despite the confusion on this score perpetuated by politicians and the media alike, why is our culture, and even our Church, so broken up about the issue?

Abortion remains as contentious as ever because its proponents believe that, *whatever the status of the embryo*, the well-being of women depends on the legal right to abortion. According to advocates of abortion rights, support for women, for women's freedom, equality, and well-being, demands legal access to abortion.

Pro-Life Feminism

But what if this pro-choice feminist claim is not true? What if the arguments feminists make in advance of this pro-abortion proposition were to fail as well?

In the balance of this chapter, I will argue that rather than serve women's best interests, abortion has harmed women, physically, emotionally, relationally, and culturally.[15] Further, I'll make the case that an authentically feminist approach would embrace the unique reproductive capacity of women, among their other abilities. An authentically feminist approach would work toward societal recognition of women's distinct sexual difference within the parameters of true freedom and equality. Unknown to many, this authentically feminist approach is also the Catholic approach.

I have not always seen things this way. Indeed, well before my journey back to the Catholic Church as an adult, I was fiercely pro-choice, and persistently accused the Church of making impossible demands: no abortion, no contraception, and no sex before marriage. Did these churchmen really believe that anyone would—or could—confine herself to this type of program? Failing to comprehend the internal logic of these teachings,[16] I looked elsewhere for life's purpose and found it, for a time, in New Age spirituality and "socialist" feminism.

After completing several courses in Women's Studies during college, I wrote the following while I was one of the leaders of our campus women's center: "The state's suppression of a woman's right to choose [was] simply a perpetuation of the patriarchal nature of our society.... To free women from [the] gender hierarchy, women must have a right to do what they please with their bodies."[17]

The story of how I came to change my mind about abortion is rather lengthy, and has been published elsewhere.[18] Suffice it to say, my unwavering support for abortion was based on my status as a feminist. Thus, two realizations were central to my eventual opposition to abortion: (1) abortion harms women's well-being; and (2) it is antithetical to a genuine feminism—one that recognizes and celebrates the uniqueness of women as women.

The pro-life feminist movement that I discovered more than a decade ago is alive and well, and growing among young women and men. Today's pro-life feminists have some feisty predecessors. America's pioneering feminists, such as Susan B. Anthony and Elizabeth Cady Stanton, fought for the right to vote and for fair treatment in the workplace. The early American feminists uniformly opposed abortion, because they saw it as an attack on women *as women*, those uniquely endowed with the ability to bear children.[19]

The suffragists worked to change political and economic institutions by insisting that the government and workplace recognize women. The 1970s feminists, still vocal today in organizations like NOW and NARAL, sought instead to change the very nature of women. They sought to mold women to fit into the male-oriented structures they were trying to enter.

Serrin Foster, president of Feminists for Life, addressed this issue in a celebrated speech, "The Feminist Case Against Abortion."[20] She describes how NARAL founders Bernard Nathanson and Lawrence Lader con-

vinced NOW's first president, Betty Friedan, that access to abortion was
necessary to attain the feminists' demands of equal opportunity in education and the workplace, as well as equal pay.[21] Lader told Friedan,
"[Employers d[o] not want to pay for maternity benefits or lose productiv-
ity when a mother t[akes] time off to care for a newborn or sick child."[22]
In other words, why endure the painstaking fight to change male-oriented
institutions? It would be far easier to convince women that, if they are to
be equal to men, they must become like men, who are by their nature less
attached to children. It is no wonder that the early American feminist
Alice Paul, author of the original Equal Rights Amendment of 1923,
called the manipulation of woman's nature that is abortion "the ultimate
exploitation of women."[23]

Since the nationwide legalization of abortion in 1973, American culture has come to rely on it as an equalizer of the sexes. Indeed, this
cultural reliance on abortion was the central—and really, the only—reasoning the Supreme Court used to uphold *Roe v. Wade* in its 1992 *Casey*
decision: "[F]or two decades of economic and social developments, [peo-
ple] have organized intimate relationships and made choices that define
their views of themselves and their places in society, in reliance on the
availability of abortion in the event that contraception should fail."[24] The
court went on to say that "the capacity of women to act in society" was
based, in large degree, on the availability of abortion.[25]

In other words, the *Casey* Court surmised, we have become comfort-
able not having to change too much in our market-driven society to allow
for women to enter colleges and workplaces on an equal footing with men.
We are not interested in ensuring women the capacity to act in society if
they are not aping men. We cannot afford to do the much more difficult
work of creating environments that welcome women who have children
(which, of course, is the great majority of women). Instead, we will just
continue to tell women what the all-male *Roe* Court told them a generation before. You choose: either your baby or yourself, your baby or your
future, your baby or your success. This is a man's world, and you had better become like a man—that is, not pregnant—if you want to succeed.

The irony in pro-choice feminist reasoning here is tragic in its proportions, and yet so rarely acknowledged. Our feminist foremothers fought
against the categorization of women as legal nonentities or, viewed more
charitably, as united in the legal personhood of their husbands.[26] Now we

are witnessing today's pro-choice feminists claim that the legal equality achieved in the modern era is dependent upon women *denying* that which distinguishes them most from men. Historically, woman was regarded as legally incorporated into man; now she is equal only insofar as she imitates man. Historical feminists fought the former. Today's pro-choice feminists conceived of the latter.

Usurping Real Solutions

More than thirty-five years after the second wave—the abortion wave—of the women's movement, studies show that women are more perplexed about balancing career and family than anything else.[27] The modern-day cause of abortion usurped a pioneering American feminism that sought to influence society to recognize the distinct dignity of women. In doing so, it forestalled solutions to the question of how women could fulfill their unique role as mothers while participating in the wider society as well.

Second only to the fight for continued access to abortion (and contraception) is the secular feminist fight for government subsidized, institutional day care. But like abortion, institutional day care is neither family-friendly nor woman-friendly; it is business-friendly.[28] Government funding of institutional day care subsidizes that option least beneficial to children, as countless studies have shown.[29] It is also least desirable to the great majority of families who would prefer that the mother or father, another family member, or a trusted person care for their children.[30] By fighting for the government to provide such day care, secular feminists again find themselves on the side of the male-oriented market: get women to work more by outsourcing the care of their children to someone less qualified and less desirable, regardless of what most women say they want.[31]

The majority of mothers say they simply want to work less. In a 2005 study, only 16 percent of mothers said that they would prefer full-time work, while 21 percent wanted to be home with their children full-time.[32] Most women with young children are eager to find ways that allow them to engage in part-time or home-based employment. In this way they can both maintain their professional lives and help support their families, but not forgo the critical work they do at home raising their children.[33]

The trouble is that most educated middle- and upper-class women discover the strong desire to care for their own children well after they have already invested much time and money in their education and professional development. They have devoted little thought along the way to how their work might interfere with raising their children well. Pro-choice feminism so shapes the corridors of academia that ambitious women (and men too) are rarely challenged to consider how their future children may affect their plans for their professional life. Indeed, the reality that a good portion of life is spent raising children is largely ignored until much later.

Such a career-focused, pro-choice feminism has driven unprecedented numbers of mothers with small children into the workforce full-time over the last few decades. Some social scientists have argued that such an exodus is largely to blame for the difficulty most *single* mothers now have at making ends meet.[34] After all, the financial power of the two-income family has driven up the price of all of life's necessities, leaving single-income families struggling to compete. While two-parent families with a single income sacrifice to allow one parent to remain at home (at least part-time) with young children, single mothers—responsible for both bread winning and child rearing—face almost insurmountable financial obstacles.

And what does pro-choice feminism proffer as a solution to this problem it helped to create?[35] Ready access to government-funded abortion. Further, they do not limit themselves to representing the poor women of the United States. They believe that all of the world's poverty-stricken women deserve ready access to free abortions—to eliminate those children conceived by non-Western women, most of whom are much more able to recognize children as a great joy. Camille Paglia, libertarian, atheist, and staunch pro-choice feminist, believes pro-life feminism may actually be the force that "saves feminism" from its current elitism: "There is plenty of room in modern thought for a pro-life feminism—one in fact that would have far more appeal to third-world cultures where motherhood is still honored and where the Western model of the hard-driving, self-absorbed career woman is less admired."[36]

Some who hold the pro-choice position do so because they think abortion provides a means to manage the burden the poor place on the rest of society. Justice Harry Blackmun, author of the Supreme Court's opinion in *Roe*, epitomized this tragic view in *Beal v. Doe*. In this 1977 case, he dissented from the court's refusal to require taxpayers to fund abortions. Blackmun wrote that the cost of elective abortion "is far less than the cost of maternity care and delivery, and holds no comparison whatsoever with the welfare costs that will burden the state for the new indigents and their support in the long, long years ahead...."[37] And so, without taxpayer funding of abortion for the poor, "the cancer of poverty will continue to grow."[38]

Contrary to the assertions of international pro-choice groups over the past few decades, population growth does not cause underdevelopment. Nor do the Western rich have the right to force contraception and abortion on families in developing countries.[39] As Pope Benedict XVI wrote in December 2008, "[W]hole peoples have escaped from poverty despite experiencing substantial demographic growth. This goes to show that resources to solve the problem of poverty do exist, even in the face of an increasing population ... population is proving to be an asset, not a factor that contributes to poverty."[40] Indeed, Europe's stark population decline, caused by an attitude that views children as burdensome, may actually sow the seeds of its economic downfall.[41]

Impact of Abortion on Women's Health

Pro-choice advocates consistently claim that abortion rights are necessary to safeguard women's health. They even claim that abortion is safer than childbirth. Yet researchers have found several harmful effects associated with induced abortion, effects that threaten the health and lives of both women and their future offspring.[42]

A 2003 landmark article in *Obstetrical & Gynecological Survey* compiled the results of several studies on abortion. These show that induced abortion increases the risk of placenta previa in later pregnancies by 50 percent,[43] and doubles the risk of preterm birth.[44]

Placenta previa occurs when the placenta implants at the bottom of the uterus and covers the cervix, putting the lives of both mother and child at risk. Pregnancies complicated by placenta previa have a higher risk of life-threatening postpartum hemorrhaging and hysterectomy (for the mother), and preterm birth, low birth weight, and perinatal death (for the child).[45]

Preterm births, in which a baby is born before thirty-seven weeks of pregnancy, accounted for 12.1 percent of births in the U.S. in 2002,[46] up from 8.9 percent in 1980. This increase occurred despite substantial attempts to lower the rate over the intervening two decades.[47] As of November 2007, fifty-nine studies from the 1960s onward showed a statistically significant increase in preterm birth after induced abortion.[48] Moreover, the risk of subsequent preterm birth increases with each abortion.[49] A 2007 article in the *Journal of Reproductive Medicine* attributed 31.5 percent of early preterm deliveries to induced abortion.[50]

Preterm birth is associated with low or very low birth weight babies. Very low birth weight babies (those born at twenty to twenty-seven weeks) have a thirty-eight times greater risk of cerebral palsy,[51] not to mention twenty-eight times greater medical costs,[52] than term babies. Moreover, many of these preemies simply do not survive.

When a woman delays her first full-term pregnancy through abortion, she also increases her risk of developing breast cancer. This is because a first full-term pregnancy, especially before the age of thirty-two, acts as a protective mechanism against breast cancer.[53] Thus, research shows that an eighteen-year-old who aborts her pregnancy almost doubles her lifetime risk of breast cancer,[54] and that risk grows incalculably high if she also has a family history of breast cancer.[55] Epidemiological studies and breast physiology have also shown that, in addition to the role it plays in delaying a woman's first full-term pregnancy, abortion itself can cause breast cancer.[56]

Studies show that women who have abortions also suffer an increased risk of anxiety, depression, substance abuse, and suicide. The number of studies revealing such a link grows annually, but here is a sampling: women who aborted their unintended pregnancies were 30 percent more likely to subsequently report all the symptoms of generalized anxiety disorder compared with women who had carried their unintended pregnancies to term.[57] Forty-two percent of women who had abortions experienced major depression—which was twice as high as women who had never been pregnant and 35 percent higher than women who had carried their pregnancies to term.[58] Women who aborted showed five times the rate of alcohol and drug abuse compared with those who carried their pregnancies to term.[59] Finally, the risk of death from suicide is two to six times higher for women who have had abortions when compared with their counterparts who went to term.[60]

Short-term complications such as hemorrhaging, uterine perforation, and infection injure thousands of women each year.[61] Though abortion-related maternal deaths are consistently underreported,[62] the Centers for Disease Control and Prevention approximates that one woman in 100,000 dies from complications associated with first trimester abortions.[63] Those performed at more than sixteen weeks' gestation have fifteen times the risk of maternal mortality as those performed during the first trimester. Black women and other minorities, who have a disproportionate number of abortions when compared to white women, also have two and a half times the chance of dying as white women.[64] Further, women are ten times more likely to die from RU-486 abortions than surgical abortions in early pregnancy.[65]

Abortion is not safer than childbirth, even though pro-choice advocates continually draw such an unwarranted conclusion from mortality statistics.[66] To start, abortion mortality statistics are notoriously unreliable, because abortion-related deaths are often mistakenly reported or counted as maternal deaths. Maternal deaths are further inflated relative to abortion-related deaths because of the conceptually different counting methods used by the CDC.[ii] Finally, abortion mortality rates reflect only those deaths that occur as a direct result of the procedure itself, failing to account for the long-term risks associated with abortion.[67]

⟶⬥⟵

One of the common arguments used in the run-up to *Roe v. Wade* was the claim that legal abortion would be safer than the "back alley" abortions that, advocates alleged, killed 5,000 to 10,000 women each year. As

---

ii. The CDC defines maternal mortality by dividing maternal deaths by *live births* rather than all *pregnancies* (thus, the equation would look like this: maternal deaths / live births). Deaths from ectopic pregnancy (the leading cause of maternal death in the first trimester) thus increase the numerator in the equation (maternal deaths) but not the denominator (live births), since ectopic pregnancies never produce a live birth. This method thus inflates the percentage of maternal deaths relative to live births. Abortion-related deaths, by contrast, are taken as a percentage of all abortions. As the director of the CDC wrote in 2004, "the measures used for abortion [related-death and maternal mortality] are conceptually different." See amicus brief of the American Center for Law and Justice in support of petitioner, *Gonzales v. Planned Parenthood* (no. 05-1382).

many now know, one of the two men leading the charge, Bernard Nathanson, obstetrician and gynecologist and co-founder of NARAL, eventually recanted this claim. He admitted that he and other pro-choice activists simply fabricated the figure to further the abortion rights cause.[68]

This is not to say that illegal abortions were safe. Though the actual data is nowhere close to the 10,000 claimed, thirty-nine women did die from illegal abortion in 1972, the year prior to *Roe*.[69] However, an additional twenty-four women died that year from legal abortion in states that had weakened their laws in the years before *Roe* came down.[70] As the medical data above reveal, legalizing abortion has not made the procedure much safer. Women still suffer serious short- and long-term complications. Even Warren Hern, noted abortionist and author of *Abortion Practice*, a leading medical textbook writes, "[T]here are few surgical procedures given so little attention and so underrated in its potential hazard as abortion."[71]

One might assume a woman's doctor would protect her from such hazards. The court in *Roe*, after all, understood the relationship between a woman and her doctor to be paramount. Yet less than 2 percent of women having abortions do so for health reasons.[72] Studies have shown that two-thirds of obstetricians and gynecologists, especially female doctors and those younger than forty, refuse to do abortions at all.[73] The vast majority of women who have abortions, then, are not contemplating a medical decision under the care and counsel of their personal physician. Most women receive little to no pre-op counseling about the nature, medical risks, and alternatives to the procedure.[74] They meet the abortion provider just minutes before he performs the abortion and are unlikely ever to see him again.

Who Really Benefits from Abortion?

Nobel Prize-winning economist George Akerlof argued in 1996 that the availability of abortion (and contraception) in the 1970s and beyond made men, not women, the real victors in the sexual market.[75] By reducing the threat of pregnancy to women, abortion (and contraception) empowered men to initiate nonmarital sex with women more readily. In turn, women lost much of the justification to wait until marriage, or at least to delay sex until their men had become mature enough to marry. Men could indulge in sex without having to provide women the connection or security they wanted, and without having to become the responsible men potential fatherhood required. As the pro-choice bioethicist Daniel Callahan once put it, "If legal abortion has given women more choice, it has . . . given men more choice as well. They now have a potent new weapon in the old business of manipulating and abandoning women."[76]

Most pro-choice feminists would deny that casual sex affects the relations between the sexes, but a few do understand how easy access to abortion impacts relationships. Radical feminist Catherine MacKinnon presciently wrote in 1987:

> [U]nder conditions of gender inequality [still present today], sexual liberation . . . does not liberate women; it frees male sexual aggression. The availability of abortion removes the one remaining legitimized reason that women have had for refusing sex besides the headache.... The Playboy Foundation has supported abortion rights from day one . . .[77]

Though some men lament the abortions of their wives or girlfriends (husbands and boyfriends, after all, have no legal rights in the abortion decision),[78] many others serve as the catalysts behind such choices. Nearly 40 percent of women who'd had abortions reported that boyfriends or husbands had pressured them into the abortion. Sixty-four percent of all post-abortive women indicated that *someone* had pressured them.[79] Access to abortion (and contraception) has freed men to expect (or demand) sex, promising women little in return, and to expect (or demand) abortion, should pregnancy unintentionally occur.

With the advent of easy access to the abortion license, women have relinquished much of the sexual power they once had over the pursuing male, the power to say no and wait until he actually committed. For many women, then, the pro-abortion euphemism, "reproductive freedom," means that women continue to negotiate all that comes with reproduction, while men enjoy the freedom of sex without consequences.[80] It's no wonder that polls show that men favor abortion rights more ardently than women do, and women are pro-life in greater numbers.[81]

A Catholic, Pro-Woman Response to the Tough Cases

Rape

Rape is undoubtedly the most grievous crime a man can commit against a woman. Owing to its heinous cruelty, many pro-life lawmakers make exceptions to their antiabortion stance in the cases of rape and incest. Since less than 1 percent of abortions are performed on women who have been raped, abortion access in the case of rape has become, *politically speaking*, a point of potential compromise.[82]

However, *as a matter of principle*, abortion, even in the case of rape, is terribly tragic and objectively wrong. Aborting an unborn child conceived through rape makes the child, rather than the rapist, ultimately responsible for the grievous violence perpetrated on the woman. Further, the often grisly procedure of abortion has been experienced by many rape victims as a second violent act perpetrated on them. Some rape victims report reliving its trauma during the abortion.[83]

Though it may be easy to sympathize with victims of rape who in their agony seek out abortion in an attempt to destroy the physical result of the tragic event, one study found that the majority of rape victims who become pregnant do not in fact choose abortion.[84] Perhaps it is because they realize that they can find greater healing and interior freedom by choosing a path diametrically opposed to the hatred and suffering they have endured.[85] By courageously embracing their unborn children through generous, self-sacrificing love, they permit a greater good to come out of great evil.

The Life of the Mother

Though a woman's life is rarely threatened during pregnancy due to advances in modern medicine, there are cases when her life is endangered. Many misunderstand Catholic teaching on this point. While a woman who sacrifices her life for that of her child undoubtedly practices an act of heroic virtue, she is not morally required to do so. The Catholic Church teaches that it is permissible for medical personnel who have been unsuccessful in their efforts to save *both* mother and child to prioritize the mother's life even if, in so doing, her unborn child does not survive.[86] Such a life-saving act however, differs from the illicit act of performing an abortion on a woman whose life *may be* threatened by continued pregnancy.

Fetal Abnormalities

Approximately 80 percent of parents abort their unborn children when prenatal screening reveals *the probability* of some sort of fetal abnormality.[87] The termination of potentially "abnormal" children ought to give all people great pause, but especially feminist- and liberal-minded people. We are a people who claim to value difference, and who make myriad efforts to assist those with disabilities. Yet many in our day are aghast when they hear of a mother who knowingly brings to term a child with genetic abnormalities.[88]

Women carrying a child expected to die in utero or soon after birth are often encouraged to abort in order to "get it over with." Yet mothers and fathers who allow the process of sickness and death to run its natural course avoid culpability in their sick child's death. Knowing that they did not cause their child's death will make it easier for them to grieve the loss of their unborn or infant child.[89] As in the case of euthanasia of the elderly, caregivers deprive themselves of the opportunity to grow in love and compassion when they accelerate the dying process of a loved one. They also deny the inherent dignity and value of their "imperfect" child (or ailing parent). Thus they would perpetuate the current cultural myth that a person's worth is found not in her status as a human being but in her ability to produce and consume.

Mothers and fathers whose unborn child will likely survive her disabilities are called to a grand, though exceptionally difficult, task of heroic love. They may discern that, even with the grace of God, they have neither the emotional nor financial resources to care for a disabled child. In such a case, scores of loving adoptive parents wait for the opportunity to nurture such children, if only birth parents would give them that chance.[90]

Ironically, aborting children with genetic abnormalities fails to help mothers and fathers to "get it over with." Research indicates that the psychological stress that genetic abortion causes both mothers and fathers is usually more severe than abortion in the event of an unwanted pregnancy.[91] The pressure to produce a perfect child, acceptable to many doctors, insurers, and society at large, is just too difficult to bear.

Catholic Feminism: Pro-Woman, Pro-Life

Over the last several decades the abortion debate has raged largely as
a rhetorical battle over rights: the reproductive rights of the woman versus the human rights of the unborn child. As the most ardent defender of
human rights in the world, the Catholic Church has especially emphasized the great injustice the judicially created right to abortion has
wrought on the human rights of the unborn.

But from the Catholic perspective, the debate over abortion is not, in
a philosophically rigorous sense, a contest between the rights of an
unborn child and the rights of a woman. Neither set of rights exists in
isolation from one another or independent of the duties that ground
them.[iii] A mother not only lacks the right to take her child's life, but as his
caretaker, she has a sacred duty to secure, protect, and nurture it. The
Catholic Church is so passionately pro-life not because she is anti-woman,
but because she understands the depth of the bond between mother and
child, a depth the woman who aborts may not even understand herself.[92]

---

iii. While the Catholic Church affirms the human person's right to life as fundamental
to all other human rights, including a women's right to self-determination, the Church has
traditionally understood all such rights as philosophically grounded in prior duties. That
is, government does not endow human beings with human rights (though civil rights, such
as the right to vote, are of government creation). Human rights, such as the right to life,
as well as the right to be free to labor, to worship, to associate (to marry and have children),
are all rights that exist prior to government. They are rights that governments, in both the
American and Catholic understandings, are created to secure.

The Church has a modern tendency to refer to human rights without mention of prior
duties. However, philosophically, the Church (but not necessarily the American founding)
understands such pre-political rights exist *because* human beings have prior duties, first to
their Creator, and then to other human beings. I have the right to worship because I have
a duty to do so. I have the right to labor because I have the duty to do so. I have the right
to life, because I have the duty to care for the life that God gave me.

Because God created human beings to live in society, with the family as its fundamental
unit, my duties to my Creator extend beyond care for myself. After myself, my greatest
duty is to my immediate family (my spouse and children, should I have them). Although
I have duties to all human beings (the Catholic principle of solidarity), my duties lessen as
they flow outward (the Catholic principle of subsidiarity). My rights are not only limited
by the rights of others (as Enlightenment thinkers would have it); my rights are also limited by my own duties to God and, secondarily, to others. See generally *Human Rights,
Virtue, and the Common Good: Ernest L. Fortin Collected Essays, Volume 3*, ed. J. Brian Benestad
(Lanham, MD: Roman & Littlefield, 1996), 191–212; see also, Mary Ann Glendon, *Rights
Talk* (New York: Free Press, 1991).

In every abortion, the Church mourns not only the life of the child and the well-being of the mother, but the sacred bond broken by a tragic act of betrayal.[93]

The overt claim in favor of abortion is that a woman has a right to self-determination, to do "what I want with my body." Apart from the medical fact that the pregnant woman carries another body in her very body, consider the underlying philosophical claim in abortion. Whether it is unacknowledged or simply not understood, the claim is that a woman has the right to be free from the duties that come with her unborn child's dependence upon her. But in denying her responsibility to her child, she begins to eat away at that which, in the Catholic view, makes us most human: the solidarity we have with other human beings. This solidarity springs, in part, from our obligations to one another. In imagining herself autonomous, free from the bonds that bind human beings to one another, that bind us especially to those put in our care, the mother who aborts acts to eviscerate her bond to the human community. The right to abortion manifests a cultural mindset that Pope John Paul II said "exalts the isolated individual in an absolute way and gives no place to solidarity, to openness to others and service of them."[94] It's no wonder that the act of abortion causes such psychic suffering for so many women.[95]

In the Catholic understanding, failure to perform a duty to God and other human beings harms not only the person to whom we owe such responsibility. When we neglect or thwart our duties to God and others, we harm ourselves as well. When a thief steals, for instance, not only the property owner is hurt. The soul of the thief suffers as well, perhaps unknown to him for a time, for he has denied the responsibility he has to respect the property of another human being, his brother or sister. He has broken the bonds he has to the human community, and in so doing has harmed himself and his own integrity. This, of course, is why Christ instituted the sacrament of Reconciliation, so that apart from the amends the contrite thief makes to the property owner, he also might heal his breach with God and the human family.

The inverse is true as well. When a benefactor assists the poor materially or spiritually, that benefactor is not only benefiting the person she has helped. Her charity lifts her up as well. By her act of kindness, her heart is transformed and made more Christ-like, indeed more inclined to act generously again. Even the best government program fails to substitute for individual human acts of love. Acts of personal generosity, of charity, then, are needed not only for the physical, emotional, and spiritual well-being of the poor. Acts of charity may be required even more for the souls of the rich.

Motherhood is perhaps the most charitable act in the world, and when unexpected, even unwanted, the opportunity for virtue grows. Motherhood, comparable only perhaps to the heroism of a soldier who makes the ultimate sacrifice, transforms because of the total sacrifice of body, mind, and heart it requires. It is a great call to love in spite of ourselves, our plans, and our own ideas of self-fulfillment. It embodies the total gift of self for which the human heart was made.

A woman becomes a mother not when she labors to bring her child out into the world, but also when God has labored to create another eternal soul in her very womb. The sacred duty of a mother to care for her child exists as soon as the child does. The task is given first to mothers, and then to fathers, who share in it equally, if only as chivalrous observers for the first nine months. The task is also given to those mothers (and fathers) who, in their own discerning charity and outright heroism, recognize that an adoptive family would better care for their child after his birth.

The responsibility to nurture and protect another human person, whether expected or not, has the power to transform us. It can pull us away from our ingrained way of thinking and call us to something more human in life. It makes us dig deeper. Such transforming potential is true of every difficult Church teaching, not just the Church's teaching on abortion. Indeed, it seems as though in the Church, God has given us a great coach whose dictates we may balk at initially, but whom we eventually recognize as a wise sage once we shore up the grit to follow her. But following her has become even more difficult in an age when we are expected to rely on our own strength alone, on our own determination to succeed. Each of the Church's teachings, difficult as it can be, requires us to go to God for the strength and the will to accomplish the plans he has set before us.

Selflessly embracing our child, who perhaps was unwanted, who is yet unknown to us, is always possible with God's grace. Whatever our situation, when we ask for grace and strength from God, we will receive it. And we can also allow ourselves to be comforted and helped by God's people. Those who staff crisis pregnancy centers and maternity homes across our nation long to give solace and guidance to women courageous enough to seek it. Indeed, solidarity among persons grows when we acknowledge our need for help, when we reject the mistaken notion that only the weak depend on others. It is a pity that many Americans have come to believe that leaving a despairing pregnant woman alone, with her legal autonomy, is somehow good for her—and even essential to her equality and freedom.[96] Authentic pro-woman solutions would assist such women to embrace the truth of their interdependence, and enable them to recognize that just as their child depends on them, so too all of us depend on one another.

When an unexpected pregnancy befalls a woman, with the myriad of complications it injects into her life, the impulse to abort, amidst the anxiety, the external pressures, the seemingly dark future, is understand-able. But when she thoughtfully and prayerfully reflects upon the human life growing within her, for whom she has been asked to care, she need only pause briefly to recognize that in such responsibility she has also been given much trust, indeed, much authority. While women are right to seek the opportunity to serve that professional engagement provides, women who are called to motherhood cannot deny the great influence they can have through nurturing and raising their children well. To do so would be to deny that which women (and men) have known throughout time—whether or not societal forces have recognized such unpaid labor as having the value it deserves.[97]

Abortion is a great challenge for the women of the world. Will we abandon ourselves to a culture that seeks to eradicate all that is feminine, the vulnerability of pregnancy that demands care and concern for others, the dependence of the unborn that inspires awe and sacrifice, the call to love most especially the weak, the needy, the oppressed? Or will we reject the falsehood with which our culture entices us, that freedom requires us to flee from those who depend on us, and embrace instead the truth that brings authentic joy: we truly find ourselves when we give of ourselves to others in love.

3

The Fullness of Sexuality:
Church Teaching on Premarital Sex

CASSANDRA HOUGH

When I tell people that my time as an undergraduate at Princeton University made me more traditional in matters of sexual ethics and more devout in my Catholic faith, they often look at me in utter bewilderment. Their confusion is understandable given the impression most people have of the college experience. The "wild" kids in high school get even wilder with their increased freedom, and even the "good" kids are expected to experiment at least a little with drinking and sex. Religious beliefs are tolerated outside the classroom as part of cultural diversity. But inside the classroom, religions are often picked apart as historical phenomena that are intriguing to study but questionable to believe. With all of our advances in science and women's rights, it is considered irrational to believe religious teachings, which are thought only to straitjacket human advancement and equality. If students regularly attend religious services, it is assumed to be more so out of habit than authentic devotion. To follow religious moral teachings, especially Catholic moral teachings, would be ludicrous. In such an environment, it is no wonder my experience seems like an anomaly.

That said, university life does challenge young men and women in their beliefs and assumptions about what is true and what is good. As an undergraduate, I was challenged to think critically about how my faith informed by behavior and my understanding of the world around me. I was either to take personal ownership of my faith, or I was to leave it. Calling myself "Catholic," while picking only those parts of Catholicism I happened to like personally, was not an option.

Given the environment described above, it was relatively easy to find arguments for why a young woman like me should reject the Catholic faith. Surprisingly, I also found a wealth of arguments (more convincing ones, to my judgment) that led me not only to take ownership of my faith, but also to embrace being a Catholic woman. Ironically, perhaps, it was the Catholic view of human love that most attracted me to the truth of the faith. Contrary to the prevailing understanding, Church teachings on sex, love, and intimacy reveal a striking understanding of the meaning and power of sex, and of women's sexuality in particular.

The Church on Sex

Of all its moral teachings, the Catholic Church is perhaps most clear, and yet most misunderstood, in its teachings about sex. Simply put, the Church teaches that marriage between one man and one woman is the only moral context for sexual intimacy (especially sexual intercourse). This is because in marriage, and only in marriage, a man and woman freely and willingly commit their entire lives to one another in mutual love and fidelity. For the Catholic, this lifelong union takes on a sacramental character: marriage is understood to signify the self-giving union between Christ and his Church.[1] Sexual intercourse then becomes the natural and most fitting physical expression of this unique, marital relationship. Already having vowed to share their lives together, a husband and wife consummate that vow by uniting as one flesh. The intimate nature of their physical union is appropriate to the intimate nature of their marital union. The Church esteems sex as beautiful and significant because of its role in consummating, or completing, the marital vows of husband and wife.

What is more, the sexual union of husband and wife shares in the creative power of God by bearing forth new human life. Non-contracepted sex between a husband and wife is good regardless of whether or not it conceives new life, because the act completes and reconfirms their marital promises. However, the Church holds that it is particularly beautiful when their physical union takes on substantial form in a third person, their child. For the Church, then, sex has both a unitive and a procreative purpose. Marriage serves to protect the deep emotional bond that exists between a sexually intimate man and woman. Further, the stability of a lifelong union provides the best context in which to raise children who may be borne of such intimacy. Thus, marriage is the only suitable, nurturing, and stable environment in which to both enjoy sexual intimacy and bring new life into the world.

In regard to human sexuality, the *Catechism of the Catholic Church* states that "[a]ll the baptized are called to chastity,"[2] and that they are to practice chastity in a way suited to their state in life.[3] For the married, this means fidelity (in mind and body) to one's spouse. For the unmarried, it means "continence"—sexual abstinence. The *Catechism* lists offenses against chastity as lust, masturbation, fornication, pornography, prostitution, and rape. All of these offenses reduce and cheapen sex by making sexual pleasure the principal goal, to the exclusion of the greater unitive and procreative purposes of sex. These behaviors contradict the intimate, sacred, and truly personal nature of sex.

Sexual Liberation: Is It Really Pro-Woman?

Over the past few decades, the sexual revolution and its advocates have challenged this traditional understanding of human love and sexuality. Feminists, in particular, have been some of the staunchest supporters of sexual liberationist ideals. Indeed, secular and Catholic feminists alike have viewed the Catholic Church's teachings on sexuality as a means to oppress women and subject them to the Church's patriarchal structure.

In her book *Eunuchs for the Kingdom of Heaven*, onetime Catholic theologian Uta Ranke-Heinemann argues powerfully that the Catholic Church has been a source of women's oppression throughout history. In the chapter "Celibates' Fear of Women," she esteems Christ as being a "friend of women, the first and practically the last friend women had in the Church."[4] Though Jesus' disciples have followed him in many ways, according to Ranke-Heinemann, they "have not followed him on this point."[5] She goes on to cite a letter attributed to Pope Clement I (A.D. 96) that was very important in clerical education. The letter instructs the men to "have nothing to do with [women]." The author concludes that Christ's openness to and respect for women was replaced by "a peculiar mixture of repressed fear, mistrust, and arrogance."[6] Throughout their formation, Ranke-Heinemann argues, priests are taught to ignore women's existence.

Ranke-Heinemann finds further evidence for her arguments in the writings and lives of the Church Fathers. John Chrysostom, in his *On the Priesthood*, describes women as the "first and foremost" influence "that weaken[s] the conscientiousness of the soul."[7] Augustine, she points out, never spoke alone with a woman, not even his own sister or nieces.[8] This "psychically disturbed" behavior, as she calls it, was later echoed in the Synod of Elvira, the fifth Synod of Orleans, and the Synod of Tours (to name a few). These synods taught that priests should not allow women, even close relatives, to stay in their houses. Ranke-Heinemann, like many other women today, takes great offense at these teachings. "To this day," she writes, "the Church's celibates believe that danger has a female face."[9]

Clerical fear of women would perhaps not be so bad for these feminist authors were it not accompanied by the active suppression of women. Dissident Catholic theologian Rosemary Radford Ruether writes in her book *Sexism and God-Talk*, "Women's capacities for spiritual equality are [to be] postponed until they reach heaven and are to be earned only by the strictest subjugation to male power in Church and society."[10]

How does she suggest women are subjugated to men? By their reproductive capacities. Ruether writes:

> Woman's body—her reproductive processes—becomes owned by men, defined from a male point of view. Women are seen as reproducing children and producing cooked food and clothes for men. Men regard this work as beneath them and they see themselves as dominating and controlling it from above. Woman then becomes both the mediator and the symbol of the domination of "lower" material processes by "higher" cultural (male) control.[11]

She finds further support for this in the writings of Thomas Aquinas, who, she asserts, concludes that while women are defective and misbegotten in their individual nature, they contribute to the overall perfection of nature through their role in procreation. She summarizes him: "It is for this and this alone that a separate female member of the human species has been created by God."[12]

Radical Catholic feminist Mary Daly joins these women in critiquing the Catholic Church with her book *The Church and the Second Sex*. She begins the first chapter by stating that those who see the Catholic Church as the enemy to securing equality between the sexes are in large part justified. She continues:

> ... the Catholic Church appears to many as the last stronghold of anachronism and prejudice, refusing to adapt its structures to the condition of modern women, still preaching to them the passive virtues of obedience, submission and meekness, while seeming to refuse or ignore the profound aspirations of half the human race to liberty and full personhood.[13]

Daly deplores the Catholic Church for its patriarchal structure and double standard in matters of sexuality. Like many of her feminist peers, Daly takes issue with the Church's stricter norms in regard to female sexual behavior. She points out that in countries where Catholicism is the privileged religion, infidelity is punished more severely for women. Furthermore, Catholicism's rejection of birth control is direct proof of the Church's denigrating view of women's sexuality. Women are reduced "to the condition of biological beast," enslaved in the patriarchal system to reproduce and nothing more.[14]

The Church's teachings on marriage and chastity are, for these feminists, the means by which the men of the Church keep women in their place. A woman's chastity is valued more than a man's because it is her chastity that binds her to him. She is taught that she needs the protection of a man, be it her father while she is young, or her husband later in life. In order to be prized by these men, she must keep her purity intact. She is a disgrace and unworthy of male attention if she offends chastity through sexual sin. Women learn immediately to value premarital abstinence and fidelity within marriage. Once married, they learn that to be a good Christian woman is to obey their husbands.

Secular feminism argues that both Holy Scripture and the holy men of the Church, from John Chrysostom and Augustine to the clergy who honor their writings today, have relegated women to a secondary, instrumental role in faith and in society. Women suffer because of the perceived dangerous and sinful quality of their sexuality, and they suffer because of the Church's patriarchal system.

Simone de Beauvoir makes such an argument in her revolutionary book *The Second Sex*:

> Patriarchal civilization dedicated woman to chastity; it recognized more or less openly the right of the male to sexual freedom, while woman was restricted to marriage. The sexual act, if not sanctified by the code, by a sacrament, is for her a fault, a fall, a defeat, a weakness; she should defend her virtue, her honor; if she "yields," if she "falls," she is scorned; whereas any blame visited upon her conqueror is mixed with admiration.[15]

The remedy for this double standard on matters of sexual behavior is, first, for women to reject the stereotypical feminine virtues of modesty, docility, and chastity. In their place, femininity is redefined to look much like masculinity: if men are free to act upon their sexual desires, women's liberation requires that women be allowed to do the same. De Beauvoir suggests as much in her concluding chapter, "Toward Liberation: The Independent Woman":

> A woman who expends her energy, who has responsibilities, who knows how harsh is the struggle against the world's opposition, needs—like the male—not only to satisfy her physical desires but also to enjoy the relaxation and diversion provided by agreeable sexual adventures.[16]

When sex has these types of benefits, why hold back? The secular feminist message says there is no need to. For a woman to hold back and deny her desires is to "repress" her sexuality. If she experiences any guilt or hesitation over her sexual choices and behaviors, it is only because she still lives in a patriarchic society where gender stereotypes continue to prevent women from exercising and pursuing their inner desires.

While almost half a century has passed since these ideas about sex and femininity first entered cultural consciousness, they remain a powerful force behind the sexual conduct and norms of today. Young women are told to separate their heart from their body. Don't get emotionally involved; don't harbor any hope for the future. To become attached to or dependent upon a man is a sign of weakness. Rather, women should engage in sex for the "sheer pleasure of it." It doesn't matter who the man is or whether both man and woman care for each other—so long as there is mutual consent, women should just relax and enjoy themselves.[17] Sentiments such as these fuel women's participation in the "hookup" culture, where "anything goes" in one's sexual choices. Such a culture treats sex and relationships casually, disconnected from love and commitment.

Are these secular (and dissident Catholic) feminists correct?[18] Are traditional teachings on sex just another way to exert power over women and make them ashamed of their sexuality and their bodies? Are the Catholic Church's teachings on chastity merely a means to keep women in their "natural" place as subordinate wife and mother? Or, do Catholicism's teachings actually promote women's dignity and freedom and allow women to get the most out of sex?

Reevaluating a Pro-Woman Sexuality

The Physical Pitfalls of Premarital Sex

To answer these questions, let's look at how the sexual permissiveness advocated by secular feminism is affecting women today. Women are told that because of widespread contraception and other means of "safe sex," they can enjoy sex without suffering negative consequences. One campus psychiatrist would beg to differ. With more than a decade of clinical experience as a campus psychiatrist at the University of California at Los Angeles, Miriam Grossman is not a stranger to the sexual choices and behaviors of college women. In her book *Unprotected: A Campus Psychiatrist Reveals How Political Correctness in Her Field Endangers Every Student*, Grossman writes of the many physical, psychological, and emotional risks associated with the "anything goes" mentality toward sex and relationships.

In her chapter "Damage Control," Grossman laments the fact that most women are unaware they have a greater risk than men for sexually transmitted infections (STIs).[19] That women are more susceptible to STIs is due to several factors. One of them, Grossman points out, is an area on the cervix called the "transformation zone." The cells in this area are more vulnerable to bacteria and viruses. With age, the transformation zone shrinks. The years during which many young women become sexually active are those very years in which they are more vulnerable to infections by virtue of their anatomy.[20]

A National Institutes of Health (NIH) publication, "Topical Microbicides: Preventing Sexually Transmitted Diseases," states other reasons
why "women are more susceptible than men to infection by HIV and
other STD-causing microbes."[21] It explains that a woman's reproductive
tract provides more surface area for infectious viruses or bacteria than a
man's reproductive tract. Additionally, intercourse can result in micro-
scopic tears in a woman's vagina that decrease her defense against infection.[22] Women are also at greater risk for delaying treatment because in
the majority of cases STIs do not cause symptoms, particularly in women.
When and if symptoms develop, they are often minor and may be confused with symptoms of other nonsexually transmitted conditions.
Therefore, many women are not diagnosed until serious problems have
developed, such as pelvic inflammatory disease (PID), which can cause
ectopic pregnancy and infertility.[23]

Fetuses and newborns can also suffer the consequences of their
mothers' STIs. The NIH reports that as many as one-quarter to one-half
of women infected with syphilis will see the death of their fetus. An
additional one-quarter to one-half of these women will give birth to
infants who are either premature or who have a low birth weight. The
report continues, "Of these births, between 40 to 70 percent of the
women will pass the infection to the infant, putting the infant at increased
risk for permanent disabilities, such as deafness."[24]

The prospect of facing infertility, ectopic pregnancy, and infection of
unborn or premature children would be quite overwhelming for most
women—if they were ever informed of these risks. Many would wonder
how they could have contracted the infection when they were sure to
"protect" themselves with a condom. Current sexual health messages
certainly laud the use of condoms as safeguards against STIs. However, a
2000 NIH report on condom effectiveness for preventing sexually transmitted diseases (STDs) was hesitant to conclude as much. The panel of
twenty-eight experts who prepared the report found the published literature to be inadequate to definitively conclude that condom use is effective
in preventing the transmission of most STDs. The panel stressed that the
absence of adequate scientific evidence "should not be interpreted as
proof of the adequacy or inadequacy of the condom to reduce the risk of
STDs other than HIV transmission in men and women and gonorrhea in
men."[25] In a study conducted in 2004 intended to supplement the 2000

NIH report, researchers did find prospective studies indicating statistically significant protection against other STDs (i.e., gonorrhea, chlamydia, herpes type 2, and syphilis), but again warned that condoms only partially protect against even those diseases.[26]

The fact is that men and women use condoms with the understanding that they are protecting themselves from infection. While consistent and correct condom use may reduce the risk of contracting STIs transmitted by genital secretions (such as gonorrhea and chlamydia), condoms are far less effective against STIs not transmitted in this manner. Take, for example, the most common sexually transmitted infection among sexually active young people, human papillomavirus (HPV).[27] HPV can be transmitted simply by skin-to-skin contact of infected areas, such as the inner thighs. Both the 2000 NIH report and the 2004 study found that no published study has concluded that condoms protect against contracting HPV.[28]

This is the difficult reality that a young woman named "Stacey" faced when she learned she had contracted HPV.[29] Grossman writes that Stacey had only been sexually active with four people, three of them in the year before her diagnosis. Although she did not always ask her partners about STIs, she did use condoms every time. According to Grossman, she was a "bright, self-disciplined young woman," who avoided cigarettes, pot, alcohol, and meat, and who rose before dawn each morning to swim thirty laps.[30] Grossman writes: "Stacey's life was about self-restraint, self-control, and self-sacrifice in the name of a healthy body. Except when it came to her sexuality."[31] Stacey thought she was acting responsibly by practicing "safer sex." She, like many other women today, took precautions by limiting her sex partners, using condoms, and getting tested. However, when we consider the *lack* of protection condoms offer in the case of HPV, combined with the prevalence of infections among sexually active men and women, these precautions do not amount to much. Even if Stacey had limited herself to one sexual partner (modest, according to today's standards), she would still be at risk. The Centers for Disease Control and Prevention (CDC) reports that one in four Americans has an STD, with almost half of all STD cases occurring among young people fifteen to twenty-four years old.[32] Additionally, at least one-half of sexually active men and women will contract a genital HPV infection at some point in their lives.[33]

For Stacey, the diagnosis brought many scary questions. In addition to wondering whether to tell her parents and her previous partners, Stacey also faced the prospect of having one of the dangerous, high-risk strands of the virus. According to the CDC, high-risk strands are those that can lead to cancer, especially cervical cancer in women. But cervical cancer does not present symptoms until it is well advanced. Even the woman who dutifully has her annual Pap test may go months without knowing she has the disease, thereby delaying treatment and ignorantly passing it on to others.

Low-risk strands of HPV are not cancer-causing but may result in genital warts that are often painful to remove.[34] While genital warts are low-risk for a woman, they may have a more devastating effect should she become pregnant. The National Institute of Allergy and Infectious Diseases (NIAID) warns that infants born to women with genital warts may develop warts in their throats (respiratory papillomatosis). While the NIAID says this condition is rare, it concedes that "it is a potentially life-threatening condition for the child, requiring frequent laser surgery to prevent blocking of the breathing passages."[35]

It is important to acknowledge that some sources indicate that the body's immune system will naturally clear an HPV infection within two years. This is true for a majority of cases. However, there are forty types of HPV that can infect the genital area. Clearing one type of HPV does not make someone immune from contracting another type.[36] Therefore, it would be naïve to think HPV is not a serious health threat.

Meg Meeker, pediatrician and author of *Epidemic: How Teen Sex is Killing Our Kids*, relates two similar cases of the consequences of STIs in her second book, *Strong Fathers, Strong Daughters: 10 Secrets Every Father Should Know*. One mother came to her shortly after the birth of her child because the infant began having terrible seizures. Meeker writes that the infant girl would "turn blue, shake all over, and her breathing [would become] so erratic that she looked like she was dying."[37] An MRI of the baby's brain showed that she was "suffering the consequences of herpes"—her brain was "punctured throughout with holes."[38] Imagine the devastation this news brought to her mother, who, never having had a herpetic sore, did not know that she had contracted the disease. In another case, Meeker treated a young girl whose advancing cervical cancer required the removal of most of her cervix. The beautiful thirteen-year-old now faced a high-risk pregnancy should she become pregnant in the future.[39]

The Emotional Pitfalls

The physical discomforts and complications caused by STIs are only part of the overall damage caused. For women, casual sexual encounters and the STIs that may result take perhaps the greatest toll on their emotional and psychological health. Consider one more of Meeker's patients, sixteen-year-old Angela. Angela did not want to lose her virginity, but she also did not want to lose her boyfriend. After one month of dating (a length of time making a relationship serious to most teens), Angela decided to exchange oral sex with her boyfriend in the back of his car. From that single event, Angela contracted herpes type 1 (oral herpes), affecting her genitalia so badly that she needed narcotics to control it. To make matters worse, her boyfriend nicknamed Angela "Miss Herpes," humiliating her before her friends and classmates. "Six months later," Meeker writes, "Angela swallowed two full bottles of acetaminophen."[40]

Angela thought she had made the right decision to exchange oral sex with her boyfriend. She thought she was retaining her virginity by having oral sex instead of sexual intercourse. Yet the depression she suffered was too much for her to handle. Certainly, much of Angela's depression was from being rejected and tormented by her boyfriend and peers. But even absent such social ostracism, contracting an STI brings a heavy emotional burden. One study found that for adolescents, diagnosis of an STI is associated with high levels of depressive symptoms within twelve months.[41]

Even when STIs do not factor into the picture, numerous studies suggest that casual sexual activity itself puts women at higher risk for depression. One such study shows that sexually active teenage girls are more than three times more likely to be depressed, and nearly three times as likely to have made a suicide attempt, as girls not sexually active.[42] One study, analyzing 8,000 teens, found that young women experienced a greater increase in depression than their male counterparts in response to romantic involvement.[43] Because depression in teen girls is almost always linked to sexual activity, Meeker considers depression itself a sexually transmitted disease.[44]

The risk of depression for sexually active, unmarried young women is built into their biological makeup. The standard sex education curriculum and literature mention little, if anything, about the hormone oxytocin. Though released in both men and women to promote bonding,[45] the hormone plays a more significant role in a woman's sexual experience. For example, oxytocin is released in large quantities during pregnancy and breastfeeding. Women become attached to their babies and are more disposed to tolerate the routine that comes with nurturing a child. A woman experiences a calm, emotional state that makes nursing her child a pleasurable activity.[46]

This same hormone is also released in large quantities when a woman has sex. In fact, Grossman points out, the release of oxytocin can be "classically conditioned" so that all it takes is a woman catching a glimpse of the man she's had sex with in order for the hormone to be released.[47] Whether a woman cares deeply for the man she is with or only just met him hours ago, her body will respond to the physical intimacy of sex in such a way as to provoke a feeling of emotional intimacy, in which she feels bonded in more than just a physical way with her partner. It is no wonder that many women are confused and tormented with thoughts of "does he care about me?" after what was intended to be a casual encounter. Women would like to believe they can be sexually intimate without allowing their emotions to get in the way. The fact is that women are more vulnerable than men when it comes to sex and relationships. This is not due to any deficiency on their part, but because of their biological and physiological makeup.

Feminism's Failure to Understand Women

Secular feminism, however, has caused women to regard any degree of vulnerability (in themselves or in other women) with embarrassment and disgust. If a woman allows herself to be vulnerable, she is being complicit with the patriarchal society that threatens to oppress her. Rather than be pitied for her weakness, a woman should actively exercise her capacity for power and influence. After all, in matters of sex, men have all too often taken advantage of women's emotional vulnerability. A man will use a woman's hopeful expectations of love and intimacy to seduce her. Once she is attached to him, she will find ready excuses for his faults and sometimes brutish behavior. Secular feminists certainly have good reason to find such situations deplorable.

However, it is ironic that having disparaged such occasions as wrong and anti-woman, secular feminists would *not* propose as a remedy that women push to eliminate such circumstances. Rather, they advocate that women turn the table on men, imitating their offensive behaviors in pursuit of equality and even vengeance. These feminists seem to desire not that men and women live together in mutual respect of each other's dignity (and vulnerabilities), but that men be made to pay for the pain women have suffered. Women should use their sex appeal and sensuality to make *men* vulnerable, to use them, and to casually leave them wanting more. In this way, women best demonstrate their power and put men in *their* place.

But the secular feminist response is just as anti-woman as the problem it reacts to, if not more so. Women following this code of sexual conduct have not rid themselves of their vulnerability in sex and relationships—they have only masked it. These women willfully put themselves in the same hurtful situations. The only difference is that instead of hoping at the outset for commitment and love, women initiate these sexual encounters with only a casual desire for pleasure, fun, or company. Although they may intend to detach themselves from emotions, hopes, and expectations, they are still engaging in behaviors that biologically dispose them to emotional and physical attachment. Trying to overcome this biological predisposition through sheer will leaves many feeling increasingly more hurt, empty, confused, and bitter. Secular feminism's casual attitudes toward sex encourage women to behave in ways that only exaggerate their vulnerability for emotional distress. Despite their desire for freedom and happiness, women cannot help but be dissatisfied with the sexual liberation lifestyle.

Secular feminism encourages women both to rigorously pursue education and careers and to "enjoy the relaxation and diversion provided by agreeable sexual adventures."[48] But how "relaxing" is it when that casual fling is accompanied by a frantic desire for him to call, or a desperate hope that perhaps one of these flings will develop into something more? How "agreeable" are those "sexual adventures" when they seem to create a deepening void, even if they do prove a point? And when a young woman has a paper due, an approaching deadline, or an important presentation, does she really want the "diversions" that accompany an STI, depression, or simply the natural release of oxytocin? With these consequences, it is no wonder that unmarried sexual activity decreases the likelihood of academic achievement.[49] One would think the same feminists who hope for women's advancement in their education and profession would want to reduce, rather than actively support, behaviors that distract them from such success.

Despite the belief that women can have sex without consequences, science seems to suggest that many consequences do in fact occur. What is more, these consequences are not easily eliminated by condom use, "safe sex," or the sheer will to push aside feelings of depression and emptiness. Women are being encouraged to make decisions about sexual behavior based on the fiction that "safe sex" protects a woman from the negative consequences of sex. This is simply dishonest when one considers the full range of consequences resulting from casual physical intimacy. The physical, psychological, and emotional consequences of casual sex threaten all sexually active women, whether they are looking to feel loved or looking for liberation. Encouraging women to act in ways contrary to their well-being is *not* pro-woman.

Not So Casual: Prenuptial Sex and Cohabitation

Up to this point, our discussion of the physical, psychological, and emotional consequences of sex have been largely placed within the context of the casual sexual attitudes and behaviors embraced by secular feminism. However, it is important to note that many of these consequences also apply when premarital sex is regarded in a more serious manner. Many women reject the casual sentiments that mark the hookup culture, but they believe that sex can be good and appropriate outside of marriage when in a loving, committed, serious relationship.

Take, for instance, the couple who are seriously considering marriage. They may have sex, believing they have sincere intentions of expressing affection or perhaps discerning whether they are "sexually compatible." Many couples today will cohabit before marriage with similar intentions of discerning compatibility for marriage. The threat of STIs and the effects of oxytocin apply in these situations as well, though admittedly STIs pose a lesser threat when the number of sexual partners is reduced. However, premarital sex, even within a committed and serious relationship, still brings with it potential risks to a woman's overall happiness.

The vast majority of women who intend to get married at some point in their lives desire marital stability. Many of these women may not know that premarital sex and cohabitation before marriage are associated with a higher risk of infidelity and divorce. For example, one study shows that women who were engaged in any sexual activity with someone other than their eventual first husband saw a 114 percent increase in their likelihood of divorce compared with women who remained abstinent until marriage.[50] Since this study shows little difference in the likelihood of divorce for women who had never engaged in premarital sex and those who did so only with their eventual husbands, one might want to conclude that engaging in sex with one's fiancé is not deleterious to future marriage. But such a conclusion would be false. First, engagement does not guarantee marriage: the only way to guarantee that one is having sex only with one's future husband is to wait until that special man *becomes* one's husband. Second, other studies find divorce to be associated with *any* premarital sexual encounter. One such study revealed that women who had their first sexual encounter with anyone before marrying were approximately 34 percent more likely to divorce than women who did not engage in premarital sex. The risk of marital disruption was reduced by about 8 percent for every year sex was delayed.[51]

Couples who cohabit may be trying to avoid divorce by testing their compatibility ahead of time. Despite their good intentions, this form of premarital intimacy is connected to higher instability rates as well. One study looked at a nationally representative sample of 1,235 women ages twenty to thirty-seven. It found that married women who had cohabited before marriage were more than three times more likely to have a "secondary sex partner" (to have an affair) than their married peers who had not cohabited. Even for those not yet married, cohabiting women were about 1.7 times more likely to have a secondary sex partner than noncohabiting women.[52] In another study, women were found to be at a significantly higher risk of divorce if they engaged in intimate premarital relationships and cohabited with someone other than their eventual spouse. This risk was highest for women who both engaged in premarital sex and cohabited with multiple partners. These women had a 166 percent higher risk than those who did not engage in any intimate premarital relationship.[53] These are discouraging statistics when we consider that it is not uncommon to find men and women having multiple sex partners and serial cohabiting arrangements before marriage. Women may think that "playing house" will give them a greater chance of marital stability. In fact, they are setting themselves up for marital strife.

Why is this? Perhaps one reason for this connection between cohabitation and marital instability is that the expectations and attitudes of couples in a cohabiting arrangement often follow them into marriage. At first glance, it seems quite sensible that cohabiting will test a couple's compatibility. However, the arrangement often makes couples especially sensitive to each other's faults and quirks (since they can "escape" them should they so desire). When cohabitation is used as a "test trial" for marriage, questions such as, "Is this fault something I can live with?" become habitual. For a marital relationship to succeed, however, couples must be more inclined to forgive (and even overlook) small faults and work to overcome larger, more important ones. For a husband and wife, the well-being of their marriage is the higher goal. For a couple that has cohabited, each individual has been in the habit of prioritizing his and her own comfort over the well-being of their relationship. It thus becomes difficult once the couple has married to make the personal sacrifices necessary to sustain a happy and healthy marital life.

Contrary to some expectations, chastity, as opposed to premarital sex and cohabitation, is the best practice for men and women striving for marital stability. Likewise, marriage is the optimal situation in which to find a happy and pleasurable sexual relationship. Compared with their cohabiting peers, married persons reported a better quality of their relationship, fewer fights and violence, and greater commitment and happiness in their relationship.[54] Additionally, greater sexual satisfaction was reported by those in married, monogamous relationships than by their single and cohabiting counterparts.[55]

All things considered, it appears that science and experience have much to offer to dispute the assertions of secular feminists, even of those who have a high regard for sex within premarital circumstances. Women who take seriously their hopes and desires for future marital stability, as well as their physical, psychological, and emotional health and happiness, ought to reject the current norm of premarital sexual intimacy, and consider an alternative lifestyle: chastity.

The Joy of Being a Catholic Woman

Authentic Feminine Strength

One finds this alternative lifestyle of chastity within the Catholic Church's teachings on sexuality. What is more, one finds reason to joyfully embrace Catholicism's teachings in light of the information provided here.

Consider again the effects of oxytocin. The feelings of attachment and vulnerability experienced by women in sex are healthy and good when they take place within a marital relationship. As husband and wife, man and woman enter into a union in which they agree to share themselves with each other, uniting on the physical, mental, emotional, and spiritual levels. This multidimensional interpersonal union of husband and wife is nourished and matures as they grow together in mutual generosity, selflessness, trust, faith, and love. Within this context, and *only* within this context, a woman is truly free to let her body respond to sex in the way it was designed to respond.

In a healthy marriage, a woman does not feel the need to assert her sexual prowess in order to prove her independence and respectability. Nor does she worry about her partner's intentions and whether or not he is taking advantage of her vulnerability. In marriage, she is *free to be vulnerable*—to trust her husband with her body, heart, and soul. She "submits" to him, yes, but this is not a submission that marks a deficiency on her part or superiority on his part, as some secular feminists would suspect.

As Saint Paul himself notes in the controverted Scriptural passage Ephesians 5, submission in marriage is mutual insofar as each spouse puts the other ahead of himself "out of reverence for Christ." Their subordination *to one another* is an expression of their loving devotion and marital fidelity. Later, when the passage goes on to state that "wives should be subordinate to their husbands as to the Lord," this passage must be read in conjunction with verse 25 to understand its full meaning (i.e., "Husbands, love your wives, even as Christ loved the church"). Saint Paul is suggesting here a *specific context* for wifely submission: that she be submissive to the Christ-like, sacrificial love of her husband. In a healthy marriage, a wife's submission to her husband is essentially an entrusting of herself to his love—a love that requires him to "[hand] himself over for her" as Christ did for the Church.

In this light, one can understand how Christian marriage is not a patriarchal system for female subjugation and abuse, but is instead a most fitting context for the feelings of attachment and vulnerability a woman naturally experiences when sexually intimate. Furthermore, one can also understand how practicing chastity—premarital sexual abstinence and fidelity within marriage—is in the best interest of women and their experience of their sexuality.

What is more, the type of strength and power secular feminists advocate women assert *over* men is no longer appealing or rational. Rather than separating men and women from one another in a struggle of ill-intentioned dominance and submission, a woman's chastity and sexual fidelity to her husband evince a unique feminine strength that brings men and women together in mutual trust, respect, and sincerity.

Saving sexual intimacy until marriage can often be difficult. It takes conviction, confidence, discipline, and a forward-looking love to reserve this gift for that special relationship. Especially today, in an age where it is the norm to do what feels right in sexual matters, it takes an incredible amount of fortitude to remain sexually committed to your spouse before marriage through sexual abstinence and during marriage through sexual fidelity. The conviction, confidence, discipline, and fortitude necessary for chastity are, in fact, all forms of strength. That fidelity and discipline are forms of strength should not be a foreign idea. Do we not admire the strength of young men and women who undergo intense physical and psychological training in the military, and who, out of fidelity to their country, put themselves in harm's way to defend their family and fellow citizens? Do we not admire the discipline of athletes and musicians who practice for hours each day in order to perfect their skills? Do we not admire the selfless commitment of a mother and a father when they sacrifice certain pleasures and comforts in order to give their children a good education? There are myriad instances such as these when we do not hesitate to value the strong character of others. Why, then, would we hesitate to admire discipline and fidelity in matters of sexuality, especially when the benefits of chastity are so numerous?

As the aforementioned studies and testimonies suggest, chastity is more conducive to women's health, happiness, and success than the sexual indulgence proposed by secular feminism. Chastity significantly minimizes the threat of STIs, the emotional stress of sexual intimacy absent authentic union and lasting commitment, and the risk of future marital instability. Chastity places sex within its proper marital context, where women are free to be vulnerable, free to be strong in their fidelity, and free to experience the full meaning and beauty of authentic sexual intimacy.

One of the major problems with the sexuality promoted by secular feminism is the disconnect made between the pleasure derived from sex and the actual meaning of sex. As F. Carolyn Graglia writes in her book *Domestic Tranquility: A Brief Against Feminism*, "The sexual revolution feminists have promoted rests on an assumption that an act of sexual intercourse involves nothing but a pleasurable physical sensation, possessing no symbolic meaning and no moral dimension."[56] Yet, once women tire of their loveless sexual adventures and hope for a love that lasts, they still continue to pursue sex, but now with the expectation that love will somehow blossom from it. The truth is, they have it backwards. Sex—and all the emotional, spiritual, and physical pleasures that accompany it—is meant to blossom from love. And not just any love—a *marital* love in which husband and wife have already grown in authentic and substantial affection for each other, so much so that they vow to share their lives together as partners in this life (and, I would add, as each other's helpers toward meriting salvation in the next).

The True Power of Eros

Pope Benedict begins his first encyclical, *Deus Caritas Est*, with a discussion of the history and nature of *eros*. In the pre-Christian world, the Greeks understood eros as a "kind of intoxication, the overpowering of reason by a 'divine madness.'"[57] Eros was celebrated as a type of "divine power" and "fellowship with the Divine." It is for this reason that fertility cults and "sacred" prostitution were popular during this time. The ecstatic pleasure experienced in sex was regarded as something supernatural—as something divine.[58]

Feminists of the sexual revolution have also raised up *eros*, or sexual desire, as a woman's "divine power." It is through a woman's sexuality that she exerts her control over men, arousing in them a type of "madness" that overpowers their reason—a type of feminine "intoxication." But this use of sexuality is hardly liberating or exalting for women. Pope Benedict reports that the prostitutes of old who would arouse this sexual intoxication "were not treated as human beings and persons, but simply used as a means of arousing 'divine madness': far from being goddesses, they were human persons being exploited."[59] Has this not been the same effect with secular feminist approaches to sexuality? In using their sexuality to exert control over men, women have only made sex more available to men, exploiting themselves, and injuring their chance of authentic intimacy. Pope Benedict labels this a "counterfeit divinization of *eros*" that "actually strips it of its dignity and dehumanizes it."[60]

Today, we often hear the expression "we're all human" as an excuse for human faults and impulses. In matters of sex, this base understanding of the human person excuses behaviors such as premarital sex, infidelity, promiscuity, pornography, and masturbation. Society today has come to consider these behaviors as most truly human, because they respond most readily to the most basic of human desires. In truth, they are corruptions of human desire, of *eros*. *Eros* is corrupted when human desire is not selflessly turned toward another, but selfishly turned in on oneself, as is the case in casual sex, pornography, and masturbation. In the former two cases, the other person is not the beneficiary of selfless love, but a mere means of satisfying a personal desire. In the latter case of masturbation, there is no other person at all. One reduces one's own sexuality to a mere tool for pleasure, disconnected from love.

The Catholic Church proposes that these responses to human desire are not at all liberating, as the sexual revolution suggests. Instead, they enslave the person in a type of addiction to sex, where one habitually submits to temptations and whimsical desires that do not serve the human good. Rather, they work actively against that which is best for the human person, and especially for women. If we come to understand what is "human" as that which is directed toward God's good will for humanity, we will find that the Catholic vision for human love and sexuality is more fully human and more fulfilling.

Contrary to secular (and some dissident Catholic) feminist arguments, the Catholic Church does not encourage women's chastity in order to subject her to male domination. The fact is, if women's purity receives any more attention than men's purity, it is out of an acknowledgement of the powerful influence women naturally have on men. Women have the profound ability to rouse both the best and the worst in the opposite sex. When women lose their concept of purity, men lose their motivation to be respectful. One male student at George Washington University told journalist Laura Sessions Stepp, "Because girls are more assertive, it's easy for us to be as*holes." [61] In contrast, when women maintain their purity with confidence, love, and faith, they inspire awe, respect, and admiration from their male counterparts. When women have high standards, men will respond accordingly.

What *is* pro-woman? A pro-woman sexuality is one that looks honestly at the female body and the female heart. It does not deny a woman's natural desire for or response to sex, but instead recognizes its beauty within the proper context. A pro-woman sexuality is one that honors both women and sex, and prescribes ways to safeguard their dignity and inherent value. The joy of being a Catholic woman is that we have these safeguards and moral standards outlined in our faith. And even more, we have the sacramental grace to aid us in our commitment to them.

4

The Liberation of Lifelong Love: Church Teaching on Marriage

JENNIFER ROBACK MORSE

Marriage is a universal human institution, defined—until recently—as the preferred context for both sexual activity and child-rearing. Until the last forty years, every society understood that some contexts for sex and childbearing were preferable to others.

Opposition to this traditional view of marriage has increased in recent times. We are told that society should not "privilege" one form of relationship or family over any others. But "privileging" is, by definition, the exact point of the marital institution: the very existence of the institution proclaims that some relationships are more socially significant, more socially productive, and more socially desirable than others. Since the Catholic Church offers one of the richest and most robust teachings about marriage, the Church has faced particularly strong criticism for her teachings.

In the current debate between the traditional view that marriage is Something, and the modern view that marriage is Whatever We Say It Is, the Catholic Church holds firmly to the view that marriage is something in particular.

The Church teaches that marriage is the lifelong, sexually exclusive, sacramental union of one man and one woman, established by the consent of the spouses, characterized by love and a common life, and ordered to the good of the spouses and the procreation and education of children.[1] In some cases, the Church teaches that the separation of spouses may be legitimate,[2] and even civil divorce can be tolerated. But remarriage (without annulment) is always forbidden.[3]

According to Catholic teaching, sexual activity outside of marriage is always wrong. This includes both adultery (sexual relations between a married person and someone other than the spouse)[4] and fornication (sexual relations between unmarried persons).[5] Obviously, then, the Church objects to nonmarital cohabitation,[6] and out-of-wedlock childbearing.

These, it is safe to say, constitute the "hard teachings" of the Catholic Church regarding marriage. Apart from her teaching on contraception, abortion, and possibly the all-male priesthood, no other teaching has caused the Church so much bad publicity and ill-feeling.

Over the past forty years, many women have become convinced that marriage is not in their best interest. Some women believe marriage is unnecessary. Others think that it is or has been harmful to them. The views of women like these, orchestrated, I will argue, by socialist and other secular feminists, have been instrumental to weakening the institution of marriage.

But the weakening of this foundational institution has also harmed women in some distinctive ways. Without a robust culture of marriage, women have been left with the burden of caring for children with far less support from men than would have been conceivable in prior ages. Married women are happier, healthier, more sexually satisfied, and more financially secure than their unmarried, cohabiting, and divorced counterparts. Moreover, the alternatives to marriage have been particularly harmful to children, quite apart from the loss of material support from their fathers. Since women on the whole care deeply about the welfare of their children, the negative outcomes to children caused by the decline of marriage must also be counted among the harmful effects on women.

Opposition to Church Teaching

Opposition to the Church's teaching hails from two main quarters. One could be described loosely as "feminist." Both within the Catholic

Church and in the culture at large, most women who call themselves feminists object to the teachings that marriage should be indissoluble and that marriage is the proper context for both sexual relationships and child-bearing.

Other objections to Church teaching come from more distinctively individualistic sources. That is, people who would not necessarily describe themselves as feminists nonetheless object to the Church's position on the relationships among the individual, the state, and marriage. These people believe that marriage is properly understood as a collection of autonomous individuals, each beholden only to himself. This means that marriage is whatever the parties involved will it to be, and society should accept anything to which these two people (or perhaps more than two people) consent. This individualist critique has led many to believe that marriage is no longer primarily an institution for raising children. Rather, marriage exists solely for the benefit of adults, to be entered into and dissolved at their shared (or not-so-shared) whim. This individualistic critique of Church teaching is every bit as potent as the feminist critique.[7] Where feminists adopt aspects of the individualist position in opposition to the Church, these two positions can be found to overlap.

Most twentieth-century secular feminists have declared marriage to be hostile to women's interests. From the 1960s to the 1990s, a chorus of self-described feminists has critiqued lifelong marriage as oppressive to women.[8] Beginning with Betty Friedan's *The Feminine Mystique* in 1968,[9] through Kate Millett's *Sexual Politics* in 1969,[10] and continuing with Germaine Greer's *The Female Eunuch* in 1971, the feminist establishment has told women that for their own good, they must refuse to marry (or, in Friedan's case, make employment rather than marriage and children their central focus).[11] As recently as 2000, feminist scholar Barbara Ehrenreich predicted that the marriage wave of the future would be:

> ... the diversity option, arising from the realization that the one-size-fits-all model of marriage may have been one of the biggest sources of tension between the sexes all along—based as it is on the wildly unrealistic expectation that a single spouse can meet one's needs for a lover, friend, co-parent, financial partner, reliably, 24-7. Instead there will be renewable marriages, which get re-evaluated every five to seven years, after which they can be revised, re-celebrated or dissolved with no, or at least fewer, hard feelings.[12]

Two assumptions underlie much feminist critique of marriage. The first is that relationships between men and women are necessarily characterized by conflict, with the continual danger that men will dominate women. The second idea is that sex and gender are fundamentally political rather than biological categories. Any observed differences between men and women are automatically suspect, presumed evidence of men's dominance over women.

It is safe to say that these are not Christian ideas.[13] These are ideas inspired more by the gospel of Marx and Engels than the Gospel of Mark and Matthew. Frederick Engels, Karl Marx's closest collaborator, equated the dominance of men over women with the dominance of capitalists over workers. He writes of an early, almost mythical period in which group marriage, without concern for parentage, was the norm. According to Engels, the transition from group marriage to monogamy marked the beginning of the subordination of women.[14]

He argues further that the economic and legal status of women is intimately connected to the organization of the household:

> In the old communistic household, which comprised many couples and their children, the task entrusted to women of managing the household was as much a public, a socially necessary, industry as the procuring of food by the men. With the patriarchal family and still more with the single monogamous family, a change came. Household management lost its public character. It no longer concerned society. It became a *private service*; the wife became the head servant, excluded from all participation in social production.
> ... Within the family, [the husband] is the bourgeois, and the wife represents the proletariat.... [T]he first condition for the liberation of the wife is to bring the whole female sex back into public industry ... [T]his in turn demands that the characteristic of the monogamous family as the economic unit of society be abolished.[15]

For Marx, Engels, and their socialist feminist followers,[16] the relationship between men and women is a special case of class struggle. Marriage is as intrinsically oppressive and unjust as private property. Getting women into the labor force, and by extension, getting their children into some form of collective care, is a priority, regardless of what women prefer.[17]

The Alternatives to the Church's Teaching Do Not Work

Although many of the radical antimarriage feminists intended that women should abstain from marriage by abstaining from relationships with men altogether, this is not a reasonable life plan for most women.[18] Most women desire some kind of sexual relationships with men at some point in their lives. So what alternatives do these feminists propose?

Since marriage is a complex social reality, there are several theoretically possible alternatives to marriage. One alternative is to have sexual relationships that are completely sterile. That is, a woman could choose a lifetime of contracepted sex, backed up by abortion in the case of contraceptive failure. As other contributors to this volume argue, this is neither a Catholic nor pro-woman alternative. Since the vast majority of women do want children at some point in their lives, the more relevant question is: what are the alternatives to marriage for childbearing?

One alternative to Church teaching is marriage that is not permanent. That is, women can get married, have children, divorce, and possibly remarry. Women can also simply choose to become single mothers. They can have children with men to whom they are not married, and perhaps do not intend to marry. Or, they can have babies with men with whom they are living but to whom they are not married.

All of these alternatives have been studied. While sometimes one alternative is preferable to another, the literature overwhelmingly reveals one conclusion: permanent marriage is far superior to each of them.

The Impact of Parental Separation on Women and Their Children

In virtually every way, children of intact married couple households do better than children from disrupted or never-formed families.[19] These children are more likely to have physical and mental health problems. Even accounting for income, fatherless boys are more likely to be aggressive[20] and to ultimately become incarcerated.[21] A recent British study offers evidence that the children of single mothers are more likely to become schizophrenic.[22] An extensive study of family structure was done in Sweden, the most generous welfare state in the world, where unmarried parenthood is widely accepted. Accounting for both the mental illness history of the parents as well as socio-economic status, the study found that children of single parents faced double the risk of psychiatric disease, suicide attempts, and substance abuse.[23]

These negative outcomes to children impact women, and not only because the care of these distressed children falls primarily upon them. When a woman becomes a mother, the well-being of her children becomes deeply important to her, no matter how independent she may once have imagined herself to be.

A recent sociological study assessed the very real human costs to the children themselves. (These statistics generally refer to all children in single-parent households, which includes those who have never been married and those who were formerly married.) The study posed this question: "What if the proportion of U.S. children living with their two married parents were as high today [in 2000] as it was in 1970?" In 1970, 69 percent of U.S. children lived with their two married parents, compared with 60 percent in 2000, a drop of 9 percentage points. Were U.S. family structure as strong today as it was in 1970, the yearly impact would be:

> 643,000 fewer American adolescents would fail a grade each year;
> 1,040,000 fewer would be suspended from school;
> 531,000 fewer adolescents would need therapy;
> 464,000 fewer adolescents would engage in delinquent behavior;
> 453,000 fewer youth would be involved in violence;
> 515,000 fewer youth would begin smoking cigarettes;
> 179,000 fewer youth would consider suicide;
> 62,000 fewer youth would actually attempt suicide.[24]

These numbers convey a sense of the tragic human price young people have paid for the modern revolution in family structure.

Now that we have established the magnitude of the general problem of parental separation, let's take a look at some of the special problems associated with specific alternatives to lifelong married love.

Divorce and Remarriage

Contrary to popular opinion, the Catholic Church does not forbid divorce, though she certainly discourages it. The Church permits separation and, in extreme cases, even civil divorce. It is remarriage after divorce that the Church prohibits. Opponents of the Church's teaching often cite the "hard line" on divorce and remarriage as an area where the Church is particularly out of touch and needs to lighten up. But the evidence does not support this view. Making remarriage work is more difficult than is usually supposed. Indeed, the probability of divorce is higher for second marriages than for first marriages.[25]

Divorce causes many problems for women. Divorced women are more likely to commit suicide than any other group of women.[26] Divorce is associated with a substantial deterioration in mental health, especially for women's mental health. Divorcing women report a greater increase in depression and hostility, and a greater decline in self-esteem, personal growth, and self-acceptance than divorcing men.[27]

Divorce causes problems for children as well. According to one study that followed the lives of highly advantaged children through their seventies, their parents' divorce reduced their children's lifespan by four years.[28] Children whose parents divorce are more likely to have psychological symptoms than children whose parents remain married.[29] Adult children of divorce have problematic relationships with their parents. The child's relationship with the father dwindles, sometimes to nothing. Adult children of divorce see less of their parents, and they describe their relationship with their parents less favorably than do children whose parents remained married.[30]

Remarriage is especially difficult for the children involved. When their fathers are more engaged in their lives, children have fewer behavioral problems[31] and have better grades.[32] But stepfathers tend to spend less time with children than do biological fathers.[33] Mothers in stepparent homes also tend to be less involved with their own children than are mothers in intact households.[34] This is not difficult to understand. The mother may feel the need to cultivate her relationship with her new partner, whereas married parents have generally established their relationship prior to having children. Children can become rivals for their mother's attention, whether the adults intend this outcome or not. This rivalry can be dangerous to children: living with an unrelated male, whether a stepfather or cohabiting boyfriend, elevates the risk of violence to children.[35]

In general, children whose parents stay married fare better than children whose parents divorce. The only exception to this is high-conflict marriages, where there is domestic violence or substance abuse. The breakup of these marriages puts an end to the stress associated with fighting and conflict. These children are better off. But in low-conflict households, divorce brings about an unwelcome disruption to the children's lives, with no compensating benefits. These are the children who suffer.[36] Similar results hold for adults: divorce increases the happiness of adults in high-conflict marriages, but not in low-conflict marriages.[37] Yet divorces in low-conflict marriages are precisely the divorces that no-fault laws make possible.[38] The percentage of divorces that arise from truly high- conflict marriages is never more than a third of all divorces, and sometimes much less than a third, depending on how conflict is measured.[39]

Multiple Partner Fertility:
A Distinctive Problem of the Underclass

Many women view living together as a stepping-stone toward marriage, with the idea that cohabiting will help them enjoy a better marriage in the future. This could not be further from the truth. A recent survey of the literature on cohabitation concluded, "No positive contribution of cohabitation to marriage has ever been found."[40]

Not only is cohabitation not good preparation for marriage, it is not a good long-run alternative to marriage. Cohabiting relationships are less stable than marriage, and this instability creates a whole series of problems. Demographers have come up with a new term to describe this situation. They call it "multiple partner fertility."[41]

We can get an idea of the magnitude of this problem with one statistic: of all unmarried urban mothers with more than one child, almost 70 percent exhibit multiple partner fertility, that is, they have children by more than one man.[42] The children of racial minorities are more likely to be born to unmarried mothers. In 2005, 37 percent of all U.S. children were born to unmarried mothers. This includes 70 percent of African American children, 48 percent of Hispanic children, and 25 percent of non-Hispanic whites.[43]

Rather than regale the reader with statistics, let me tell the story of a hypothetical young woman named Lucy. Not all of the outcomes that happen to Lucy happen to each and every unmarried mother. Lucy's story is a composite of the outcomes that are systematically more likely to happen to unmarried women, or to cohabiting women, than to married women. (I have omitted the hazards associated with drugs and alcohol, so as not to cloud the marriage issue.) Telling Lucy's story illustrates what multiple partner fertility looks like in the lives of ordinary people of modest means.

Lucy has graduated from high school, has a job as a dental assistant, and lives with her boyfriend, Izzy. Lucy becomes pregnant. It isn't entirely clear whether this is an "accidental" pregnancy. She has been on the Pill, but she missed one or two. (The failure rate for the Pill for low-income, cohabitating women younger than twenty is 48 percent.)[44] Lucy is glad to be pregnant. She has always wanted to be a mother.

Izzy isn't so happy. He isn't ready to be a father. Pregnancy was not part of the deal. He feels cheated. They quarrel frequently, and he sometimes hits her. (Domestic violence is more common in cohabiting couples than in married couples.)[45]

As her pregnancy proceeds, Lucy becomes less and less interested in sex, and Izzy becomes less and less interested in her. He has sex with a former girlfriend. (Cohabiting couples are more likely to have "secondary sex partners.")[46] He feels entitled, since he isn't "getting any" from Lucy, and after all, she cheated him by becoming pregnant in the first place. They quarrel some more, and he moves out for a while. By the time baby Anna is born, Izzy has moved back in with Lucy.

Now Lucy isn't so happy. In fact, she becomes depressed. (The presence of children increases a cohabiting woman's probability of depression. Children do not affect a married woman's probability of becoming depressed.)[47] Izzy is caught up in the excitement for a while. But the combination of sleep deprivation, a needy infant, and a preoccupied and depressed Lucy are more than Izzy can handle. He moves out for good when Anna is six months old. (Cohabiting relationships are less stable than married relationships.)[48] He never offers to contribute support to the care of Anna. (Never-married fathers are much less likely to pay child support than fathers who were once married to the child's mother.)[49]

Lucy finds that she can't handle the demands of her job and the care of her baby by herself. She goes to court to try to get Izzy to pay child support. The court orders him to pay an amount that is nowhere near enough for Anna's needs. He does not have a very good job, so Lucy seldom collects even the small amount the court has ordered. (Cohabiting men earn half the income of married men.)[50] In the meantime, Izzy does not feel like working at a normal job with a normal payroll, since his wages are garnished for Anna's care. He works under the table at informal jobs, keeping for himself the little income he makes.

Lucy moves back in with her mother. Everything goes smoothly until Lucy becomes lonely. She becomes involved with Tom, who has a decent job and thinks Lucy is pretty and the baby is cute. Lucy leaves her mom and moves in with Tom.

Lucy becomes pregnant again. Tom becomes less and less tolerant of Anna, who is a toddler by this time, but Tom is very happy when their new baby is a boy. Of course, baby John takes much time and energy from both Anna and Tom. Anna feels neglected, cries a lot, and misbehaves. Lucy is exhausted. Tom helps her with the new baby, but he is not interested in Anna. Both parents begin to show a preference for little John. (Men spend less time with their partners' children than with their own biological children. The presence of a stepfather decreases the time a mother spends with her children.)[51] Anna's behavior deteriorates. Lucy and Tom quarrel about Anna's poor behavior.

One night, Lucy takes baby John and Anna and slips out. She goes back to her mother. Tom is furious. He wants her back, and he wants his son back. Lucy refuses. She gets a court order for child support; he gets a court order for visitation rights. He is trying to be a good father, as he understands it. His visits with his son are anguished. The little boy doesn't understand what is happening. He wants to go home with his daddy. (Parental divorce increases a boy's probability of depression, regardless of the quality of parenting. Nothing seems to compensate for the sense of sadness that boys experience at the loss of their fathers from the home.)[52]

Meanwhile, Lucy finds a new boyfriend, Joe. She, Anna, and Johnny move in with him. You guessed it: she gets pregnant again. The new boyfriend does not like little John, the reminder of Lucy's past relationship with Tom. One day while Lucy is at work, Joe slaps John. Lucy asks him how Joe got a bruise on his thigh. Joe says he fell. Lucy wants to believe him. The second time she comes home to find a new bruise on Johnny, Joe admits that he slapped him. (Children are more likely to be abused by their mother's boyfriend than by anyone else.)[53] According to one study, children living in a household with an unrelated adult are fifty times more likely to die of inflicted injuries than children living with two biological parents.[54]

At the same time, Anna's behavior is deteriorating. She hasn't seen her own father since infancy. Neither Tom nor Joe has been very interested in Anna. (Children in cohabiting stepparent households are more likely to feel sad and lonely, and have poorer self-control.)[55]

By this time, Anna is in first grade, and she frequently misbehaves in school. Lucy gets a call from the principal, Mr. Knowles. He tells Lucy that he is concerned about Anna. Mr. Knowles thinks Anna needs a father figure, and would benefit from counseling. (Fatherless girls become sexually active earlier than girls who are with their fathers.)[56] They also get their periods earlier.[57]

Lucy gets angry and says there is nothing wrong with her daughter. Her boyfriend Joe is a perfectly fine father figure. In her heart, though, she knows all is not well with Anna. The girl still wets the bed almost every night. Joe complains about the odor, and makes fun of her. Lucy can't really stand up to him. She doesn't want to lose him, and she needs his income.

Little Anna is on course for abusing drugs and alcohol, for teen pregnancy, and for a lifetime of multiple partner fertility herself.[58] Little Johnny is at a higher risk for violence, delinquency, and drug use.[59] If Lucy had married one of those men and stuck with him, her life chances and those of her children would be greatly enhanced. Some of her children might have had the problems associated with stepfamilies. But at least the subsequent children would have the benefit of both parents, married to each other. Without marriage, the fathers of Lucy's children are unlikely to contribute much, if anything, to the care of their children.

One might object that some of these problems are associated with teen pregnancy and poverty. That is partly true. But the deeper truth is that channeling sexual behavior and childbearing through marriage creates wealth rather than dissipates it. Men behave differently when they marry, and especially when they become married fathers.[60]

One might also object that Lucy's case of switching from partner to partner is extreme and atypical. But once we jettison permanence and exclusivity as serious social norms, we are on weak ground in trying to say that Lucy shouldn't have ditched her boyfriends quite so casually. If a husband is an unnecessary accessory to childbearing, why isn't it okay to have multiple children, each with different fathers? If one divorce without cause is acceptable, why aren't multiple divorces? In other words, once we've discarded Catholic principles, alternative principles are not so obvious.

One might object that women of higher income and education will not face as many and as serious problems as Lucy. Perhaps a more highly educated, wealthier woman could cohabit, raise children, and do just fine. In some cases, this may prove to be correct. After all, wealthier people have more resources to face all kinds of life challenges than those of lower income. Indeed, every problem of the poor is exacerbated by the failure of marriage.

The Benefits of Marriage

Now that we have gone through the alternatives to marriage, we can see that marriage really does offer significant benefits to women, as well as to children, men, and the overall society. In fact, the subtitle of a recent book, *The Case for Marriage*, says it all: *Why Married People Are Happier, Healthier, and Better Off Financially*. We might also add that married people live longer,[61] have lower suicide risks,[62] and have better and more frequent sex.[63]

Marriage is a wealth-creating social institution. This is partly because two people working together can produce more wealth and accumulate more assets than either of them could do living independently. Studies show that by retirement age, married couples accumulate twice as much wealth per person as unmarried people, either single or divorced.[64]

Part of the reason married couples can accumulate more wealth is that men behave differently after marriage, especially if they become fathers. The late University of Virginia professor Steven L. Nock has shown that married men work harder and longer and in a more focused way. They are less likely to engage in destructive behaviors like excessive drinking. And according to Nock's statistical inferences, this is more than a selection effect. That is, it isn't just that more capable and stable men tend to get married, although this is true to some extent. Marriage itself changes men's behaviors.[65]

But probably the most important reason that marriage produces wealth is that marriage is the most basic and fundamental unit of social cooperation. A man and a woman come together spontaneously (needing no coaxing!) and create a child (or children) together. They work together for the benefit of the child, to raise him or her to adulthood. They both have an interest in the child's well-being. They both have particular knowledge of the child's unique needs. Their union, their cooperation, is socially productive. Working together, they bring a child into being, which neither of them could do completely on their own. The outcomes for children are far better when the parents work together. We can interpret this evidence as an illustration of the benefits of their cooperation.

Such cooperation between husbands and wives also solves one of the most vexing problems of the modern age: balancing work and family. This problem is particularly acute for college-educated women, since they are the most likely to have embraced the feminist goals of income equality and personal independence. Such goals have proven difficult to achieve, however, for women who also desire to have children.

Equalizing the incomes of men and women requires equality in all the behaviors that go into generating people's wages. The presence of children is the single most salient factor in the income differences between men and women.[66] Women tend to leave the labor force to take care of their children. Whether they leave completely, or whether they take reduced hours in a "scenic route" career path, the market punishes deviations from full-time employment. Since pregnancy and child-rearing affect the earnings of men and women differently, the feminist goal of income equality requires removing the sting of that difference.

Thus, a central tenet of the feminist platform has been convincing women that before they get married and have children, they must pursue an education and career. Only when one is well-established professionally is it safe to consider children. Implicit in this strategy is the notion that men are unreliable; a woman must plan on being able to support herself (and her children) on her own. Such a feminist life plan has persuaded many women to shape their work lives into the mold created by male career paths. Yet, traditional male career trajectories demand the most intense investment early in life, which also happens to be the time that women's bodies are most suited for pregnancy.

Many highly educated women (including myself) defined our goal as equal participation in a labor market designed for men, that is, for people who don't give birth. And so, we educated women have made a bargain. We are allowed to participate in the public sphere as long as we chemically neuter ourselves during our peak childbearing years. If we finally do have children, we agree to place them in commercial care when they are very young and most vulnerable. If we are unlucky and unable to conceive when we are finally ready professionally and financially, we may agree to undergo assisted reproductive technology, which includes artificially overstimulating our ovaries.[67]

Lifelong married love allows us to step out of this destructive pattern and meet our many life goals at different times of our lives. In a stable marriage, women are free to accept the reality that our fertility peaks during our twenties. We are free to get married and have children, and allow our husbands to support us as much as they can. We are free to remain at home full-time or work only as much as is necessary. As our children mature and require less of our time and attention, some of us might go back to school for an undergraduate or advanced degree, and then perhaps work our way into the professions. At that juncture in life, we may then be able to help support our children through college, and help provide for joint retirement with our husbands. And, since women live longer than men, we might opt to work longer, and let our husbands spend some time with our grandchildren.

This vision requires that marriage be a lifelong institution for mutual cooperation and support, rather than the unenforceable noncontract it has become. It turns out that a lifelong commitment shared by spouses makes women far happier anyway.[68] This is the exact opposite of the feminist vision, which replaced marital stability with the goal of employment stability.

Christian Marriage: The Humane Alternative

We can now see why the Church's teaching is superior to the alternatives. Though the Catholic Church is not a utility-maximizing or income-maximizing institution, following the natural law brings with it the natural consequences that people are on average better off. Violations of natural law are likely to result in negative results, sooner or later. These negative consequences can be observed by anyone who looks at the evidence in a systematic way. This proves to be particularly true in the area of marriage and sexuality. No matter what the civil law allows, we pay a steep price for violations of the natural law.

The tragedy today is that so many women up and down the socio-economic ladder have come to believe that marriage is somehow not in their best interest. By engaging in sex outside of marriage and child-rearing without husbands, women accept too little for themselves and for their children. But Catholic teaching offers them a better way.

Contrary to popular opinion, the Church's teaching is not simply a list of prohibitions: the Church is trying to steer people toward the positive good of lifelong married love. Pope John Paul II was a master of refocusing Church teachings on sexuality and marriage away from the prohibitions and toward the positive good. His justly celebrated theology of the body[69] reveals how all of the "negatives" so often associated with Church teaching actually point toward the "positive" of lifelong married love. Man and woman are meant for love, union, and communion with one another. According to the *Catechism of the Catholic Church*, "Sexuality is ordered to the conjugal love of man and woman. In marriage, the physical intimacy of the spouses becomes a sign and a pledge of spiritual communion."[70]

God had something specific in mind when he created us as gendered beings. Male and female are two different ways of being human. And our gender is intrinsic to our person, not merely an attribute. A woman is more than a list of feminine attributes and behaviors. Being a woman is essential to the person.[71]

The Church's teaching about marriage includes a teaching about the nature of the human body, and the nature of the human person. Our gendered nature helps us to be aware of the fact that we are intrinsically limited and interdependent. We cannot create new life by ourselves. We need a partner. We moderns sometimes resent the reality of this limitation. Catholicism teaches that interdependence is a good thing, not a bad thing as the modern world so often supposes. In fact, our interpersonal communion elevates us to the highest level of our humanity. As John Paul puts it: *"[M]an became the image of God not only through his own humanity, but also through the communion of persons. . . .* Man becomes an image of God not so much in the moment of solitude as in the moment of communion."[72]

The human body is a great good that reveals God. Catholic teaching about sex and marriage flows from this view of the human body. Part of our modern dilemma is that we tend to view the body in an instrumental

fashion. Following Descartes, the philosopher known for positing mind-
body or "Cartesian" dualism, we imagine that we can use our bodies as
we wish, because we believe that our bodies are not intrinsic to our identity. We rather imagine that the real person is the mind, occupying a body,
and driving around in it, using it as we might use a car. John Paul's theology of the body is a brilliant response to this Cartesian dualism, and a
profound defense of the significance of the human body.[73]

Many modern people do not like to think about the human body, and
with it, human sexuality, as having any natural ends. They treat the procreative powers of sexuality as nothing more than optional add-on features that you can have if you like that sort of thing and are willing to pay
extra for it.[74] But children are a central feature of the Church's understanding of marriage. If we could reproduce without sex, if human offspring were born as fully formed independent creatures, and if children
weren't helpless for long periods of time, we wouldn't need an institution
like marriage. But human reproduction does require a man and a woman,
and children are dependent for a long time. The bearing and rearing of
children is intrinsically a cooperative endeavor. Catholicism embraces this
fact and declares that this form of human cooperation called marriage is
uniquely blessed and beloved by God.

The Church's teaching about marriage and sex is also a teaching about
society, because the Church views marriage as the foundational institution for the rest of society. Marriage is a little society, which contributes to
building up the wider society. The modern view that treats marriage as
nothing but the "property" of the two individuals is itself a radical
redefinition of the purpose and meaning of marriage. In the Catholic
view, marriage and human sexuality are *fundamentally social*.[75] As the
Catechism puts it:

> In creating man and woman, God instituted the human family and
> endowed it with its fundamental constitution. . . .[76] The family is the
> *original cell of social life*. It is the natural society in which husband
> and wife are called to give themselves in love and in the gift of life.
> Authority, stability and a life of relationships within the family con-
> stitute the foundations for freedom, security and fraternity with
> society. The family is the community in which, from childhood, one
> can learn moral values, begin to honor God and make good use of
> freedom. Family life is an initiation into life in society.[77]

The Catholic Church also has a definite view of the family in relationship to the state: the family is prior to the state, and the state has obligations to respect the family.

> A man and a woman united in marriage, together with their children, form a family. This institution is prior to any recognition by public authority, which has an obligation to recognize it. It should be considered the normal reference point by which the different forms of family relationships are to be evaluated.[78]

By contrast, some in modern society believe that marriage is purely the creation of the state, which can define and redefine marriage at will. For example, the Massachusetts Supreme Court explicitly asserted the priority of the state over marriage when it created same-sex marriage in the Commonwealth.[79]

Lifelong Married Love Is Possible, and Worth the Effort

It goes without saying that married life can be a serious challenge: living with another flawed human being for a lifetime cannot be otherwise. But the solution is not to throw up our hands over our disappointments and problems with our spouses. The solution is to enter more deeply into relationship with them, to prayerfully work out our problems together, and to grow in love and fidelity, mutual respect and forbearance. The sacrament of Matrimony offers Catholic spouses special graces to do so.

We can manage the differences between husbands and wives by enhancing their cooperation. For the woman of modest means, lifelong cooperation between herself and one husband enhances her wealth, health, and happiness, as well as dramatically improving the life-chances of her children. For the educated woman, following a different career path from her husband can become an opportunity for both of them, rather than a liability. The protections of marriage enable both spouses to reach their individual and shared potential through specialization and mutual support.

The best way to ensure that husbands and wives cooperate with each other over the course of their lifetimes is to foster the stability of a social institution that creates a set of mutual rights and responsibilities. That social institution should have legal recognition and protection, so that at least the most basic of those rights and responsibilities are legally enforceable, and not so easily evaded when times get tough. That social institution should also be supported by the culture because of the positive good it offers both parents and children.

That social institution, of course, is marriage. It is the distinctively Catholic vision of marriage: the lifelong, sexually exclusive union of one man and one woman, established by the consent of the spouses, characterized by love and a common life, ordered to the good of the spouses and the procreation and education of children.

Women deeply desire a new way of understanding their role in society and of living out their lives as wives, mothers, and workers. Marriage isn't the problem for women. Marriage is the solution.

5

The Gift of Female Fertility: Church Teaching on Contraception

ANGELA FRANKS

It is startling for those living in a society that so relies on contraception to learn that, for nearly two millennia, every Christian denomination prohibited the use of contraception, even within marriage. This common front first cracked in 1930 when, at the Lambeth Conference, the Anglican Church made a limited exception for the use of contraceptives by husband and wife.[1] Within the half-century that followed, the pro-contraception view mutated from an anomalous exception into the dominant strain of conventional opinion.

Accordingly, dissent from the Catholic Church's prohibition of contraception is common coin, even (or perhaps especially) among Catholic theologians. Stephen Pope, a Boston College theologian, told a television reporter, "I would say the encyclical [*Humanae Vitae*, affirming the Church's teaching on contraception] was one of the worst things that happened to the Catholic Church in the twentieth century."[2] In fact, it is easier to find a theologian who dissents from this teaching than to find one who agrees. Such birth-control boosterism is especially predominant among theologians who matured in the hothouse of dissent in the 1960s,

1970s, and 1980s. It might even be argued that the average Catholic young adult appreciates the Church's teaching on sexuality, marriage, and the theology of the body[i] more deeply than does the average Catholic theologian.[3]

Many points are pressed by these older, dissenting Catholic theologians against Church teaching, some of them taken straight out of the secular feminist, anti-Catholic handbook. First, they say that to reject contraception is to indulge in anti-woman bias. Thus, Luke Timothy Johnson, a New Testament scholar, insists that the Church's teaching on contraception must reflect a "pervasive sexism."[4] In other words, the Church forbids contraception because she just doesn't like women that much. Despite Church teaching to the contrary, as recent encyclicals make explicitly clear, these theologians (and anti-Catholic feminists) believe that the Church doesn't respect women's freedom or equality. If she did, she would obviously allow women to contracept.

Second, these theologians argue that the Church narrowly focuses on the physical act of sex itself (claiming "physicalism") and neglects to attend to the attitudes present in the relationship as a whole, such as a couple's "general" openness to children. They hold that the Church should overlook what happens in individual acts of sexual intercourse and instead focus on what they take to be "good [for] the relationship [as a whole]."[5]

In addition, there is the cliché that the Church is simply against sex. The dissenting theologians assert that the Church and the celibate males making up her hierarchy are deeply suspicious of sexual pleasure and the hearty enjoyment of it by married couples. Complaining about Pope John Paul II's theology of the body, Johnson writes, "I would welcome from the pope some appreciation for the goodness of sexual pleasure—any

---

i. The theology of the body refers to a collection of addresses Pope John Paul II gave between September 1979 and November 1984. In his theology of the body, the Pope presented the Church's teaching on human sexuality as part of God's loving plan, which seeks the happiness of each human being. John Paul argues that human sexual differentiation into male and female is good, bearing the intrinsic meaning that we can only be fulfilled in making a sincere and definitive gift of self. For most people, this means that the path to happiness runs through the lifelong, life-giving sexual love of marriage. The addresses were first published as *The Theology of the Body: Human Love in the Divine Plan* and then retranslated by Michael Waldstein and published as *Man and Woman He Created Them: A Theology of the Body.*

bodily pleasure, come to think of it!"[6] Rosemary Radford Ruether goes so far as to make the upside down charge that the Church's alleged negativity concerning sexual pleasure is the cause of pornography.[7]

Lastly, many theologians agitate for Church endorsement of contraception simply because a majority of Catholics (in the white, wealthy populations of Europe and North America) state that they approve of contraception, in percentages roughly similar to non-Catholics.[8] Those who cite this fact generally do not go on to make the explicit argument that might makes right (or, at least, superior numbers among bourgeois sectors of the world make right). Perhaps a straightforward assertion of this strategy of Church-governance-by-poll-numbers might strike too many Catholics outside the individualistic West as being incompatible with larger truths about what it means to be Catholic.

In truth, it is not the Church that maintains an anti-woman, anti-sex bias. Rather, the Church is the incomparable witness to the dignity of women, as well as to the full reality of sex. I will show this by providing the too-often absent historical context for the debate about contraception, as well as offer data regarding the damaging effects of contraceptives. I will then elucidate the reasoning behind the Church's teaching. I will show that the pro-contraception attitudes that most contemporary people have internalized are not eternal truths. Rather, as with any ideology, these conventional attitudes have a history. The happiness of women and girls, indeed of all society, depends on a critical evaluation of these attitudes.

The contraceptive mindset cannot avoid scapegoating women's bodies as the cause of both personal and societal problems. By contrast, the Church, with critical and prophetic clarity, points out that selfish desire, not the female body, is the source of our problems. It is only this latter approach that presents viable ways of actually meeting the real challenge of female oppression.

The Mindset of the Original Birth Controllers

Much of the theological debate surrounding contraception often takes place in a breathtaking vacuum of historical ignorance. While the story of explosive dissent over contraception has been told many times, it is usually framed in parochially Catholic terms: Pope John XXIII convened a

commission to study birth control, and its advisory report to Pope Paul
VI was leaked in 1967. The majority of the commission voted to change
the Church's teaching on contraception, making its case in the Majority
Report, as well as in a rebuttal to the commission's minority paper (the
Majority Rebuttal). The Pope rejected the majority's recommendations
and issued *Humanae Vitae* (*Of Human Life*) in 1968, which reaffirmed traditional teaching but unleashed a firestorm of protest and dissent.[9]

The larger historical context is missing from this account: why was
there such a revolution in elite and public opinion about birth control, and
what ignited it? The Catholic debate would not have been possible if it
weren't for the widespread reexamination of the morality of birth control
that began to be debated in America in the 1920s.

In order to understand this history of contraception, necessary for a
critical appraisal of the now-dominant contraceptive ideology, one must
understand Margaret Sanger (1879–1966), the American birth-control
pioneer.[10] Sanger was a committed neo-Malthusian. The neo-Malthusian
movement followed the now-discredited population theories of Thomas
Malthus (1766–1834). Malthus had erroneously argued that population
growth would inevitably outpace food production. The "neo" part of the
movement involved promoting population control not through sexual
abstinence, for which Malthus had argued, but through contraception.
Neo-Malthusians were also eugenicists. Eugenics is the belief that some
people (the "unfit") are genetically inferior and should not perpetuate
their "subpar" genes by having children. Opinion varies about who counts
as "unfit": for example, the Nazis insisted that Jews were unfit, while others (such as Sanger) never evinced anti-Semitism. But all eugenicists agree
on three categories of "unfitness": the poor, the physically disabled, and
the mentally or intellectually disabled. Neo-Malthusians tied together
Malthus's population control with eugenics. One of the neo-Malthusian
eugenic slogans was "quality, not quantity"—that is, eugenic quality, not
population quantity.

Sanger developed a worldview that I call the "ideology of control,"
which promoted three types of control: birth control, population control,
and eugenic control. All of these were put in service of Sanger's other
passion, an untrammeled pursuit of sexual pleasure. Sanger insisted that
women would be liberated through a free-ranging sex life coincident with
eugenically limited reproduction. She was not the only, or even the first,

person to link these concerns, but she was the most important because she institutionalized them in her powerful organizations.[11] She founded America's first birth-control clinic in 1916, the earliest incarnation of the organization now called the Planned Parenthood Federation of America.

The extent to which eugenic control conjoined with sexual libertinism prompted Sanger's promotion of birth control is seen in her 1920 book, *Woman and the New Race*. Its opening line declares: "The *most far-reaching social development of modern times* is the revolt of woman against sex servitude."[12] This "sex servitude" is the biological slavery of women to their reproductive systems.[13] Moreover, "involuntary motherhood" was bad not just for individual women but for the whole world. As a neo-Malthusian, Sanger saw the single greatest cause of society's ills—tyranny, war, famine, injustice—to be the fertility of women, which leads to overpopulation.[14] If overpopulation is the world's central problem, birth control becomes the central solution, one that also leads women to a new freedom. (And Sanger's concern wasn't some generic overpopulation; it was the overproduction of the "unfit": Sanger claimed that birth control was "nothing more or less than the facilitation of the process of weeding out the unfit, of preventing the birth of defectives or of those who will become defectives.")[15]

Let's be precise: what oppresses women, according to Margaret Sanger? Misogynist attitudes or social structures? The lack of basic civic rights, such as the right to vote? No, the answer is much simpler and more chilling: the female body. Thus Sanger places the blame for female oppression squarely on ... women themselves.

Sanger's equation of contracepted sex with freedom and world progress has an even darker and harder side to it. Sanger uses the language of freedom ("voluntary motherhood"), yet her ideology of control assumes that free choice in reproduction extends only one way, namely, to the choice against children. *Woman and the New Race* makes explicit the limits of Sanger's support for freedom. "As [woman] has unconsciously and ignorantly brought about social disaster, so must and will she consciously and intelligently *undo* that disaster and create a new and a better order. The task is hers. It cannot be avoided by excuses, nor can it be delegated."[16]

In fact, Sanger says that women have a "duty" to use contraception. Through birth control, she argues, women would free themselves from "sex slavery" and prevent society from having to bear the burdens of their children. They *owe* it to society.[17] Sanger insists that it was not enough to reform society in other ways. Political or social reforms are mere "palliatives" compared to the fundamental duty of women to use birth control for their own and society's well-being.[18]

It is illuminating to compare Sanger's ideas about what oppresses women with its main rival theory, against which Sanger subtly argues in *Woman and the New Race*. At Sanger's time, there was already a well-established feminist movement in America. This movement began in the middle of the nineteenth century and had a much broader agenda than Sanger's. Its main program was the pursuit of female suffrage. It was not diverted by interest in sexual "liberation." Unlike Sanger's cramped focus on contraception and sex, the suffragist movement embraced a variety of issues, such as the education of women, property rights, and divorce law.[19] In fact, few feminists in Sanger's day supported contraception. Even a free-love feminist such as Tennessee Claflin would write that the "washes, teas, tonics, and various sorts of appliances known to the initiated [were a] standing reproach upon, and a permanent indictment against, American women.... No woman should ever hold sexual relations with any man from the possible consequences of which she might desire to escape."[20] In *Woman and the New Race*, Sanger condemns the efforts of the suffragist movement as mere window dressing, hiding the more fundamental problem: female fertility and its negative effects.

Sanger's views may not seem very startling to twenty-first century readers. After all, women have internalized the now-dominant message that their biology enslaves them. In fact, contraception and abortion have been made synonymous with "reproductive health." For example, Brazilian theologian Ivone Gebara has deplored the Catholic prohibition of contraception, saying, "It is impossible to [have] reproductive health if you don't allow [condoms and birth control]."[21]

But "reproductive health" ought to refer to having a healthy reproductive system. Healthy reproductive systems are fertile. When disease or injury disrupts the functioning of a woman's reproductive system, she goes to a doctor to restore it—unless, that is, the disruption is deliberately caused through birth control. Then the disruption is viewed as furthering her "reproductive health." Charles Chaput, archbishop of Denver, spells out the underlying logic: "At the heart of contraception, however, is the assumption that fertility is an infection that must be attacked and controlled, exactly as antibiotics attack bacteria."[22]

Indeed, we usually take pills when we are sick, not when we are healthy. Contraception must be the only case in which a person takes a pill solely in order to thwart the natural purpose of a bodily system, all in the name of "health." The practice indicates that we have bought Sanger's line: reproduction is fundamentally unhealthy, both for women and for society. Ardent feminist Germaine Greer fears this war against the female body:

> More and more it seems that women themselves are coming to regard their wombs as a burden they have been lumbered with on behalf of the race.... If men flee the female, we will survive, but if women themselves treat femaleness as a disease we are lost indeed.[23]

At War with Fertility

If the world's problems are caused by female fertility, then governments have a right and even an obligation to encourage, or coerce, women to limit their reproduction.[24] As we have seen, Sanger's conjuring of a female "duty" to prevent overpopulation is an implicit rejection of the basic human freedom to bear as many children as one desires. She is more explicit elsewhere: "Possibly drastic and Spartan methods may be forced upon society if it continues complacently to encourage the chance and chaotic breeding that has resulted from our stupidly cruel sentimentalism."[25] Among these "drastic and Spartan methods" was forced eugenic sterilization, legalized nationwide in *Buck v. Bell* by the U.S. Supreme Court in 1927.[26] *Buck v. Bell* allowed the forced sterilization of over 60,000 Americans.[27]

There are more recent expressions of this coercive mentality. Beginning in the 1970s, the population-control movement popularized the fertility-as-disease equation. Warren Hern, an influential population-control activist and late-term abortionist, asked, "Is pregnancy really normal?" In 1993, he theorized that human population growth was "carcinogenic."[28] A similar mindset can be seen in research for an "anti-pregnancy vaccine." Such a vaccine would trigger the body's immunological response against the new life by attacking pregnancy-related hormones or else the eggs, sperm, or the new life, as a regular vaccine triggers the body's responses against a disease.[29]

In China, the attribution of female fertility as the cause of social problems is writ large in the country's one-child population policy, which has led to uncounted numbers of forced sterilizations, abortions, house demolitions, and imprisonments. Peru recently sterilized some 340,000 of its citizens, often in forced operations on its minority Indian population. A government subcommittee that investigated the crimes determined they were genocidal.[30] These countries reproduce the attitudes seen in India in the 1970s, when the country ran horrific compulsory-sterilization programs. D. N. Pai, a Harvard-educated doctor who was director of family planning in Bombay in the 1970s, explained the situation to the *New York Times* in 1976: "If some excesses appear, don't blame me.... You must consider it something like a war.... There has been pressure to show results. Whether you like it or not, there will be a few dead people."[31] Pope Paul VI in his encyclical *Humanae Vitae* feared such a result would follow from popularizing contraception. If couples can use it to promote their supposed good, why not whole nations?[32]

Though the enthusiasm of one such as Pai might make Catholic apologists for contraception nervous, they nonetheless embrace the population-control justification for contraception. The March 1974 issue of the mainstream Catholic journal *Theological Studies* was dedicated to the population question, with contributions from well-known theologians such as J. Bryan Hehir, Margaret Farley, RSM, and David Hollenbach, SJ. According to the contributors, the "overpopulation crisis" necessitates, at the very least, an avoidance of making a public case for *Humanae Vitae*.[33] Indeed, Hollenbach devotes his entire dissertation to the argument that the right to procreate is not absolute and may be limited by the state, rejecting as simple-minded the Church's insistence that people be free of governmental coercion in this matter.[34] (In his research, he must not have discovered the fact that state-mandated population-control programs always brutally target the poor. Population control simply cannot be squared with the preferential option for the poor.) Hollenbach presumed, of course, that the Church's teaching on contraception was wrong.[35] More recently, Daniel Maguire of Marquette University has recycled the "duty" argument of Sanger by insisting that contracepting is the "service we owe this earth" in order to halt overpopulation.[36]

The overpopulation argument is based on numerous fallacies. Population density cannot be said to cause economic problems, environmental devastation, or war; political and economic systems have much more to do with these problems than the number of people.[37] Mary Eberstadt summarizes the truth drolly when she writes, "Less than half a century later, these preoccupations with overwhelming birth rates appear as pseudo-scientific as phrenology. Actually, that may be unfair to phrenology."[38] In fact, despite the mounting evidence pointing to the sociological and economic dangers of decreasing birth rates, population controllers continue to push contraceptives upon the unwilling, especially nonwhite, poor—even though, for example, Kenya's population density stands at 59 people per square kilometer, while Belgium's is 341.[39] When was the last time we heard the population-control establishment worrying about the fertility of the world's rich?

At War with Oneself

The "war" that is fought against female fertility is not restricted to what happens in health clinics in the developing world. It is carried to the very psyches of women and girls everywhere. If we are telling women that their own bodies are the cause of their problems (and those of the world as well), how can we expect them to be at peace with themselves?

Lest this claim seem extravagant, let's look more closely at some of the explicit and implicit messages that impress upon women and girls the need to turn against their bodies in order to be liberated. An ad for the first birth-control pill assumed women are enslaved by their bodies:

> From the beginning woman has been a vassal to the temporal demands ... of the cyclic mechanism of her reproductive system. Now to a degree heretofore unknown, she is permitted *normalization* ... of cyclic function. This new method [of] control is symbolized in an illustration borrowed from ancient Greek mythology—Andromeda freed from her chains.[40]

The ad copy lays out with astonishing explicitness what most women only unconsciously think: I am imprisoned by my body, especially by my fertility, and I need to control it, bend it to my will, in order to be free. My body, especially my fertility, is not a gift but a burden. This ideology is echoed in the Majority Rebuttal of the pope's birth-control commission in 1967: "biological fecundity" (that is, female fertility) "is subject to many *irregularities* and therefore ought to be *assumed into the human sphere* and *be regulated* within it."[41] Translation: let contraception "normalize" the disconcerting power of not-quite-fully-human female fertility (technological control yielding a masculine regularity), and we'll all be better off. But is this the way to respect women and their bodies: to make male physiology and sexuality the norm (indeed, "the human sphere") to which women must conform themselves?

If it sounds far-fetched that such abstractions could affect everyday women, consider this: how many women do you know who seem at home in their bodies? Modern Western women and girls are too often in a state of undeclared war with their bodies, seeking to remake them until they fit the dominant cultural standards of attractiveness. During the past forty years or so, those standards have gradually come to emphasize thinness to an extreme degree. As fertility has become more and more optional and undervalued in women, so have cultural elites located female beauty less in fertile Rubenesque voluptuousness and more in prepubescent skin-and-bone youth.

A second sign of the internalized war women and girls undergo is the degree to which they are willing to accept all manner of side effects and dangers in the cause of suppressing their fertility. One might compare the mechanism of the Pill to that of killing a mouse with a cannonball. Unlike barrier methods, which put a physical obstacle between the sperm and the egg, hormonal contraception disrupts the body's whole hormonal system for the sole sake of preventing ovulation. Despite being commonly dispensed to women and girls as though they were aspirin, hormonal contraceptives pose significant, though incompletely assessed, health risks, especially for the young. We almost never reflect upon this risk, even as organic food becomes more and more popular among the well-off. Critical thought on this subject, as reflected in this former Pill-user's account, is all too rare: "I was eating organic vegetables, drinking hormone-free milk and using chemical-free cleaners. I knew deep down that birth control pills did not fit into my parameter of healthy living."[42]

Some side effects and risks of oral contraceptives have been documented. One only has to read the Pill's package insert to see them enumerated. Some are almost amusing, if you like ironic humor: loss of libido, for example, an effect that could be long-term.[43] (Take this medication as your ticket to sexual freedom, and hopefully you won't lose your sexual desire along the way. But then, was the point of the sexual revolution, radicalized in the "hookup" culture, ever really the satisfaction of female desire?) Some side effects are more serious, such as blood clots. It was the incidence of strokes and fatal blood clots among the early cohorts using oral contraceptives that caused some feminist backlash against the drug in the early 1970s.[44] Recent research indicates the risk for heart attack or stroke doubles for women on low-dose pills.[45] Another study showed the risk for cervical cancer doubling among women using the Pill for five or more years.[46] Fortunately, for many of these conditions, the risk dissipates after discontinuing use of the Pill.[47]

The cavalier way in which women are expected to expose themselves to health risks for the sake of sterility indicates a wider problem. Women and girls internalize the war against their bodies by accepting the dominant, masculine utilitarian calculus as determining their value. Female bodies become reduced to their possibilities for providing enjoyment to men. But when female fertility is valued, women's bodies are recognized as having a larger purpose beyond male sexual fantasy. That purpose, of course, is the bearing of children, which transcends the often selfish pursuits upon which men and women fixate in a culture of consumerist desire. While sex accomplishes many things beyond procreation in a relationship, maintaining an openness to children prevents sex from becoming narcissistic. Children point one to the future, to the great unknown, to projects and plans bigger than just me or even us. If children are taken out of the equation, then it becomes easy to reduce women's bodies to what is useful in the here and now.

But *is* there a better use for female bodies than the pursuit of pleasure? A twentieth-century cultural analyst, Michel Foucault, enunciated the dominant paradigm: sex is about bodies and pleasures.[48] Because fertility doesn't matter any more, it doesn't matter whether the bodies are male or female; they are all just raw material for anonymous couplings. This is the depersonalized view of the body that reigns in the age of "hookups" and "friends with benefits," the age of contraception and same-sex "marriage." It is a world in which female fertility just doesn't fit. It is also a world in which the female body is ripe for exploitation by male pleasure-seekers—provided, of course, that the body is suitably sterilized first.

That this turn of events is degrading to women is acknowledged by all but the most obtuse contemporary feminists. Eberstadt observes that numerous feminists have complained about the current sexual regime, but she notes that "there is no auxiliary literature of grievance for men— [who], for the most part, just don't seem to feel they have as much to grieve about in this new world order. . . ."[49] In fact, the male voices opposing such exploitation have usually been religious ones. For example, Pope Paul VI predicted in *Humanae Vitae* that contraception would lead husbands to "lose respect for their wives." As a result, they would be tempted to "use their wives as instruments for serving their own desires. Consequently, they will no longer view their wives as companions who should be treated with attentiveness and love."[50] Likewise, Mohandas Gandhi wrote, "As it is, man has sufficiently degraded [woman] for his lust, and artificial methods, no matter how well-meaning the advocates may be, will still further degrade her."[51]

But such voices are too rare. Easily obtainable sexual gratification from perpetually available women and girls: no scoundrel would have dared dream up this world simply delivered into his lap by *Sex and the City* "feminism." And what happens to a whole society when everyone agrees that the female body is better off sterile?

What a Contracepting Society Looks Like

Contraception was from the beginning touted as the answer to a host of societal problems, from the old neo-Malthusian bogeyman of overpopulation, down to marital unhappiness and child abuse. But have such extravagant claims come true?

Has contraception helped marriage? Contraception, after all, is sold as promoting the deeper union of the spouses. But divorce has skyrocketed to around 40 to 50 percent of all marriages since contraception became a widespread marital practice. If contraception increases bonding between spouses, then at least some amelioration of the divorce rate among those using contraception (that is, almost every married couple) should be evident. But no data indicate such an effect. In fact, demographer Robert T. Michael has argued that half of the rise of the divorce rate between 1965 and when it leveled off in 1976 "can be attributed to the 'unexpected nature of the contraceptive revolution' ... especially in the way that it made marriages less child-centered."[52] More generally, given the deepening of love that it is supposed to foster, contraception should help prevent fatherless homes, in which the security provided by two married, biological parents is lacking. The evidence points to the contrary. Nobel Prize-winning economist George Akerlof has documented how the "choice" for women to contracept beginning in the 1960s has significantly *raised* the rates of unwed motherhood and child abandonment by fathers: "The sexual revolution, by making the birth of the child the *physical* choice of the mother, makes marriage and child support a *social* choice of the father."[53]

Has contraception prevented "unwanted children" from being conceived, thus supposedly reducing child abuse? Again, the correlative data is not good for theologians who promote contraception: in 1960, 749 children were believed to be abused in the U.S.; by 2006, more than 900,000 children were determined to be abused or neglected.[54] Much of this increase is surely due to better reporting of incidents. But if contraception is such a panacea for the problem of unloved children, should not *some* decrease in child abuse be detectable as the rate of contraceptive use increased dramatically?

What about preventing abortion? This possibility is still raised by some Catholics as a pious reason to support contraception. Speaker of the House Nancy Pelosi has repeatedly promoted "preventing unintended pregnancies and reducing the need for abortion through increasing access to family planning services and access to affordable birth control."[55] Yet it is astonishing that few people who make this claim attempt to provide any empirical support for it. Pelosi doesn't reckon with the reality that contraception closes the partners' hearts, here and now, to a child. They think they have made an arrangement: sex but no child. No thought goes into what might happen if a child is conceived. So, when a child comes—as one so often does, given the fact that sex tends to produce what it is meant to produce—the adults are not mentally open to her. They have contracepted their hearts. We shouldn't be surprised that increased promotion and use of contraceptives among adolescents are linked to *more* abortions, not fewer.[56]

So what does a contracepting culture look like? It looks a lot like our culture: more divorce, more unwed parenthood, more abuse, more abortion, less commitment, less trust, less love. Looking at this aggregate of social ills, one sociologist has written, "The shifts in sexual and familial behavior to which dissenters would like the church to accommodate herself have been revealed in study after study to be social catastrophes."[57]

Could these catastrophes have been foreseen? In fact, they were—by Pope Paul VI. We have already noted two of his predictions that have come true: coerced contraceptive use inflicted by oppressive governments, and the increased degradation of women (including an increase in marital infidelity). The Pope made another prediction: a general lowering of sexual morality was to be expected.[58] If one doubts whether this has occurred, just ask any young person about "sexting" (sending sexually explicit messages or photos by cell phone) and the hookup culture as a whole.

It is important to understand that neither Pope Paul VI nor I would want to claim that birth control is wrong *because* it has bad effects. Human actions are right or wrong because of the acts that they are, not because of their effects. But bad actions usually lead to bad effects, because they are not good for us. We were made for true love, and anything less fails to make us truly happy.

From Contraceptive Control to Life-Giving Love

The reigning ideology tells us that the unkempt contours of female fertility must be scoured away by a masculine, mechanizing ideology in order to fit into the smooth cogs of the sexual revolution. But is the only paradigm that applies to female fertility one of technological control? Or is there another way to approach female fertility that appreciates rather than scapegoats it, while not requiring women to produce dozens of progeny?

The Catholic Church's countercultural way of cherishing female fertility is spelled out in *Humanae Vitae*. There Pope Paul VI notes that, rather than asking women to have as many children as they are physically able to bear, the Church proposes "responsible parenthood": intelligent openness to welcoming many children. Many considerations might enter into the discernment of whether having a child at a given time is prudent—if such discernment is carried out in a spirit of generosity.[59]

This intelligent, active discernment is the opposite of the eclipse of the question of children facilitated by hormonal contraceptive use. With contraception, one may decide against having children at a certain time and never deliberately revisit the original decision. Technological *control* does

not require self-knowledge and *self-mastery*, but merely the ability to follow directions on a package.

Resorting to technological autopilot means one can go along without
seriously engaging the question of the larger meaning of one's life. Why am
I here? What is that wise and loving plan of God for my life that is the reason
for my existing at all? Has my fertility been entrusted to me to freely and
deliberately serve God's overflowing desire to bring more human lives into
existence? How do my "private" actions affect the body politic?

Discerning "serious reasons" for delaying childbirth through "responsible parenthood," as proposed by the Church in *Humanae Vitae*, is conducted within this infinite horizon of divine wisdom and love, and of the
common good of society. This is a world away from birth control, which
reduces the horizon of my consciousness to *my* plans for *my* life, a meager
thing compared to the greatness God has in store for each of us. The
Church never wants any of us to settle for less than the nobility and gran-
deur of true love.

There may indeed be serious reasons to delay conceiving a child at a
given time, but one must be open to reconsidering that decision at any
point if it seems that God's wise and loving will is leading a couple onto a
new path. The discernment of responsible parenthood is, in other words,
an interior openness to letting God's generous, life-giving will into the
bedroom—even if it is not convenient—for God wants only each person's
happiness, the fulfillment of our freedom in a love without limit.
Responsible parenthood is one thing; it is quite another to control inconvenient fertility through technological routinization.

The decision to postpone childbearing requires such careful discernment because children are good for a marriage. What really makes us
mature people able to sustain an intimate, permanent relationship is the
ability to love definitively, without reserve, without thinking first of one's
own advantage. A person capable of true love can give and take, can compromise, can communicate without defensiveness or nastiness, and so
forth. But, in the usual case, what teaches a married couple such
selflessness is having children.[ii]

---

ii. Infertile couples bear a great cross, which if accepted as God's will, will take them
along another path leading to fruitfulness of a spiritual order. Nevertheless, every time
they engage in the marital act, they are still saying with their bodies, "I love you totally. I
give everything of myself to you." They are not holding their fertility back, as with contraception.

Before children, it was possible for me to live with my husband as I might live with a really congenial roommate. He had his schedule; I had mine. Marriage was a wonderful and challenging thing in many ways, but it did not ask us to give of ourselves extravagantly most of the time. When our first child came, however, I experienced for the first time the genuine neediness of another person. I had to bend my schedule and my life to her, as did my husband. This newfound ability to give of ourselves, while often painfully won (colic and all), was the most important growth that we experienced in our lives. It was also the single best thing that ever happened to our marriage. We experienced what is true for every human being: self-gift, while difficult, makes us flourish.

We did not have children right away in our marriage. Initially we were both in graduate school, and we thought we had serious reasons to delay having children at the beginning of our marriage. (I was in my third tri-mester with our first child while taking my doctoral comprehensive exams.) So, what could we do if contraception was off-limits?

Just prior to Paul VI's time, a scientific breakthrough in the under-standing of the cycles of female fertility had laid the groundwork for a new method of natural family planning (NFP). NFP depends upon judg-ing the signs of fertility given by the woman's body and either abstaining from intercourse during fertile times (in order to avoid pregnancy) or engaging in the conjugal act (in order to achieve pregnancy). When used properly, it is 99 percent effective in avoiding pregnancy—as effective as the Pill—and much more effective than artificial reproductive technolo-gies in achieving pregnancy.[60]

Many people do not understand the distinction between NFP and con-traception. Surely, they say, the intention is the same, and thus NFP is just "Catholic birth control." Indeed, faithful Catholics are often hesitant about NFP because they worry about what might constitute a sufficiently serious reason to postpone childbearing. It is significant that the teaching documents of the Church deliberately avoid providing a list of reasons that would count as "serious." The pope cannot, nor does he have the least desire to, decide if a family is ready to have a child at a given time; only the couple's prayerful discernment of God's wise and particular will for them can do that.

My personal observation is that natural family planning weeds out less-than-serious reasons. Instead of routinely popping a pill every day, the

NFP couple have to discuss their decision to postpone having children. This discussion may even occur over several days every month! When a reason becomes less than serious, the method invites a couple to begin engaging in the marital act on days that are on the outer edge of fertility, and so on. NFP of itself places a couple in a deliberate, and joint, vocational discernment of God's loving will. This is far different from the birth-control routine. The former is always nimble, always open to God's will, while the latter tends to foster an avoidance of the question of children. The proponents of birth control may speak of "family planning" and "planned parenthood," but, ironically, birth control tends to suppress a free and deliberate approach to children.

Act, Intention, and Object: A Quick Primer in the Philosophical Underpinnings of NFP

This fundamental difference between the NFP and contraceptive patterns of life flows from a difference in the *kinds* of acts involved. Without understanding this, it is hard to fully grasp why NFP is not "Catholic birth control." If a couple uses natural family planning, depending on the woman's point in her cycle, they will either engage in the marital act, or not—both of which are of course, in and of themselves, perfectly licit things to do. The contracepting couple does something entirely different: they engage in deliberately sterilized acts of sex. This is a different *kind* of action.

It is no small part of the difficulty in intelligently distinguishing between NFP and contraception that the notion of *kinds* of things, let alone of kinds of *actions*, has fallen into disfavor. In our relativistic culture, we tend to think that things do not have inherent meaning, but rather that they gain their meaning from the value one places on them in terms of one's own desires. The "realist" view, by contrast, holds that things have *real* natures that are intelligible, that is, a discoverable design that intelligibly fits into the whole system of other natures. Realists claim, for instance, that marriage has a real nature—one man and one woman publicly and faithfully committed to each other for the exclusive sharing of their life together, ordered to the procreation and education of children. Relativists will say that marriage is whatever we define it to be, according to our desires.[61]

Along with losing the recognition that there are real kinds of *things*, we are also losing the sense that some *actions* are of such a kind as to be always encouraged and other actions to be always resisted. Every properly human action, that is, every free human action, will be either good or bad. Any free human act will either advance us along the path of our flourishing, the path of happiness, or along the path of disintegration, or unhappiness. In performing any free act, we either make ourselves better or we make ourselves worse.

When, in this relativist culture, we think of actions as good or bad, we instinctively think of our *personal intention* as decisive. Thus, "it may not be the best thing to tell a lie, but he just didn't want to hurt her feelings. His intention was good, so what he did was all right." It is certainly the case that intention has much to do with the badness or goodness of an act. But intention is not the most basic factor; what is most basic is the *object* that makes an act into a certain *kind* of act.[62]

In and of themselves, certain kinds of actions are good (such as giving money to the poor); some are indifferent (such as crossing the street), and some are evil, always and everywhere (such as rape and murder). An action is good, indifferent, or evil by virtue of what is technically called the "moral object." If someone were to ask you whether "taking" is wrong, you would have to ask, "taking what?" The "what" would be the moral object. "Taking" is not a specific *kind* of moral act. But taking something against the reasonable will of its owner *is* a recognizable kind of moral act: stealing. This is distinct from the issue of intention. One can steal with a good intention, but that good intention does not change stealing from *being* a bad act, which in and of itself it is, into *being* a good act. Intention does not change the nature of the act. The ends (intention) do not justify the means (the kind of act performed).[63]

Suppose I have a good intention: to feed my family. But what is the *kind* of moral act I perform as a means to that end? I could either hold up a convenience store, or I could get a job and work hard to earn money. The intention is the same; are the acts the same? Hardly. One is a bad kind of act, and the other a good kind of act.

So let's look again at the kinds of action involved in contraception and NFP. The intention may be exactly the same: to avoid having children at this point in time. Does that mean that NFP is simply another form of birth control? We could only say this if we focused solely on the intention of the actors. Though intention is important, the more basic reality is the kind of act involved. What *kind* of act is contracepted sex; what *kinds* of acts are involved in NFP?

Pope Paul VI notes in *Humanae Vitae* that sex, the marital act, has two "meanings": the intimate unity of the spouses and the generation of children, called the unitive and procreative meanings respectively.[64] With contraception, the moral object of the action is the deliberate blocking of the possibility of children in an otherwise fertile sexual act. That is, when a couple contracepts, whatever their good intention, they distort the nature of the sexual act by severing its unitive and procreative meanings. If we thus deform sex, which inherently *means* the union of lifelong and life-giving love, we cannot expect to flourish as a result. Intentions and desires are not all there is to reality.[65]

When NFP is used to avoid pregnancy, the couple either abstains from the conjugal act during the fertile period or engages in it during the infertile time. These actions, or nonactions, do not involve deliberately taking away the procreative meaning of an otherwise fertile conjugal act. Instead, the couple *honors* that meaning, and thus the given nature of sex, *precisely by abstaining during the woman's fertile period.*

Cultivating Ethical Maturity: NFP's Path to Self-Mastery

It is important to understand that being able to redirect one's drive for intimacy into nonsexual expressions for a time is not a bad thing. Rather, it fosters human flourishing—and thus it is morally good. Periodic abstinence heals and integrates one's desires. Through such self-mastery comes real freedom, which is the freedom to give generously of oneself, without limits. What passes as freedom in a consumerist culture—being able to pursue whatever desires happen to strike one's fancy—is in fact the very opposite of freedom: we can't help but follow our urges. Morally good action instead leads toward freedom from the compulsion and unhappiness involved in being internally enslaved to every passing desire. A genuinely free and mature person is able to say no to immediate desires, when necessary, in order to pursue things that are more lasting and valuable—such as better health, achievement in athletics or the arts, or professional advancement. We have all made sacrifices of immediate gratification for the sake of such goods. When we can say no to the satisfaction of lesser desires for the sake of higher desires, we come to love better.

In cultivating such ethical maturity, natural family planning places fertility regulation within the wide horizon of God's wise and loving plan for the happiness of each human being. Instead of *external*, technological control severing the two meanings of the sexual act, as happens with contraception, NFP promotes the interior *self*-control, or better, self-integration, necessary for one to be able to make a sincere and total gift of self.[66] NFP provides training in true love, and true love is the only path to happiness. Contraception opposes human happiness by elevating immediate self-gratification to the position of primacy in sexual decision-making. Sexual desire and pleasure are great things, but they are meant to serve true love.

And that is why, finally, contraceptive sex is not good for us: because self-centeredness is not good for us. It makes us unhappy, while self-giving leads to true, deep happiness, the kind of happiness you see in those close to God. For sex to be self-giving, both meanings of sex have to be present. When the procreative end of sex is deliberately thwarted through contraception, the ability of the spouses to unite in a total self-gift (the unitive meaning) is thwarted as well. The ramifications of this can be seen in the roughly 50 percent divorce rate among the general public, while the divorce rate among NFP-practicing couples is between 0.2 percent and 4 percent.[67] Openness to life and spousal bonding *do* go hand in hand. In fact, the bonding is so powerful precisely because sex is meant to be total surrender to the other person, including surrender to the possible fruitfulness of one's mutual love. It is this openness to the future, to something greater than just "us," that actually makes sex so thrilling.

This big picture of self-gift is what dissenting theology and conventional feminism miss. Recall the charge of physicalism, the accusation that Catholic teaching on contraception focuses obsessively on the mechanics of the physical act of sex rather than the relationship's openness to children as a whole. But it is precisely the point of Pope John Paul II's theology of the body to show that sex is not simply about bodies bumping together. By placing sex within the big picture of true love in all its breadth, John Paul makes clear that sex is a deeply *personal* act, one of the most personal we will ever perform. The stakes are so high with sex because at issue is the future of true love, of society, of God's plan for our greatness and happiness.

Saint Thomas Aquinas, the thirteenth-century theologian, argues that sins against God, such as blasphemy, are objectively the worst, but sins involving lust are in some ways the most dangerous, because they ensnare us the most.[68] We are not brains in a vat, tenuously connected to bodies that can do their own thing. Rather, our bodily acts form *who we are*. If a man develops selfish patterns of sexual desire, then *he* is harmed—not just his body—and the spiritual pleasures of true, personal love become a closed book to him. After all, how many times do I have to rob a convenience store before *I am* a thief? It would be supreme silliness for me to sit in court and declare, "I am fully committed to respecting private property and living justly. Sure, I robbed three Quick-E Marts, but don't call me a thief! Those were just the acts I did with my body, not with my mind!"

In fact, we cannot decide which acts we are going to let affect us in our innermost core. It would make no sense for the Church to say, "Stealing is wrong. But as long as you don't let this particular act of theft affect your overall commitment to justice, then one act of theft is okay." Likewise, the Church cannot simply decide that individual acts (how many?) of contracepted sex are not going to hurt one's relationship with one's spouse and with God. If we *act* selfishly in our sexual life, we *become* selfish, and no amount of wrangling about the Church's teaching on contraception can change that.

"An Act of Giving, Not Taking"

Margaret Sanger and the dominant culture give one answer to the question of what is bad for us: female fertility. By contrast, the Church argues that it is not the female body that oppresses women and girls, but rather that deformed desire is at the heart of all sin—and thus all oppression.

If deformed desire is bad for us, healed desire, put in the service of self-giving love, is good for us. How do we develop such love? As we have seen, the periodic abstinence involved in natural family planning heals desire in a way that contraception cannot. Desire is in itself not immoral; by nature, we are creatures who physically desire, because we have bodies with senses that detect what is pleasurable. But desire must be fully human: it has to be directed by our intelligence and freedom. Some training of sexual desire is necessary in order that it find its right place: *eros* in the service of *agape*, that is, erotic love put in the service of charity.[69] Here NFP can play a central role.

As my husband can testify, NFP demands something profoundly countercultural: that men learn to measure their sexual desires by the rhythms of the female body. Such a request is unheard of in a society in which male desire appears to set the guidelines—especially in the "hookup" culture. Indeed, such a reorientation of desire is more revolutionary than any secular feminist project.

In reflecting on the internal chastity that came with practicing NFP, Fletcher Doyle, author of *Natural Family Planning Blessed Our Marriage: 19 True Stories*, noted how profoundly it altered his relationship with his wife for the better. "She became even more beautiful to me," he said. "Now, more than ever before, I had to consider her in her entirety as a human person and avoid the trap of thinking of her as someone to take care of my needs ... [m]y life with my wife became more an act of giving rather than taking."[70]

Perhaps it was for this reason that Pope John Paul II recommended the periodic abstinence of NFP as intrinsic to marital spirituality, regardless of a couple's childbearing plans.[71] This abstinence helps form one's desires in the virtue of chastity, which in turn renders one capable of seeing one's spouse the way God sees him or her. Chastity gives spouses "a singular *sensibility for all* that in their vocation and shared life carries *the sign of the mystery of creation and redemption*: for all that is a created reflection of God's wisdom and love."[72] Reverence for the procreative meaning of sex means reverence for the female ability to bear new life and, thus, reverence for the female body in its holistic truth—as opposed to reducing the female body to the status of a sexual object. The Church, through NFP, promotes the reorientation of male desire toward such reverence for the female body. This cherishing of women and girls in their personal wholeness would be a genuine sexual revolution.

Reverence for the other disrupts the frantic pursuit of pleasure that withers our ability to love generously. As we have seen, in a contracepting culture, the single-minded pursuit of sexual pleasure to the exclusion of new life leads a man and woman to close their hearts to that future *beyond their control* that they would face together as mother and father. By controlling births, our culture hopes to control, to tame, and to commodify the extravagant claims of love—to measure them according to our mea-ger measure.[73] Contraception was sold as something that would build up love, yet it narrows love into a cramped selfishness that causes both personal heartbreak and social injustice.

In stark contrast to this contraction, the reality is that we human beings are called to greatness. We are made in the image of God, made to know and love him and each other in a love without limit. God is supremely selfless, giving of himself constantly. We are made for no less. That is why the Second Vatican Council could say that the likeness between us and God "reveals that man, who is the only creature on earth which God willed for itself, cannot fully find himself except through a sincere gift of himself."[74] This kind of love—a no-holds-barred, self-giving, God-trusting love—is an arduous adventure. It is not "safe." But it is the only kind of love that is worthy of the dignity of men and women, made for the greatness of union with God. And it is the only kind that will make us truly happy.

6

The Church's Best Kept Secret: Church Teaching on Infertility Treatment

KATIE ELROD

WITH PAUL CARPENTIER, MD, CFCMC

Infertile. It is a ugly word and certainly not one I wanted to hear from my doctor in 2001. I was thirty-one years old, and a year earlier I'd had a miscarriage at twelve weeks. I was heartbroken, but determined to find a treatment. I asked what I could do. My doctor responded that I should relax for a while, and jokingly suggested that I might spend more time with a friend of mine and a patient of hers who seemed to get pregnant at the drop of a hat. Angry and taken aback, I walked out of that doctor's office and never returned. I had to endure four more years of infertility, miscarriages, and pain before I gave birth to my son in 2005.

This is the story of my struggle with infertility. During this difficult time, I came to understand that the diagnosis of infertility is more common than one might think, and that its treatment can be fraught with risk. But, to my great joy, I found the answer to my medical problems within an institution not so well known for being at the cutting edge of science and medicine: the Catholic Church.

Infertility Today

A woman is diagnosed as infertile when she has had intercourse for twelve months or more and has not become pregnant.[1] According to the National Center for Health Statistics, 12 percent of all sexually active women and 15 percent of married women experienced impaired fertility in 2002;[2] the U.S. Department of Health and Human Services reports that 33 percent of couples in which the woman is thirty-five or older and is seeking to become pregnant suffer from infertility.[3]

So often taken for granted, the conception of a child is a sophisticated process that depends upon many factors. If any one factor is impaired, infertility could result. The capacity to achieve a pregnancy relies on the following: the ability of the man to produce healthy sperm and the woman healthy eggs; unblocked fallopian tubes; the existence of good cervical fluid through which the sperm can reach and fertilize the egg; the receptivity of the endometrium (i.e., the uterine wall) to the implantation of the newly created embryo; the quality and ongoing health of the embryo; an adequate hormonal environment for the embryo to develop; and other factors.

Most doctors consider infertility a disease in and of itself. However, appropriate analysis reveals that infertility is actually a symptom of many possible underlying diseases or conditions. Some of these diseases and conditions are congenitally or medically unavoidable; others may be avoided by the lifestyle choices a woman makes early in her life.

Ovulation disorders cause approximately 40 percent of female infertility problems.[4] When healthy, the female reproductive system depends on a delicate balance of progesterone and estrogen levels, which rise and fall throughout each menstrual cycle. If a woman's hormone levels are below average or the hormones are not produced at the right time in her cycle, conception is unlikely to occur; if it does, the embryo will not successfully implant in the uterus, resulting in miscarriage.

One in ten women are thought to suffer from another ovarian dysfunction called PCOS (polycystic ovarian syndrome).[5] PCOS patients experience a cluster of disorders that include high levels of male hormones called androgens, the growth of ovarian cysts in each ovary, and the inability of the ovary to produce mature follicles capable of ovulating.

Female infertility can also be caused by blocked fallopian tubes as a result of endometriosis or other conditions. Endometriosis is a medical condition in which tissue similar to the inner uterine lining locates itself elsewhere in the woman's reproductive system. It was once thought that such tissue could cause a toxic environment inside the pelvis, preventing an egg from being released from the ovary or the embryo from being implanted. New evidence suggests that endometriosis and ovarian dysfunction are simultaneous consequences of a complex interplay of immune dysfunction[6] and abnormalities in the production of estrogen and prostaglandins.[7] Together these often lead to pain, poor ovulation, and poor implantation, and are often accompanied by premenstrual tension symptoms. The numbers of women suffering from this disease is high: as many as 5 million American women of reproductive age have endometriosis,[8] while 30 to 50 percent of women suffering from infertility have the disease.[9]

Several lifestyle choices increase a woman's chance of becoming infertile. If she smokes or is overweight, she is more likely to have trouble conceiving. A 1998 study concluded that in smokers, infertility rates are higher, conception rates are reduced, and time to conception is delayed.[10] A 2007 study showed that women with regular cycles, and no other obvious fertility problems, still have difficulty achieving a pregnancy if they are overweight. This study also found that the more overweight the woman is, the lower her chances of pregnancy.[11]

A third significant lifestyle factor that causes infertility is the type and number of sexually transmitted diseases (STDs) a woman has had. The most common female STDs—chlamydia and gonorrhea—are infections of the cervix and fallopian tubes. If left untreated, such infections can cause infertility. The incidence of chlamydial infections has increased annually since the late 1980s. In 2007, more than 1 million cases were reported in the United States. According to the Centers for Disease Control and Prevention (CDC), this is the largest number of cases ever reported for *any* condition, corresponding to approximately 370 cases per 100,000 people, an increase of 7.5 percent from 2006.[12]

Chlamydia is a bacterium that can be easily eradicated by antibiotics. If left untreated in its earliest stages, however, an infection can lead to

pelvic inflammatory disease (PID). This is a serious condition that dam-
ages the reproductive tract, often scarring and blocking the fallopian
tubes. Scarring may prevent fertilization from occurring, and it also
greatly increases the chance of an ectopic pregnancy and chronic pelvic
pain. PID is one of the major causes of infertility among women of reproductive age, because many women who have chlamydia experience no
symptoms and so fail to properly treat the STD. Up to 40 percent of
females with untreated chlamydia infections develop PID.[13]

Another STD, the human papillomavirus (HPV), is an extremely common sexually transmitted disease.[14] The virus infects and can cause serious abnormalities of the cervix that can lead to cervical cancer. Treatment
can involve freezing or excising part of the cervix, which can decrease or
sometimes totally eliminate future cervical fluid production.[15] Without
cervical fluid, sperm are trapped in the vagina and will die within hours,
unable to travel to the fallopian tubes to fertilize an egg.

Another lifestyle choice that affects a woman's ability to conceive due
to the poor production of cervical fluid is the use of the birth control pill
and similar hormonal contraceptives. These drugs expose the woman's
body to various combinations of potent artificial hormone-like substances
that interact with her natural hormone receptors. These artificial hormone receptor interactions disturb the natural function of the body,
inhibiting ovulation, decreasing cervical fluid, and thinning the lining of
the uterus.[i 16]

Advanced age is the final, and increasingly common, lifestyle cause of
infertility in women. Many women today are delaying childbearing well
into and beyond their years of fertility. Fertility in women peaks at age
twenty-two, and declines as a woman ages, especially after thirty-five.[17]
By age thirty, a woman has only a 20 percent chance of becoming pregnant in a given month, and by age forty, it falls to 5 percent.[18] Despite this
biological reality, the average age of first-time mothers in the United
States has increased from about twenty-one years old in 1970 to just over

---

i. These artificial hormones often stifle future cervical fluid production by suppressing
estradiol receptors in the cervical fluid glands of the cervix. If these receptors are sup-
pressed, then even if the ovary is able to regain its ability to produce normal levels of
estradiol, the cervix will be unable to respond to those hormones due to the lost or dimin-
ished sensitivity of the receptors.

twenty-five in 2005.[19] More than 20 percent of mothers are over thirty-five when they have their first child.[20]

This aging of first-time mothers is a result of a culture that has come to value the establishment of a career or education above the establishment of a family—at the often-painful expense of a woman's fertility. In 2002, the American Society for Reproductive Medicine, the largest association of fertility experts, sought to notify women of the biological facts of female fertility so they could make informed choices about their reproductive lives. But critics, including the National Organization for Women, lashed out at the effort, claiming the advertising campaign was exaggerated and offered partial information.[21]

Jennifer Roback Morse, an economist and contributor to this volume, who herself delayed childbearing for an academic career and suffered from infertility as a result, agrees that women are not receiving the information they need about their fertility. Despite the undeniable success of women in the workforce, she argues, "the typical career path is geared towards the needs of men, not women."[22] The years one must work to secure partnership in a law firm or tenure at a university are the same years a woman is at her peak fertility. The cultural expectation that women should forge careers along the traditional path of men, when women's window of opportunity to bear life is far shorter than their male counterparts, makes one question just how pro-woman the career-centric feminist movement has really been.

Diagnosis and Treatment for Infertility: Putting the Cart before the Horse

Since infertility has many causes, conventional treatment is varied. However, the key to any successful fertility treatment, which not only brings about a healthy, full-term baby, but also heals a woman's underlying pathology, is proper diagnosis. Unfortunately, even before a woman walks through the fertility clinic's door, she has a 25 percent chance of walking out with an "unexplained infertility" diagnosis.[23]

Typically, an infertility doctor will ascertain that the woman's fallopian tubes are not blocked, her partner's sperm is healthy, and her ovaries are going through some ovulatory phases and producing some progesterone.

Some women will then be treated with ovary-stimulating drugs and/or minor surgeries that correct tubal blockages and cauterize endometriosis. If correctly diagnosed, almost 50 percent of these women will have a successful pregnancy from these conventional treatments.[24] But for a large minority of infertile women who undergo this preliminary testing (and even some of these conventional treatments), the cause of their infertility will remain uncertain. Their diagnoses will be recorded as unexplained, and they will be encouraged to seek extraordinary means to achieve a pregnancy.[25]

Many factors can influence a fertility doctor to begin extraordinary infertility treatment without a proper diagnosis. Foremost among them is that assisted reproductive technologies are extraordinarily profitable, and virtually unregulated by either federal or state governments. The average cost of one IVF (in vitro fertilization) cycle is $12,000,[26] and success, if it occurs at all, rarely comes in the first cycle. Profits are estimated at $1 billion annually,[27] with increasing numbers of women seeking IVF.[28] The industry also provides "spare embryos" to researchers involved in genetic manipulation and embryonic stem cell research.[29] Lucrative markets exist for gametes (eggs and sperm), as well as genetic screening and selection.[30] Given the confluence of enormous profits with the strong desire of patients to bear a child, it is deeply troubling that regulation is so lacking.[31] Brooks A. Keel, professor of biomedical sciences and associate vice president of research at Florida State University, explains: "A fertility doctor can literally set up a lab in his garage and hire his son or daughter to run it, and it would be perfectly legal.... A woman gets more regulatory oversight when she gets a tattoo than when she gets IVF."[32] Due to its lack of regulation, the industry has been dubbed the "wild wild West" of reproductive medicine.[33]

Assisted Reproductive Technology

Assisted reproductive technology (ART) is not formally defined but could be considered the group of procedures that go *beyond healing* the body to include those treatments that are artificial,[34] domineering, or ex vivo (outside of the body). The ex vivo procedures are biological processes that usually are accomplished naturally within the body, but can now be conducted outside of the body through these artificial techniques.

ART attempts to procure a baby by using fertility drugs and invasive techniques to take control of the woman's body, rather than assisting the woman's natural reproductive capacities by discovering and then healing the pathologies that have caused the woman's infertility.

Accounting for almost 99 percent of the procedures that handle sperm and eggs outside the womb, IVF dominates fertility medicine because it exerts almost complete control over every part of the reproductive process and is more effective than other ex vivo procedures such as GIFT and ZIFT.[35] IVF involves several steps:

— pumping superovulatory drugs into the woman's body in order to harvest as many eggs as possible;

— extracting the woman's eggs;

— collecting sperm or using sperm already collected and/or frozen;

— joining the sperm and eggs in a petri dish;[36]

— monitoring the growth of the newly created zygotes in the laboratory under a microscope;

— taking cells from the zygotes for chromosomal analyses (in order to try to determine sex and some genetic traits);

— transferring some of the embryos into the woman's uterus through the cervix.

Those embryos that are not transferred are frozen to be implanted at a later time, left in cryostorage indefinitely, used by another couple or for experimentation, or thawed and destroyed.[37] To say this callous treatment of nascent human life is morally problematic would be an understatement.[38] Putting aside the moral objections for now, however, in vitro fertilization has proved itself to be potentially harmful to both women and the children conceived through the procedure.

In Vitro Fertilization—Potentially Harmful to Women and Their Children

The physical and emotional ramifications a woman can suffer during and after an IVF cycle are significant. Perhaps such consequences could have been foreseen had IVF undergone rigorous testing prior to its introduction to women in 1978. The National Institutes of Health conducted no initial studies of IVF, and the procedure was performed on women even before primates or other animals. This caused one embryologist to remark that "women were [perhaps] serving as the model for nonhuman primates."[39] IVF is still under-studied, but medical research is beginning to reveal that the procedure poses significant health risks to both women and the children conceived through IVF.

Though the American Society for Reproductive Medicine recommends the implanting of two to five embryos, depending on the age of the woman, no regulations exist that limit the number of embryos transferred into the uterus.[40] Thus, the vast majority of women undergoing IVF treatment are given superovulatory fertility drugs in order to stimulate their ovaries to produce several eggs at once. A common side effect of superovulation is "ovarian hyperstimulation syndrome" (OHSS), which can result in the dramatic enlargement of the ovaries. Mild to moderate symptoms include abdominal discomfort, nausea, and vomiting, while more severe complications include ovarian ruptures, cysts, and cancers.[41] Though mild to moderate OHSS is more common,[42] as many as 5 percent of women suffer from severe ovarian hyperstimulation.[43]

Further, according to former chief medical officer of the Food and Drug Administration, Suzanne Parisian, the long-term risks from hyperovulatory drugs are largely unknown:

> Although it is common practice in IVF facilities to extract eggs as part of infertility treatment, many of the drugs used during these procedures have not been adequately studied for long-term safety, nor do some of these drugs have FDA approval for these specific indications....
>
> Pharmaceutical firms have not been required by either the government or physicians to collect safety data for IVF drugs regarding risk of cancer or other serious health conditions despite the drugs having been available in the United States for several decades.
>
> ... studies to date have not ruled out a possible link between stimulation drugs and an increased risk of ovarian cancer.[44]

The FDA has on file more than 6,000 complaints regarding Lupron, a drug approved by the FDA but *not* approved to hyperstimulate the ovaries, including twenty-five reported deaths.[45] Indeed, the FDA has specifically labeled Lupron "pregnancy category X," indicating that it should *not* be given to women expecting to become pregnant.[46] Lupron's original purpose and FDA-approved use: to treat men with advanced prostate cancer.

What about the health of a baby conceived in an IVF procedure? Are babies fertilized in a petri dish just as healthy as those conceived in the womb? Not nearly. A 2002 study in the *New England Journal of Medicine* concluded that infants conceived with the use of in vitro fertilization have twice the risk of major birth defects, such as chromosomal or musculoskeletal abnormalities, as naturally conceived infants. The study begins, "In vitro fertilization was introduced into practice with little formal evaluation of its effects on the health of the children conceived with this procedure."[47] Additional studies have found an association between the use of ARTs with a heightened risk of other diseases and malformations.[48]

IVF babies are also at a greater risk for miscarriage. Since women are often undiagnosed or misdiagnosed at the outset, the underlying ovarian, uterine, and pelvic pathologies often do not receive adequate attention during ART. Thus embryos are placed into an unhealthy womb. In 2001, 6.7 embryos were lost to miscarriage for every baby that was born.[49]

Even if a baby conceived through IVF is carried to term, she is still much more likely to be born at a lower birth weight than her naturally conceived peers. Due to the often excessive implantation of embryos into the uterus, 35 percent of all IVF babies are multiples, mostly twins. There is a direct link between multiple births, prematurity, and low birth weight in infants.[50] Fifty percent of premature multiples are at *risk* for severe complications such as respiratory distress syndrome, and they have a higher rate of death in the first month.[51] Multiple pregnancies also heightens *the mother's* risk of high blood pressure, anemia, preeclampsia, uterine rupture, placenta previa, and abruption.[52] As they mature, premature babies are at greater risk for developmental problems, cerebral palsy, and blindness.[53] In recent years, researchers have found that some of the premature babies conceived through ART are not multiples. ART-assisted singletons also have a higher risk of prematurity and thus low birth weight, with all of the usual consequences.[54]

IVF doctors often advise their patients who have conceived multiples to "selectively reduce," that is, abort, one or more of the fetuses.[55] Though the purpose is to sacrifice one or two of the siblings to increase the odds that the others will survive, the procedure carries a risk of losing all the fetuses.[56] One study found a 16 percent rate for both miscarriage and prematurity following one type of "selective reduction,"[57] while an alternative method is associated with a higher risk of infant mortality.[58] It is simply devastating for a woman who has so longed for a child to be advised to participate in ending her nascent child or children's lives (even in an effort to save the others). This can place a great psychological burden on her.[59]

An infertile woman is already emotionally burdened even before she undergoes any type of infertility treatment. A 1993 Harvard Medical School study found that women who suffer from infertility are just as distressed as women diagnosed with cancer.[60] After she found out that her scarred fallopian tubes would prevent her from ever conceiving, one woman remarked, "I might have jumped out of the hospital windows if they hadn't been hermetically sealed.... That may sound shocking, but the psychology of infertility is pernicious and crushing."[61] In addition to an infertile woman's sense of being broken, most are also feeling physically ill in one way or another. Many describe pelvic pain, painful intercourse, premenstrual dysphoric disorder, unusual bleeding, hirsutism, acne, sleep difficulties, low energy, and other symptoms. In this emotionally and physically sensitive state, many women are vulnerable to doctors who advertise quick results from an IVF procedure.

Secular feminists have been some of the most vocal critics of in vitro fertilization because of their belief that the procedure objectifies women: (1) it exploits their desires (or anxieties) about motherhood; (2) it exposes their reproductive capacities to (male) technological manipulation and control; (3) it fragments and then reconstructs their bodies; and (4) it depersonalizes and disintegrates them as persons.[62] This feminist critique makes good sense because, philosophically speaking, women undergoing IVF procedures *are* objectified. They are used, treated as a *means* to the desired end (even if it's the woman's desired end): a live and healthy baby.

The source of a woman's objectification resides in the utilitarian nature of IVF. It does not restore her reproductive health, but bypasses, usurps, and overrides the woman's natural fertility cycle by using an aggressive technique solely focused on producing a child—often at the cost of a woman's physical and emotional health.

A baby conceived through IVF can come at a great price to a woman's well-being. Fortunately, it doesn't have to be this way. The Catholic Church in her concern for the whole person has, through her teachings, encouraged an effective and holistic treatment for infertility. One successful and restorative treatment using licit means is called Natural Procreative Technology. NaProTECHNOLOGY, to which the latter half of this chapter is dedicated, treats not only infertility, but also many other reproductive health issues facing women, such as premenstrual syndrome (PMS) and postpartum depression.

The Church's Loving Response— Donum Vitae *and* Dignitas Personae

The Church wrote her first official response to the practice of ART in the now famous document, *Donum Vitae* (1987). According to *Donum Vitae*, when medicine deviates from the principles inherent in the Hippocratic Oath—staying true to the art of healing and aiding in the person's inclination toward wholeness[63]—women, babies, and families are likely to suffer. This suffering originates in a misunderstanding of the nature of the human person and the intrinsic meaning and dimensions of procreation.

The Church unequivocally states that an inalienable dignity belongs to every human being from the moment of his or her conception. The origin of this proclamation is both anthropological and theological. From the anthropological point of view, the Church teaches that:

> The body of a human being, from the very first stages of its existence, can never be reduced merely to a group of cells. The embryonic human body develops progressively according to a well-defined program with its proper finality, as is apparent in the birth of every baby.[64]

Every child, born or unborn, created as a result of loving married intercourse, or in a petri dish to be transferred to the womb, left indefinitely in cryostorage, or used in scientific experimentation, shares equally in this inalienable human dignity.[65] Moreover, each child is equal in dignity to his or her mother. This is why the *desire* for a child, albeit a very real and natural desire, can never become a *right* to a child at any cost. "No person can claim the right to the existence of another; otherwise the latter would be placed on a lower level of value than the one who claims such a right."[66]

When a woman contracts with a third party to create a child through IVF, she is regarding the baby as an object to be procured or a commodity to be bought. This artificially created child, though ardently desired and of equal value to those naturally conceived, exists solely as the object of the woman's will. By electing to artificially create another human being, she has taken the place of God, giving herself an authority, a responsibility, over another person that does not befit a mere human being.[67]

Besides objectifying the child, by transforming her desire for a child into a right to a child at any cost, the woman inadvertently objectifies herself. Her desire for a child can never supersede her duty to respect herself as an integral whole, an embodied soul. For decades, feminists have fought against the traditional notion that women are just bodies, bodies made for making babies, and that's all. From lipstick ads to workmen whistling at women walking by, feminists fight against any objectification of a woman's body that separates it and parts of it from her whole person. Yet IVF does precisely this. Through IVF, doctors invasively use a woman's body and its reproductive parts (her ovaries, eggs, uterus), as an instrument for engineering another person. If prostitution is an act in which a woman (and her client) uses her body for a lower good (i.e., money and pleasure), IVF is an act in which a woman (and her doctor) uses her body for a higher good (i.e., a baby). Whenever wrongful, or in this case, objectifying, means are used to reach even a great end, the act becomes wrongful or objectifying. By objectifying herself, treating herself, her body, as an object to be invaded and manipulated, a woman violates her inherent human dignity. She buys into the discredited idea that she has value as a woman only if her body can produce a baby.

The theological teaching of the Church confirms this anthropological understanding. The Church claims that every child has dignity, royalty even, because she was made in the image and likeness of God—indeed, that she is a child of God. We are not just creatures of God, but God has claimed us as his own children (see Jn 1:12).

Human persons are like God not only because we have been endowed with reason and free will, but also because we are designed to find meaning and fulfillment in communion with and service to others. As John Paul II taught: "God in his deepest mystery is not solitude, but a family, since he has in Himself fatherhood, sonship, and the essence of the family, which is love."[68] God is his own family, in which each of the three divine persons of the Trinity serves and loves the others. This Trinitarian God created the whole universe out of love, and loves each of his creations infinitely.

As children of this communal God, we are created to love as God does, finding happiness in acts of love and service to one another. The highest human expression of this divine communal love is found within sexual intercourse between a husband and wife. For John Paul, the conjugal act is itself an icon of the inner life and love of the Trinity.[69] The act in which God designed human beings to be conceived, then, is sacred, because it mirrors the way in which God loves. As a result, a child made in the image and likeness of God deserves to be conceived in an act that reflects his inherent dignity.[70]

Despite varied worldviews, today most people of goodwill acknowledge that there is more to sex than just pleasure and procreation. The Church teaches that the conjugal act has two meanings: the unitive meaning and the procreative meaning. These two meanings are equal and inseparable. Therefore, in addition to the pleasure sexual intercourse offers, as well as the possibility of conceiving children, sex between a man and a woman binds and seals them to each other in an emotional, primordial, and even spiritual way. This intense bonding is its unitive meaning.

The unitive dimension of sex originates in the vulnerability inherent in sexual intimacy, wherein each person offers him or herself as a gift to the other without reserve. In lovemaking, then, the spouses should treat each other not as a means to an end (whether that end be pleasure or even procreation), but as ends in themselves. Paraphrasing John Paul II, the theologian Christopher West writes, "if the only reason a couple is having sex is to transmit life, then they may be in danger of using each other rather than loving each other."[71] The body should not be treated as a tool to produce an end, even an end that is objectively good, because the body itself "is a constitutive part of the person who manifests and expresses himself through it ... in the body and through the body, one touches the person himself in his concrete reality."[72]

When a couple decides to use IVF to satisfy the desires inherent in the procreative aspect of sex, and so bypass the unitive aspect of conjugal love, the body is then being put to use for "biological fertility" alone, instead of for the broader and richer phenomena of "conjugal fecundity."[73] *Donum Vitae* explains:

> The origin of the human being thus follows from a procreation that is "linked to the union, not only biological but also spiritual, of the parents, made one by the bond of marriage." Fertilization achieved outside of the bodies of the couple remains by this very fact deprived of the meanings and the values which are expressed in the language of the body and in the union of human persons.[74]

Reverence for the rich meaning of sex assumes and also preserves the reverence for the female body in its holistic truth. Once respect for the conjugal act dissipates, a woman is reduced to being viewed as a vessel that simply gestates a fetus, rather than an essential partner in the cocreation of an immortal soul.

At the end of *Donum Vitae*, the Church implores scientists to "continue their research with the aim of preventing the causes of sterility and being able to remedy them so that sterile couples will be able to procreate in full respect for their own personal dignity and that of the child being born."[75] Thankfully, Catholic doctors and scientists have found a way to help infertile couples bear their own children. I am personally grateful for this treatment for infertility, called NaProTECHNOLOGY.

NaProTECHNOLOGY: What Is It and Does It Work?

NaProTECHNOLOGY (NPT) stands for Natural Procreative Technology. NPT is described on the NaProTECHNOLOGY Web site as:

> [A] new women's health science that monitors and maintains a woman's reproductive and gynecological health. It provides medical and surgical treatments that cooperate completely with the reproductive system. Thirty years of scientific research in the study of the normal and abnormal states of the menstrual and fertility cycles have unraveled their mysteries.[76]

Even though it utilizes highly advanced surgical techniques and employs low doses of fertility medication, NPT is natural because its primary goal is to restore a woman's reproductive health. Once that is done, conception can take place naturally through the life-giving, lovemaking action of husband and wife.

Obstetrician-gynecologist Thomas Hilgers, the founder of NPT, began his investigation of fertility patterns in women while in medical school in the late 1960s. With the help of nurses Sue Hilgers, Ann Prebil, and K. Diane Daly, Hilgers developed the Creighton Model Fertility*Care* System (CrMS). This system teaches women to chart their menstrual cycles using their own biomarkers, primarily observations of cervical fluid. These biomarkers directly reflect the function of a woman's hypothalamus, pituitary, and ovaries. They also reflect the impact of stress, sleep quality, adrenal and thyroid health, nutrition, and cervical and endometrial responsiveness. Thus, these markers act as a window into the comprehensive physical well-being of the woman.

The CrMS can be used to either achieve or avoid pregnancy. With the assistance of a trained instructor, a woman who uses the CrMS can clearly recognize her fertile window each month. She and her husband can then determine whether to engage or abstain from intercourse depending on their family's needs. Alongside the sympto-thermal and Billings methods, the Creighton model has revolutionized family planning. The guesswork and inaccuracy that previously accompanied the rhythm or calendar method are replaced by a highly accurate, individualized, scientific method, offering couples a reliable means of regulating births. In addition to family planning benefits, the CrMS also makes possible a recorded history of a woman's reproductive health. Being completely aware of her biomarkers, a woman charting her menstrual cycles can often recognize that she is suffering from a pathology before any tests are done. Hence, the CrMS has developed into a complete system of health care called Fertility*Care*.

Over the years, Hilgers found that a consistent profile of biomarkers, such as limited cervical fluid and short luteal phases, and/or brown menstrual spotting, became evident for women who suffered from infertility. Using his skills as a board-certified laser laparoscopist and reproductive medicine specialist, his professional attention expanded from family planning to properly diagnosing and treating the causes of infertility, as well as other female reproductive problems, such as PMS and PCOS (polycystic ovarian syndrome). He and his collaborators called this system of diagnosis and treatment NaProTECHNOLOGY.

NaProTECHNOLOGY begins with the premise that infertility and many other women's health issues are a result of disorders that disrupt normal ovarian and uterine function. Thus, these disorders can also interfere with the normal processes of conceiving and/or sustaining a pregnancy. Infertility is not treated as a disease in and of itself, but rather as a symptom caused by one or more pathologies in the woman's body. If not treated, these illnesses can have many short- and long-term health problems such as PMS, miscarriage, ectopic pregnancy, pelvic adhesive disease, ovarian cysts, chronic pelvic pain, and increased risk for breast, ovarian, and uterine cancers. In short, a woman's overall health can directly influence and even determine the health of her reproductive system.

A Fertility*Care* physician is trained to heal and restore a woman's reproductive health beginning with a thorough and accurate diagnosis. In NPT, an "unexplained" infertility diagnosis is rare. My Fertility*Care* physician boasts that no one has left his office without a proper diagnosis. He has found that 60 to 80 percent of his infertile patients have some degree of ovarian dysfunction and many of those patients have endometriosis.

Ovarian dysfunction is uncovered not only by medical history and observations, but also through timing the blood work that measures hormonal levels precisely with specific events of the woman's menstrual cycle. (The standard protocol of fertility doctors is to indiscriminately send all their patients in for blood work on the same days of a menstrual cycle.) However, when a woman is using the CrMS to chart her biomarkers, she knows when she is about to ovulate and on which day she has ovulated, and she can recognize the duration of the post-ovulatory phase. The timing of those days is not the same from one cycle to the next or from one woman to the next. Yet, in order to know whether the ovary is functioning properly, it is imperative that the blood work reveal hormonal levels at specific points in the menstrual cycle.

Many women suffering from endometriosis are asymptomatic.[77] Yet the CrMS charting reveals clues to the NPT physician that endometriosis may be present. Only a laparoscopy can reveal the distinct, inflamed tissue of endometriosis (it does not show up on ultrasounds, CT scans, or MRI scans). Therefore, the charting of a woman's cycles, combined with the knowledge base of the NPT physician,[78] can help to select the most appropriate patients for surgery. Furthermore, a Fertility*Care* physician can guide the patient to select a surgeon who has the necessary skill set to perform this procedure effectively—with minimal post-operative adhesions, which may also jeopardize the patient's future fertility.[ii]

---

ii. Many fertility surgeons cauterize or burn away the endometriosis tissue during the laparoscopy. Hilgers and others have found that this technique is not effective and can cause the endometrial tissue to grow again or can lead to adhesion formation. Instead, the NPT version cuts out the tissue, or vaporizes it with a laser, to prevent recurrence. Fertility*Care* physicians often remark that one of the best determinants that a patient probably has endometriosis is that she has had a laparoscopy in the past, even if her doctor had not seen endometriosis at the time of the laparoscopy.

An Illustration of NPT at Work: My Story

After having been diagnosed as infertile in 2001, and having had two miscarriages the following year, I visited a fertility clinic in the summer of 2003. I fervently hoped that a specialist in reproductive endocrinology would be able to diagnose my problem. My fallopian tubes were checked (and were open, as they'd been previously), and my husband's sperm was considered healthy and motile. My follicle-stimulating hormone (FSH) was at a good level (meaning I had plenty of time left on my biological clock), and the estrogen and progesterone levels in my blood were considered normal (within the range of fertility).

I will never forget the optimism in my doctor's voice when she related the news, "Everything looks great." The next step, she said, would be to take the drug Clomid to stimulate my ovaries to produce more eggs—and to have an interuterine insemination, or IUI.[79] My husband and I were confused, so I asked the obvious. "Why should I take Clomid if my estrogen levels are normal? And why should I have an IUI if my husband's sperm is normal?" The doctor stammered a bit. I pressed on. "I don't understand why you are offering me techniques to get pregnant. If all of our tests are normal, then why are we having such a hard time getting pregnant and staying pregnant? Why override my reproductive system with drugs, and a syringe and catheter full of my husband's sperm, when the cause of my infertility is still unknown?"

After we left the clinic, rather dejected and frustrated, my husband suggested that I call the archdiocese's natural family planning office to see if they knew of a Catholic reproductive endocrinologist. I scoffed at first, but to my surprise and humility, I discovered that two doctors in Massachusetts practiced something called NaProTECHNOLOGY.

The same day I called the doctor's office, I also found out that I was pregnant again and was miscarrying. I left a message with his nurse relating some of my story. Dr. Paul Carpentier called back, and his first words to me were, "I am so sorry. I wish I could have treated you before you achieved this pregnancy. It sounds like you are suffering from ovarian dysfunction. And if that is not treated, you will continue to risk having miscarriages." I was shocked on two levels: a doctor who cares, and who thinks he already has an answer to my infertility?

After charting my cycles using the CrMS and having my blood drawn many times over the course of several menstrual cycles, I sat down with Carpentier for two hours to discuss my situation. Using charts of female anatomy and hormonal levels, he described in detail how the female reproductive system is supposed to work and how slight changes to it can dramatically impact a woman's fertility. He answered all my questions honestly and completely. For the first time, I felt free from the crippling diagnosis of infertility. I was confident that everything that could be done would be done to heal me. If I still could not get pregnant at that point, then at least I would be at peace.

My blood work revealed that I had ovarian dysfunction, like many of his patients. My ovaries were producing eggs, but not mature and healthy ones; my hormones were subfertile, not infertile. I was confused by this diagnosis since the previous fertility doctor had indicated that my hormonal levels were fine. Carpentier explained that the fertile range for female hormones is not well appreciated by most doctors.[80]

The first step in my treatment was to increase the production and quality of my cervical fluid with natural, over-the-counter enhancers such as vitamin B6 and guaifenesin.[81] After that proved insufficient, Carpentier put me on a very low dose of Clomid. Most fertility doctors prescribe at least 50 mg of Clomid for each of five days; I was given 25 mg for each of three days. We then monitored my ovaries' response, and the Clomid dose was adjusted to try to achieve adequate ovarian function. When that was inadequate, we suspected something was suppressing my ovarian responsiveness. Carpentier referred me to an endometriosis specialist for laparoscopic exploration. The laparoscopy revealed that I had Type 1 (early) endometriosis; the surgeon cut it out then and there. Three months later, I became pregnant with my son, T.J. When I reached my fifteenth week of pregnancy, my husband and I danced a jig of thanksgiving.

But am I just one of the lucky few? How effective is NaProTECH-NOLOGY? In 2008, the *Journal of the American Board of Family Medicine* published a full-fledged study of NPT as an effective infertility treatment.[82] The study reported that after twenty-four months of *basic, non-surgical* NPT treatment,[iii] 52.8 percent of previously infertile women

---

iii. All couples were taught to identify fertile days through the Creighton Model FertilityCare System, and most received medication to support hormone and/or mucus production, including clomiphene (Clomid).

experienced a live birth.[83] The number of twins born in the study was only 4.5 percent, and more than 88 percent of the babies had a normal birth weight.[84] None of the patients experienced ovarian hyperstimulation syndrome.[85] Importantly, 33 percent of the women who sought NPT treatments in this study had already failed ART. Thus, the study involved a more difficult cohort of patients than those presenting at most ART clinics.[86] Even more significantly, this study tracked the success of medical (or non-surgical) NPT alone.

During 2004, the Pope Paul VI Institute, under the direction of Hilgers, recorded the success rate of NPT, *employing both medical and surgical techniques*. The rate of pregnancy for infertile couples was even higher: 45 percent achieved a pregnancy after twelve months of treatment; 60 percent at twenty-four months; and by thirty-six months, 70 percent of the women had given birth.[87]

In addition, unpublished data of Carpentier's NPT practice over twenty years reveal that 64 percent of couples that followed a NPT treatment regimen for a year successfully conceived and gave birth.[88] Furthermore, the babies conceived by Carpentier's NPT patients were ninety-six times less likely to be lost to miscarriage than the embryos implanted by IVF centers.[89] Because NPT treatment strives to heal the woman's reproductive system rather than override it, the embryo that implants in its mother's womb is allowed to mature in a much healthier environment.

On the whole, NaProTECHNOLOGY is the optimal treatment for infertility, because it heals the underlying pathologies that have surfaced as symptoms of infertility. Once a woman's reproductive health is restored, many other common reproductive ailments, such as PMS and postpartum depression, disappear. More important, NPT is a powerful treatment because it engages the woman holistically, treating her as an active participant in her own reproductive health. Women's reproductive capacity is no longer regarded as either wholly mysterious or a system to be manipulated, but as a gift that deserves to be respected and understood. It is no accident that the book *Taking Charge of Your Fertility*, which advocates a fertility awareness technique based on the Creighton model (but not associated with the Catholic Church), has become a national bestseller and is even endorsed by the pro-choice, secular feminist authors of *Our Bodies, Ourselves* and *Women's Bodies, Women's Wisdom*.[90] The book's author, women's health educator Toni Weschler, refers to women's fertility as "miraculous."[91] Indeed, she is right.

When women's fertility is reverenced for the miracle it is, a woman's *in*ability to conceive or bear a child does not become an occasion for technological incursion. Instead, it becomes an opportunity to discover the way toward healing, restoration, and wholeness. For many, the Catholic Church may be the last place they thought they would discover such a treasure; for me, it confirmed my understanding of the fundamental symbiosis between faith and science. For when reproductive technology allows itself to be ordered by respect for the human person, it discovers avenues for inquiry that not only produce results, but are also in accord with human dignity. And sometimes that "result" is the creation of a new baby to love.

Part III

WOMEN IN THE CHURCH, THE HOME, AND THE WORLD

7

Embodied Ecclesiology: Church Teaching on the Priesthood

SARA BUTLER

Reserving priestly ordination to men in the Catholic Church is controversial and surely concerns women. But one could argue that this topic does not belong in this book because it differs significantly from the other questions examined, and has to be settled on different principles. For all the other controversies the Catholic apologist can propose arguments from reason and experience. The Church may have pronounced on them and have provided evidence from Scripture and tradition to elucidate her answers, but her teaching appeals first and foremost to principles accessible to philosophical and scientific reasoning. In the controversy over women's ordination, however, the Church appeals first and foremost to evidence from Scripture and tradition.[1] While it is possible to advance arguments from reason and experience to explain why it is *fitting* to reserve priestly ordination to men, the critical judgment relies upon matters of faith; it should be acknowledged clearly at the outset that this is an "in-house" matter.[i]

---

i. Of course it is a matter of concern within other Christian communities as well. The churches of the Christian East (e.g., the Orthodox, Oriental Orthodox, and Assyrian

When Pope John Paul II formally addressed this question on Pentecost, 1994 (in *Ordinatio Sacerdotalis*),[2] he maintained that the Church has no *authority* to change the universal and unbroken tradition of reserving priestly ordination to men because she must remain faithful to the will of Christ. The will of Christ on this matter, he said, can be known from these sources: first, the Sacred Scriptures, which record Christ's example of choosing men as his apostles; second, the Church's constant tradition of choosing only men in imitation of his example; and third, the constant teaching of the magisterium (that is to say, of the pope and the bishops exercising their teaching office). The Pope did not appeal to any particular theory about the nature of women and their capacity, or lack of it, to exercise leadership. He did not compare women's traits to men's and argue on this basis that only men are suited for this office. When he declared that this teaching was to be definitively held by the Catholic faithful, he did not even call to mind the theological arguments related to sexual complementarity that many Catholics find persuasive. For example, he didn't mention that it is fitting for the priest to be a male because he serves as an "icon" of Christ the Bridegroom vis-à-vis the Church his Bride. The Pope appealed only to the norm that Jesus Christ established in calling twelve men to be associated with him in his mission and to represent him, and to the example of the apostles, who did the same in choosing fellow workers.

Right from the start, then, it is important to acknowledge that the resolution of the question of women's ordination is inextricably linked to Catholic doctrine concerning Holy Orders, the constitution of the Church and her sacramental structure, the normative role of the apostolic tradition, and ultimately the divinity of Christ. Reason alone cannot demonstrate the "necessity" of a dispensation that is the sheer gift of Christ to the Church. Nor can those who do not share this understanding of the Church, the sacraments, the priesthood, and the nature of Christ (and that would include many other Christians and most people of goodwill who are not Christians) be expected to be persuaded by arguments that depend upon these Catholic doctrines. Still, by inviting both Catholics and

---

churches) maintain the tradition of reserving priestly ordination to men, but many Christian communities springing from the sixteenth-century Reformation now ordain women. We are concerned here with the official teaching of the Roman Catholic Church.

non-Catholics to enter into the inner logic of this teaching, I hope to show that it is based, not on an outdated view of women, as many suspect, but on a set of beliefs foundational to Catholic Christianity.

It is well known, of course, that some Catholic theologians continue to dispute this teaching.[ii] They remain firmly convinced that women should have access to priestly ordination as a matter of strict justice. The arguments they propose often sidestep or call into question the Church's settled teachings on the matters mentioned above. Those who are unfamiliar with, suspicious of, or uncommitted to the Church's teaching tend to find these objections reasonable, however, and accept them on "common sense" grounds. Many critics of the Church's teaching assume it is rooted in an outmoded conviction—supported, perhaps, by some difficult passages from the Letters of Saint Paul[iii]—that women are, by nature or as a result of the Fall, inferior to men or different from them in ways that render them unsuited to public leadership. When they are assured that Catholic teaching promotes women's human rights and equal dignity with men, they ask why women, solely on account of their sex, are prevented from assuming leadership roles in the Church. They think that the positive doctrinal claim concerning women's equality is virtually canceled out by the tradition of a male-only priesthood.

Three premises are hidden in this familiar reasoning: first, that the ministerial priesthood[3] is the subject of a right; second, that it is essen-

---

ii. From 1975 on I was an advocate of women's ordination. After about 15 years of serious engagement with the question, in light of my study of the theology of the body and repeated opportunities to address it in theological and ecumenical dialogue, I became convinced of the truth of the Catholic Church's teaching. See my book *The Catholic Priesthood and Women* (Chicago: Hillenbrand, 2006), x–xi.

iii. The problematic passages, taken together, are called the "Pauline ban." First Corinthians 14:33b–35: "As in all the churches of the saints, the women should keep silence in the churches. For they are not permitted to speak, but should be subordinate, as even the law says. If there is anything they desire to know, let them ask their husbands at home. For it is shameful for a woman to speak in church." First Timothy 2:11–14: "Let a woman learn in silence with all submissiveness. I permit no woman to teach or to have authority over men; she is to keep silent. For Adam was formed first, then Eve; and Adam was not deceived, but the woman was deceived and became a transgressor." First Corinthians 11:3, 8–9: "But I want you to understand that the head of every man is Christ, the head of a woman is her hus-band, and the head of Christ is God... A man ought not to cover his head since he is the image and glory of God; but woman is the glory of man. For man was not made from woman, but woman from man." (Scripture citations are from the *Revised Standard Version*.)

tially a leadership role in the Church; and third, that there is no credible theological obstacle to the ordination of women priests once outdated views of women's nature or their subordinate role vis-à-vis men are set aside. We need to closely look at each of these premises. Before we address them, however, it is important to establish that the explanation the Church gives for reserving priestly ordination to women does not rely on antiquated and prejudicial views of women.

Official Church Teaching Does Not Rely on Antiquated Views of Women

The idea that women might claim the right to be ordained as priests took hold during the 1970s. The more general question of equal rights for women had gained attention in the United States a decade earlier. It was given impetus by the popular revival of liberal feminism with Betty Friedan's *The Feminine Mystique* in 1963[4] and, for Catholics, by the Second Vatican Council's teaching on the equal dignity of the sexes (1965).[5] Following the pattern established by the civil rights movement, women demanded legislative protection for their "equal rights" with men. Where African Americans had insisted on the need to overcome *racism* so they could achieve full participation in public life, liberal feminists now insisted on the need to overcome *sexism*, so they could achieve equal opportunity with men in education, business, culture, public life, and ultimately, in the Church. The political controversy over the Equal Rights Amendment to the U.S. Constitution (introduced in 1970), the U.N. International Women's Year (1975), the Episcopal Church's decision to ordain women to the priesthood (1976), and the opening of new pastoral and liturgical roles to the laity in the Catholic Church were several factors that moved this topic onto the agenda.

In this context, and in that of the newly established ecumenical dialogues, people began to ask "Why are women not eligible for priestly ordination in the Catholic Church?" The question had been considered before, either from practical or speculative interest, but the tradition of reserving priestly ordination to men was so well established that the Church's pastors had never before found it necessary to state the reason for it. In the absence of an official formulation of doctrine, scholars and advocates for change (including ecumenical dialogue partners) consulted the theories proposed by theologians and reported in the manuals used for seminary education. Finding them to be unsatisfactory and inconclusive,[6] they undertook a new evaluation of the scriptural evidence and considered afresh the patristic and canonical sources and the opinions of the medieval Scholastic doctors. They not only studied the evidence; they also speculated about motives that might have determined this tradition of sacramental practice.

Under the direction of the famous theologian Karl Rahner, Haye van der Meer wrote an influential book on the topic. He suggested that the Church's practice was no more than an unexamined way of acting dictated by historical and cultural prejudices regarding women, rather than serious theological reasons.[7] On the basis of his assessment, many Catholic theologians became convinced that there were no longer any genuine theological obstacles to ordaining women priests.[8] Van der Meer's scholarly inquiry lent credibility to the suspicion that the real obstacles were the historically conditioned views that women are by nature inferior to men, in a state of "subjection" to men as the result of the Fall, or different from men in ways that exclude them from public leadership roles.

In response to the line of reasoning opened by van der Meer's book, the Congregation for the Doctrine of the Faith issued *Inter Insigniores*, a *Declaration on the Question of the Admission of Women to the Ministerial Priesthood* (1976).[9] *Inter Insigniores* evaluates the ways in which theologians and canonists understood and sought to explain this doctrine over the years.[10] In agreement with van der Meer, *Inter Insigniores* acknowledges that some of the arguments these theologians advanced appealed to outdated views of women's nature and status, e.g., that women are in a "state of subjection." *Inter Insigniores* states explicitly that the judgment affirming the Church's practice as normative relies not on theological arguments of this sort, which must be abandoned, but on a tradition that traces this practice to the example of Jesus Christ.[11]

Inter Insigniores, in fact, does not base its teaching on speculative *theological arguments* at all.[iv] It relies, rather, on certain *fundamental reasons*, namely, the constant tradition itself, universal in East and West, of admit-

---

    iv. The official Commentary on *Inter Insigniores* reminds theologians that the Church's authoritative determinations pertain to the doctrinal affirmation, not to the arguments proposed to explain it.

ting only men to priestly ordination; the will of Christ, known from his example in choosing only men to belong to the Twelve; the practice of the apostles who faithfully followed the Lord's example in handing their office on to others; and the fact that this tradition has always been regarded as normative for the Church. In giving priority to the *fundamental reasons*, *Inter Insigniores* recognizes the importance of a fact: Jesus chose only men as apostles. This fact is that which gave rise to the tradition of reserving priestly ordination to men, and so also to the magisterial declaration that the Church has no authority to change it. *Theological arguments* follow after the fact; they attempt to show why the fact is meaningful, or "fitting."[12] They employ analogical reasoning to show that the Lord's dispensation in this matter clarifies and confirms other doctrines and finds a place within God's plan of salvation.[13]

Since there is no "saying" of the Lord to explain why he did not choose women, it is necessary to study his deeds as reported in the Gospels in an effort to understand his reasons—and his deeds reveal his high estimation of women. *Inter Insigniores* endorses the findings of contemporary historical-critical scholarship (often, feminist scholarship) when it calls attention to Jesus' unconventional and even revolutionary behavior with respect to women. He actively promoted the dignity of women, breaking with the social customs and religious legislation of his day by including them in his company and in his parables, opposing the traditions that discriminated against them,[v] pardoning them, healing them, conversing with them, teaching them, sending them on missions, and entrusting them with the message of the Resurrection. Later, Pope John Paul II would refer to this as the "Gospel innovation."[14] The Lord, by his example and his teaching, confirmed the truth about the essential equality of women and men in the order of salvation, a truth that came to explicit formulation in Saint Paul's statement that those who are baptized into Christ are no longer divided by race, sex, or social condition (Gal 3:28).

Some advocates of the ordination of women suggest that this evidence favors their cause,[15] but *Inter Insigniores* makes the opposite case. It maintains that since Jesus displayed such extraordinary freedom in the

---

v. Jesus' teaching in defense of women's dignity must also be kept in mind, namely, his prohibition of "adultery in the heart" (Mt 5:28) and of divorce (Mk 10:1–12; Mt 19:3–9).

face of contemporary religious and societal expectations, it follows that he would likewise have been free to call women who belonged to his company to the apostolic office. The fact that he did not do so—that he did not even entrust his Mother with the apostolic charge[vi]—strongly suggests that his choice of men was deliberate, and has been taken as evidence of his will.[16] If Jesus disregarded the customs of his day in his relationships with women, he also acted with sovereign freedom when he called only men to be his apostles. If he was free from constraint in the one case, he was free from constraint in the other.

No One Has a Right to Priestly Ordination

The Church does not defend her practice by appealing to the view that women are inferior to men by nature, subordinate to them by reason of the Fall, or different from men in ways that exclude them from leadership roles. On the contrary, she upholds the equality of women with men in all that pertains to fundamental human rights. Contemporary Catholic teaching firmly supports women who seek "equal rights" in the social order so that they may secure the same opportunities for self-expression, self-fulfillment, and advancement that men have, and in order to influence culture and contribute to the common good.[17] Many wonder, then, why women do not enjoy "equal rights" in the Church's own life. Why are they prevented from serving the Church as priests and bishops? Some feminists suspect that this policy has been established and maintained by men for the sake of securing their own power and privilege vis-à-vis women.[18]

To respond to this query, it is necessary to recognize that the Church is original in her nature and structure and therefore different from other societies. According to Catholic teaching, the Church is the community of the New Covenant called together by God through Jesus Christ in the

---

vi. That he did not even choose his Mother is part of a very ancient argument. *Ordinatio Sacerdotalis*, no. 3, makes reference to this: "Furthermore, the fact that the Blessed Virgin Mary, Mother of God and Mother of the Church, received neither the mission proper to the Apostles nor the ministerial priesthood clearly shows that the non-admission of women to priestly ordination cannot mean that women are of lesser dignity, nor can it be construed as discrimination against them. Rather, it is to be seen as the faithful observance of a plan to be ascribed to the wisdom of the Lord of the universe."

power of the Holy Spirit. The Church seeks the eternal salvation of its members, who are served by the apostolic ministry instituted by Christ and handed on by the sacrament of Holy Orders. Bishops, and priests as their coworkers, carry out the teaching, sanctifying, and shepherding ministry in the Church by Christ's authority and in his place and "person," that is, as his "ministers."[19] Given this belief, it is evident that questions regarding the Church's ordering cannot be resolved by an appeal to democratic principles.

Still, it is necessary to explain what the radical equality of the baptized means if women do not have equal opportunity with men for advancement in the Church, as equal opportunity is generally understood in the social order. In the first place, this radical equality has to do with access to salvation. It means that those who belong to Christ and to the Church have a common dignity, a common grace of adoption, and a common vocation to holiness. They have "one Lord, one faith, one baptism" (Eph 4:5). Among the Christian faithful, the Council asserts, "[t]here is ... no inequality on the basis of race or nationality, social condition or sex...."[20] Stated positively, a "true equality" exists among the faithful, and canon law makes no distinctions on the basis of sex when it considers their dignity, the activity common to all the faithful, their duties, and their rights.[21] Each member, however, cooperates in building up Christ's Body, the Church, according to his or her own *condition* and *function*.[22]

Distinctions exist among the Christian faithful, of course, but they are made on the basis of their "condition" and "function," not their sex. Of these, one distinction is fundamental, for it structures the Church and belongs to her constitution, namely, the distinction between lay persons and clerics, or "sacred ministers."[23] Because the priesthood is reserved to men, it may seem that this distinction is based on sex, but most men are laymen, not clerics. "Nonordained" women (which describes all Catholic women) and "nonordained" men (which describes almost all Catholic men) have the same canonical rights and responsibilities.[24] All share in Christ's priestly, prophetic, and kingly offices.[25] All can, in principle, be called upon to carry out the same functions and exercise the same offices and lay ministries in the Church,[26] on the basis of their Baptism. Some functions, however, are reserved to priests and bishops by reason of their ordination. Not only women, but all laymen, too, are excluded from the exercise of these functions.

The Catholic Church holds that this distinction between the laity and the clergy is of "divine institution," that is, it is rooted in the will of Christ. The ministry entrusted to bishops and priests by the sacrament of Holy Orders is called "apostolic" because it has its origin in the ministry Jesus entrusted to the apostles.[27] According to the Gospels, Jesus' call of the apostles was a defining moment in his public ministry. After praying all night, he chose "those whom he willed" (Mk 3:13–14; Jn 16:70). He called them by name to belong to the Twelve (a symbolic number related to the twelve patriarchs of the Old Covenant),[28] and they remained visible as the group of men he associated with himself in the work of establishing the New Covenant. "These men," Pope John Paul II points out, "did not in fact receive only a function which could therefore be exercised by any member of the Church; rather they were specifically and intimately associated in the mission of the Incarnate Word himself."[29] The priestly ministry is thus more than a social role or "leadership position" in the Church. It is the apostolic ministry, conferred by a sacrament, that authorizes the priest to act in the person of Christ[30] with respect to other members of the Church.

Given this understanding, it can be seen that Christ's call to some members of the Church to exercise the apostolic ministry on behalf of others does not derogate from the radical equality of the baptized.[31] The ordained are called to mediate Christ's gifts in word and sacrament to the rest of the faithful and to govern the ecclesial community. The ordained do this not in their own name or by reason of their gifts and talents, but in the power and "in the person" of Christ. By their ordination, they receive the authority to do this from Christ's Holy Spirit. They do not take this office upon themselves, but must be called by Christ and by the Church. Ordination, then, is not a matter of social advancement. Nor can anyone, man or woman, claim it as a "right," as if without it one would be deprived of some advantage with respect to one's salvation.

In the technical expression used by the Council, the difference of "condition" between the laity and the ordained is a difference "in kind," not only of "degree."[32] Pope John Paul II expresses this in somewhat different language when he writes that the ministerial or "hierarchical" priesthood exists for the service of the "hierarchy of holiness."[33] Priestly ordination places a man at the service of the rest of the baptized, just as Christ placed himself at the service of his people. The priest is to make the gifts of

Christ in word and sacrament available to them so that they may grow in holiness. The ultimate goal of the Christian life is to be a saint, not to be a priest.[34]

Women Have Access to Leadership and "Full Participation" in the Church

Those who think Catholic women suffer an injustice in being excluded from the priesthood sometimes lament that they are thereby barred from "full participation" in the Church, and that the leadership gifts they might have offered to others are squandered or "lost." These comments are not concerned with the eschaton, when what matters is being a saint, but with life as it is presently ordered and conducted in the Church. It appears to them that men alone can aspire to the "higher" and more important roles, while women are relegated to the "lower" and less important ones, with the result that women remain "second-class citizens" in the Catholic Church. In light of the fact that most men are not called to the priesthood either, the fallacy in this reasoning should be evident: if women are "second-class citizens" in the Church, so are most men. Is it then the case that the laity are "second-class citizens"?

I have already pointed out that the Church is original in her nature and structure. In addition, the priesthood is ordered to, and at the service of, the rest of the Christian faithful and of the Church as a communion. Two additional points may be necessary, however, to fill out the picture. First, the laity are not simply the passive objects of clerical ministry, or collaborators in that ministry in some auxiliary capacity. They have their own vocation.[35] Second, the Catholic discussion of the ordination of women has been influenced, and sometimes distorted, by the debates and decisions of Christians in denominations that stem from the sixteenth-century Reformation.

Lay people participate in the saving mission of Christ and his Church by reason of a commission from the Lord himself, given through Baptism and Confirmation and nourished at the Eucharist. First, they participate "[a]s sharers in the role of Christ the priest, the prophet and the king ... [they] have their [own] work ... in the life and activity of the Church."[36] The *Catechism of the Catholic Church*, §§ 901–913, offers a helpful description of lay participation in Christ's triple office. Under the *priestly* office it first mentions the offering of daily activities as "spiritual sacrifices accept-able to God through Jesus Christ," the worship of holy actions, and the consecration of the world itself to God. Parents are said to exercise the office of sanctifying in marriage and family life. But the lay ministries of lector and acolyte, and the other forms of lay participation in liturgical worship are also incorporated under this heading. Laypeople exercise Christ's *prophetic* office when they announce the Gospel in direct procla-mation and by the witness of holy living; but the services of lay catechists, theologians, and communications specialists are also noted, along with their obligation to contribute to the correct expression of the faith and to the pastoral care of the faithful. The laity share in the *kingly* office of Christ through acquiring mastery over sin in their own lives and by work-ing to overcome evil and to instill moral values in social institutions and culture. They also share in it by cooperating with their pastors in the ser-vice of the ecclesial community through the exercise of various ministries and through collaboration in particular councils, diocesan synods, pasto-ral councils, and so on.

Second, the laity are the chief protagonists of the Church's mission in the world. They are called to work within the social order, bringing their faith directly to bear on the realities of marriage and family, work, culture, politics, peace, and relations among nations. This is an ecclesial vocation, distinct from the vocation of the clergy. As the Council said, "[T]he laity, by their very vocation, seek the kingdom of God by engaging in temporal affairs and by ordering them according to the plan of God."[37] By fulfilling their ordinary duties in the spirit of the Gospel, by their work, and by the witness of their faith, hope, and charity, they announce Christ to their neighbor. In those places to which they alone have access, they are the Church. In other words, the lay faithful have the indispensable role of "incarnating" the Gospel, bringing it to bear on the common human tasks of living in dignity, harmony, justice, and peace—that is, of evangelizing the culture. Women are called to participate in this great undertaking alongside men and in ways specific to them as women.[38] Since the Council, many laywomen, singly or in lay ecclesial movements and other associations, have discovered new opportunities for this sort of "full par-ticipation" in the Church and her mission.

Some consecrated religious men and women (e.g., monks and nuns, brothers and sisters) also belong among the lay faithful, inasmuch as they

are not ordained. But their vocation is characterized by their "eschatologi-
cal" witness of freely surrendering even the legitimate goods of this world
for love of Christ Jesus and for the sake of God's reign. Their vocation,
then, differs from the "incarnational" vocation, with its positive relationship to secularity, of the rest of the lay faithful. They are called first and
foremost to "the contemplation of divine things and assiduous union with
God in prayer."[39] Members of active apostolic congregations share in the
Church's mission according to the inspiration of their founders. Women in
these religious congregations are well known for the extraordinary leadership they have offered in direct service to the Church's life and growth and
also in bringing the Gospel, healing, and liberation to suffering humanity.
The example of women religious demonstrates in a particularly vivid way
that "full participation" in the Church's life is not defined by priestly ordination, nor with having an official ministerial role, but with living the
Christian life to the full according to one's proper vocation.

The questions about leadership and "full participation" in the Church
are closely connected with the second point mentioned above, namely,
the influence of contemporary Anglican and Protestant debates and decisions regarding the ordination of women on the Catholic discussion.[40]
Most of the mainline Protestant denominations began to consider the
question some years before it became an issue for Catholics. These
denominations looked at the ordination of women as a "justice question,"
and were able to resolve it positively by means of a reconsideration of the
biblical doctrine of woman. First, they gave prominence to Galatians 3:28
as the key for interpreting the teaching of Saint Paul: "There is neither
Jew nor Greek, there is neither slave nor free, there is neither male nor
female; for you are all one in Christ Jesus." Second, they highlighted the
Gospel evidence concerning Jesus' relationships with women. Thus they
concluded that there is no biblical obstacle to ordaining women. Because
the more conservative Evangelical denominations were not so confident
that this reinterpretation of the Pauline texts was legitimate, they generally did not proceed to ordain women. In both cases, the determining
factor seems to have been the assessment of the "biblical doctrine of
woman." This, as we have seen, was also thought to be the critical issue
in the early years of the Catholic debate.

The sixteenth-century reformers, of whom Protestants are the heirs,
denied that Holy Orders is a sacrament, that is, by the Catholic definition,

an "efficacious sign of grace, instituted by Christ and entrusted to the Church, by which divine life is dispensed to us."[41] While they regarded Baptism and the Lord's Supper as sacraments, they thought of ordination as an ecclesiastical rite by which a Christian is commissioned to pastoral office for the ministry of word and sacrament.[42] According to this understanding, ordination to the ministry represents a difference of "degree" rather than a difference "in kind." In other words, the person who is ordained moves into a "leadership role" in the Church on the basis of his or her spiritual gifts and the call from the community. Accordingly, it requires only a change of discipline, not doctrine, to admit women to ordination. Indeed, in the liberal Protestant view, it would be unjust to bar women members from ordination.[43]

In distinguishing this Protestant view from the Catholic view, it is important, then, to recall certain elements that belong to the Catholic doctrine of the priesthood. These are the Catholic belief that Holy Orders is a sacrament *instituted by Christ*,[44] and that it is an *efficacious sign*, that is, that the priest's ordination grants him the grace to represent, or act in the person of, Christ the Head of the Church. The "fundamental reasons" the Catholic Church gives for reserving priestly ordination to men thus depend upon these other doctrines: that Christ founded the Church, that he intended to institute the apostolic ministry, and that he instituted the sacrament of Holy Orders by which it is conferred.[45] Most ecumenical dialogue partners who have proceeded to ordain women do not give the same account of the origins of Christian ministry. So it is not surprising that they do not find the "fundamental reasons" persuasive. And if these are not firmly in place, the "theological arguments" are generally thought to be inconclusive.

Some Catholic theologians who have adopted similar methods also raise critical questions about the institution of Holy Orders by Jesus Christ.[46] Their question is not whether *women* should be priests, but whether *anyone* should be ordained. That is, they question whether Jesus intended the apostolic charge to be passed on to others, whether he instituted the ministerial priesthood, whether priestly ordination is a sacrament, and whether the Church should be hierarchically structured. In raising these questions they introduce doubts about the Church's "settled" doctrine. Pope John Paul II, well aware of these currents of thought, pointed out that the question of the priestly ordination of women pertains to the very constitution of the Church.[47]

A Male Is the Fitting Sacramental Symbol
of Christ in the Ministerial Priesthood

Those who accept the Church's teaching concerning the Lord's institution of the apostolic ministry and of the sacrament of Holy Orders by which it is conferred may still feel puzzled by its reservation to men. Granted that Jesus established this norm, it remains to search for an answer to the question, "Why?"

"If women are equally capable of performing priestly functions, why did the Lord choose men and not women for this role?"

"What is there about the priesthood that requires the male sex?"

These questions lead to a consideration of the "theological arguments" that *Inter Insigniores* proposes in order to illuminate the "fact" that Jesus called only men to belong to the Twelve, and thereby indicated his will for the priesthood.

"Theological arguments" are also called "arguments from fittingness." They are proposed in order to illumine our minds concerning divine revelation, not to demonstrate or prove that things *had to be* this way. Here, we are concerned to understand the significance of a fact of salvation history that is held to establish a permanent norm for the Church. Since many people find the norm to be in serious tension with the Church's teaching about the equal dignity and rights of women with men, it is necessary and useful to conduct this inquiry.

The popular notion holds that women should be ordained because they are capable of carrying out priestly functions as well as men. But this view overlooks the relevance of the Catholic doctrine that sacraments (including the sacrament of Holy Orders) are *signs*, natural signs that refer believers to events in the economy of salvation. In order for a sacrament to be an effective sign of the grace that Christ is giving, the sign itself must be perceptible to the faithful—we must be able to recognize what the sign points to with ease.[48] For example, washing with water at Baptism signifies cleansing from sin, regeneration, and participation in the mystery of Christ's death and resurrection.

According to Saint Thomas Aquinas, persons as well as material elements contribute to the making of sacramental signs.[49] Thomas uses the example of the Anointing of the Sick: the "subject" of the sacrament must be a sick person, because the sacrament is an efficacious sign of healing. Today, we might think of the sacrament of Marriage: the "subjects" of this sacrament must be a man and a woman, because Christian marriage is a "sacrament" of the love between Christ and his Church (Eph 5:32). The priest, likewise, is not just the bearer of certain *functions*; he also *participates in the sacramental sign* that refers believers to events or mysteries in the economy of salvation. If only a male can be ordained to the priesthood, his sexual identity clearly must have some relevance for the constitution of the "sign."[50]

In the Church, the priest is a sacramental sign or "icon" of Jesus Christ.[51] Pope John Paul II alludes to this when he states that the apostles and their successors were given the mission of "representing" Christ.[52] This doctrine goes back to Saint Paul (2 Cor 5:18–20), was made explicit by Saint Cyprian of Carthage (A.D. 258), and has remained firmly in place until our time. Not until Saint Bonaventure (A.D. 1274), however, was the theological argument from gender correspondence developed as a reply to the question of women's ordination. For Bonaventure, because Christ the Head and Mediator is male, the priest who represents him must be male.[53] Bonaventure adds to this a theological argument based on the long-standing tradition of regarding the bishop as the "spouse" or "bridegroom" of his diocese: since a priest may be called upon to accept the episcopacy, only a male should receive priestly ordination.[54] Crucial to this theological argument is his suggestion that the sacramental symbolism of the priesthood reflects the bishop (or priest) in *relationship with* the Church.

Bonaventure's theological argument seems to provide the structure for the theological arguments presented in section 5 of *Inter Insigniores* and developed further in Pope John Paul II's apostolic letter *On the Dignity and Vocation of Women*. The fact that "the Word became flesh" (Jn 1:14) as a male is taken to be theologically significant. Christ is the New Adam, the new Head of fallen humanity, and the author of the New Covenant. The Covenant that God made with the Chosen People is depicted in the prophetic literature as a marriage, a mutual commitment of love (Is 54:5–8, 10). In the Old Testament, God's love is compared to a man's love for a woman; in fulfillment of the promise, Christ identifies himself as the Bridegroom[55] and establishes the New Covenant in his blood, laying down his life for love of the Church, his Bride (Eph 5:25).[56] The self-giving love between spouses in marriage is the premier symbol of the union Christ has with his Church.

The priest represents Christ in his relationship with the Church and acts in his person (*in persona Christi*), especially in the celebration of the Eucharist, the sacrament of the New Covenant, which perpetuates Christ's sacrifice. The celebration of the Eucharist can be seen to express "the redemptive act of Christ the Bridegroom toward the Church the Bride."[57] The sacramental significance of the priest's male sex thus comes to light when he acts in the person of Christ the Bridegroom with respect to the Church his Bride. This theological argument from the nuptial analogy leads to the following conclusion: "in actions which demand the character of ordination and in which Christ himself, the author of the Covenant, the Bridegroom and Head of the Church, is represented, exercising his ministry of salvation ... [Christ's role] must be taken by a man."[58]

Many critics suppose that the Church appeals to this nuptial symbolism to justify reserving priestly ordination to men.[59] In doing so, they mistake the theological argument from fittingness for the more critical fundamental reasons. Some also seem to make the mistake of thinking that sexual complementarity is significant only for reproduction. They are not inclined to discover how Christ's male sex, and therefore the priest's, contribute to the sacramental symbolism. This represents, however, a failure to appreciate that sexuality is a constitutive dimension of the person. Being a man or a woman is central, not simply incidental, to one's identity and defines one's capacity for relationships, that is, for "making a gift of self."

The nuptial analogy compares Christ's love for the Church—expressed in the sacrifice of the Cross—to a man's love for a woman. If Christ's role as Head and Bridegroom of the Church must be taken by a man, this is due not to any "personal superiority" of men to women "in the order of values." It is due only to "a difference of fact," that is, the difference of sex, which God wills from the beginning (Gen 1:27) and which is ordered to the communion of persons. On the basis of these arguments and the appeal made to the nuptial analogy, it is correct to conclude that *Inter Insigniores* replaces the theological argument from women's inferiority with a theological argument from the significance of sexual complementarity.[60]

Women Suffer No Injustice

The Catholic Church has only recently found it necessary to assert that she lacks the authority to admit women to priestly ordination and to explain why she believes this to be the case. In so doing, the magisterium has explicitly rejected theological arguments that relied on a flawed view of women and has produced a new body of teaching that promotes the vocation and dignity of women and of the lay faithful. The Church's doctrine on the reservation of priestly ordination to men does not depend, however, on theological arguments, old or new. Rather, it depends on a constant and universal tradition, traced to the will of Christ and the practice of the apostles, and faithfully maintained as a norm.

Do women have a right to ordination, and does exclusion from the priesthood prevent them from exercising leadership and participating fully in the life and mission of the Church? To the first question, I point out that no one has the right to ordination. To the second, I explain that the equality of the baptized refers to access to salvation, not access to priestly ministry. The vocation to priesthood comes from God. Those who do not receive this call suffer no injustice; God calls them to live out their Christian vocation in a myriad of other ways. Those who do receive the call to priestly ordination, receive it in order to render to the rest a specific service, namely, Jesus Christ's own ministry of teaching, sanctifying, and governing.

Today, the Church invites theological reflection on why Christ called only men to priestly ordination. The Church proposes theological arguments that link the fact of the Incarnation with the biblical symbolism of Covenant. This entails a nuptial symbolism that displays God's plan for our salvation in Christ in terms of self-giving, sacrificial marital love, a love that calls forth a response. This sacramental symbolism draws on the difference between the sexes not to disparage women. Rather, it shows that the male priest is a living sign who makes visible Christ's own spousal relationship to the Church.

Dueling Vocations:
Managing the Tensions Between
Our Private and Public Callings [i]

Elizabeth R. Schiltz[1]

A couple of times each year, some popular media outlet seems to run an article, or someone publishes a book and makes the rounds of the talk shows, about the extraordinary fact that women with great educations and credentials continue to choose to give up their jobs, or to scale back in their professional ambitions, in order to devote more attention to raising their children. Whether it's called "the opt-out revolution"[2] or the "mommy track,"[3] this "phenomenon" always occasions a flurry of impassioned arguments as another skirmish erupts in the "mommy wars."

A particularly virulent outbreak in this war erupted in 2005 after the journalist Linda Hirshman published an article called "Homeward

i. This chapter differs in an important respect from the preceding chapters in which authors offered reasons in support of definitive Church teachings on matters of faith and morals. The subject matter addressed here does not lend itself to such a defense because the Church has no official teaching on the matter. Guided by the Church's social doctrine and a variety of other encyclicals, the author offers her unique perspective on the timely issue of "balancing" work and family (Editor's note).

Bound."[4] Using census data, Hirshman documented the decline from 1976 to 2004 in the numbers of women with infants working full-time. Then, focusing on "elite" women, she cited studies finding that only 38 percent of female Harvard MBAs from the classes of 1981, 1986, and 1991 were working full-time. Moreover, 43 percent of women with children who had graduate degrees or degrees from prestigious colleges had taken time off from work, primarily for family reasons. Even more striking than these statistics, according to Hirshman, was the persistent absence of women in "elite workplaces":

> If ... women were sticking it out in the business, law, and academic worlds, now, 30 years after feminism started filling the selective schools with women, the elite workplaces should be proportionately female. They are not. Law schools have been graduating classes around 40 percent female for decades—decades during which both schools and firms experienced enormous growth. And, although the legal population will not be 40 percent female until 2010, in 2003, the major law firms had only 16 percent female partners, according to the American Bar Association.... The Harvard Business School has produced classes of around 30 percent female. Yet only 10.6 percent of Wall Street's corporate officers are women, and a mere nine are Fortune 500 CEOs. Harvard Business School ... has a 20 percent female academic faculty.[5]

Hirshman reasoned that workplace discrimination and the conscious rejection by women of the fiercely competitive atmosphere of "elite" occupations might explain some of this data. But she argued, "It defies reason to claim that the falloff from 40 percent of the class at law school to 16 percent of the partners at all the big law firms is unrelated to half the mothers with graduate and professional degrees leaving full-time work at childbirth and staying away for several years after that...."

But it was not Hirshman's conclusion that women were leaving work to stay home with their children that provoked the strong reaction to her article. Rather, it was that Hirshman did not merely *observe* this phenomenon—she *challenged* it. She argued that it was *wrong* for so many of "the wealthiest, most-privileged, best-educated females in the country" (women in a position to have their wedding announcements published in the Sunday Styles section of the *New York Times*) to "stay home with their babies rather than work in the market economy." It was wrong, she argued, because it is "bad for them, is certainly bad for society, and is widely imitated, even by people who never get their weddings in the *Times*."

To avoid the fate of these wealthy, privileged, well-educated brides of the *Times* who had chosen to stay home with their families, Hirshman provided very specific career advice for "women who want to have sex and children with men as well as good work in interesting jobs where they may occasionally wield real social power." She offered three specific rules. First: "Prepare yourself to qualify for good work," by getting practical college degrees. Second, "treat work seriously," by shedding yourself of "self-important idealism about the kinds of intellectual, prestigious, socially meaningful, politics-free jobs worth [your] incalculably valuable presence." In other words, make career decisions that translate into making more money, rather than less. She advised, "Money is the marker of success in a market economy; it usually accompanies power, and it enables the bearer to wield power, including within the family." Third, "don't put yourself in a position of unequal resources when you marry."

Hirshman fleshed out this last rule with three specific marriage strategies. First, simply refuse to do more than your fair share of the housework. Hirshman wrote:

> Never figure out where the butter is. "Where's the butter?" [writer] Nora Ephron's legendary riff on marriage begins. In it, a man asks the question when looking directly at the butter container in the refrigerator. "Where's the butter?" actually means butter my toast, buy the butter, remember when we're out of butter. Next thing you know you're quitting your job at the law firm because you're so busy managing the butter. If women never start playing the house-hold-manager role, the house will be dirty, but the realities of the physical world will trump the pull of gender ideology. Either the other adult in the family will take a hand or the children will grow up with robust immune systems.

Second, marry either a man with less social power than you (the safest bet—someone significantly younger or older than you) or, she argues, a socially liberal man who is genuinely committed to gender equality. Either choice will increase the odds that, when work and family needs start to conflict, you will not automatically be the one who sacrifices work. Third, do not, under any circumstances, have more than one baby.

Hirshman's views are shared by many secular feminists who argue that women must either entirely refuse to engage in the largely unpaid and socially undervalued work of caring for children and the household, or insist that men do an equal share of this unpaid labor, in order to achieve equality in the workplace.6 (One of the most radical of these feminists, Katherine Franke, uses the term "repronormativity" to criticize what she considers to be an unreasonable cultural bias toward considering reproduction by women to be "inevitable and natural."7)

Clearly, Hirshman did not claim to provide a Catholic account of any of the topics she addressed in her article. The propositions she advances would appear to have almost nothing in common with the Church's views on women, families, human flourishing, work, or children. However, on one of Hirshman's most central points, she and the Church are in complete agreement.

Over the years, the Church has demonstrated an increasing recognition that it is, indeed, detrimental to society if women with children do not participate in the public sphere including, but not limited to, paid jobs. Unlike Hirshman and her feminist sisters, though, the Church is emphatic in its insistence that the work that women do in the private sphere, including (but, again, not necessarily limited to) raising their children and caring for their families, are some of the most important services women can provide to the world.[8]

I believe the Church realizes that its teachings on these two points are in tension. Further, I believe this tension manifests itself in a broader context than just that experienced by working mothers who strive to balance work and family. I also believe that this tension is, in fact, inherent in the precarious balance between the private vocation and the public vocation to which each of us is called, whether male or female, parent or childless.

By our private vocation, I mean our calling to live according to a Christian understanding of the web of relationships into which we are all personally imbedded. The most significant of these relationships is typically the relationship we have with our spouse and then the other members of our family, but the web extends to relationships with our coworkers, fellow parishioners, neighbors, the members of any religious orders to which we might belong and, most importantly, to God. Our Christian vocation demands that we conduct these relationships in accordance with Christian principles, prayerfully seeking to love and serve others with a spirit of self-sacrificing generosity.

By our public vocation, I mean our responsibilities to live and witness as Christians in and to the various social institutions to which we belong— the Church, our local communities, our places of employment, our country, and our world.

The flashpoint in most discussions of the tensions between our private and public vocations is typically the conflict between our responsibilities to our families and to our professional—paid—work. Today, these two vocations are clearly at a particularly tenuous balance. The market for paid work, as currently structured, makes demands on many of us that are not particularly conducive to living out our private vocations as primary caregivers of children or elderly parents. But our private vocations also include our relationships to God and others in our lives. And our public vocations also include our commitments to institutions and enterprises other than our paying jobs, such as volunteer work, apostolic activity, and social and political advocacy.

Most of this chapter will focus on the work/family tension, as experienced particularly by women, because that is the most pressing manifestation of this tension as well as the one most directly addressed by the Church's teachings. But, I will argue, the way in which the Church is coming to understand the tensions between work and family, and the resources that the Church offers to help navigate such tensions, ought to be more generally applicable to a broader understanding of our private and public vocations.

Using Hirshman's article as an example of common secular feminist arguments, I will first explore the commonalities between the positions of many of these feminists and that of the Church regarding the need to construct social policies that facilitate women's participation in the workforce. Then, again using Hirshman's article as an example, I will explore the points at which the Church's conception of family, work, and human flourishing diverges from that held by many—but not all—secular feminists. I will conclude that the Church's conception of family, work, and flourishing offers Catholics a set of extremely useful tools for navigating not just the tensions between our family responsibilities and our paid work, but also the broader tensions between our private and our public vocations.

The Church's Position on the Importance of
the Public Vocation of Women

According to Hirshman, it is detrimental for society not to have more "elite women" represented in the workplace because:

> ... elites supply the labor for the decision-making classes—the senators, the newspaper editors, the research scientists, the entrepreneurs, the policy-makers, and the policy wonks. If the ruling class is overwhelmingly male, the rulers will make mistakes that benefit males, whether from ignorance or from indifference. Media surveys reveal that if only one member of a television show's creative staff is female, the percentage of women on-screen goes up from 36 percent to 42 percent. A world of 84 percent male lawyers and 84 percent female assistants is a different place than one with women in positions of social authority.

In Hirshman's view, the choices these "elite women" make become the model for other women in society. As a result, "even if women don't quit their jobs for their families, they think they should and feel guilty about not doing it."

Increasingly over the past decades, the Catholic Church, through the writings of Pope John Paul II and Pope Benedict XVI in particular, has begun to express the same sort of concerns.[9] While never neglecting to emphasize the crucial role that women who are mothers must play in preserving families, Pope John Paul II also displayed a growing awareness that the presence of women in public life is critical to the transformation of culture. He devoted much of his 1988 apostolic letter *Mulieris Dignitatem (On the Dignity and Vocation of Women)* to arguing that women possess a particular "genius," a particular ability to appreciate each human person's obligation to love every other human person. Through their "feminine genius," women have special access to the truth that we are each loved by God and created in the image and likeness of God.[10]

In his 1991 encyclical *Centesimus Annus*, John Paul wrote that this truth—the truth to which he argued women have some sort of special access—is "the main thread ... and the guiding principle of ... all of the Church's social doctrine."[11] A quick glance at the table of contents of the *Compendium of the Social Doctrine of the Church*[12] demonstrates just how central a role the Pope thought women must play if their particular

genius is to be brought to bear on the multitude of concrete social problems facing our world. After all, the Church's social doctrine encompasses
the teachings on the principles of the common good,[ii] the universal destination of goods,[iii] subsidiarity,[iv] and solidarity.[v] This social doctrine is
concretely applied in social policies concerning the family, marriage, the
rights of workers, economic life, the political community, the international community, the environment, and world peace.

John Paul II repeatedly emphasized that women's particular genius
was required across the breadth of the Church's social concerns, for the
"establishment of economic and political structures ever more worthy of
humanity."[13] He recognized that "[w]omen will increasingly play a part in
the solution of the serious problems of the future: leisure time, the quality of life, migration, social services, euthanasia, drugs, health care, the
ecology, etc."[14] He claimed that women involved in education "exhibit a
kind of affective, cultural and spiritual motherhood which has inestimable
value for the development of individuals and the future of society."[15] And

---

ii. The common good refers to "the sum total of social conditions which allow people,
either as groups or as individuals, to reach their fulfillment more fully and more easily. The
common good does not consist in the simple sum of the particular goods of each subject
of a social entity. Belonging to everyone and to each person, it is and remains 'common,'
because it is indivisible and because only together is it possible to attain it, increase it, and
safeguard its effectiveness, with regard also to the future." Pontifical Council for Peace and
Justice, *Compendium of the Social Doctrine of the Church* (2004), no. 164 (italics and citations
omitted).

iii. "God gave the earth to the whole human race for the sustenance of all its members,
without excluding or favoring anyone. This is the foundation of the universal destination
of the earth's goods." Ibid., no. 171 (italics omitted).

iv. "Just as it is gravely wrong to take from individuals what they can accomplish by their
own initiative and industry and give it to the community, so also is it an injustice and at
the same time a grave evil and disturbance of right order to assign to a greater and higher
association what lesser and subordinate organizations can do." Ibid., no. 186 (citation
omitted).

v. "Solidarity must be seen above all in its value as a moral virtue that determines the
order of institutions. On the basis of this principle the 'structures of sin' that dominate
relationships between individuals and peoples must be overcome. They must be purified
and transformed into structures of solidarity through the creation or appropriate
modification of laws, market regulations, and juridical systems. Solidarity is also an
authentic moral virtue, not a 'feeling of vague compassion or shallow distress at the mis-
fortunes of so many people, both near and far. On the contrary, it is a firm and persevering
determination to commit oneself to the common *good*. That is to say the good of all and
of each individual, because we are all really *responsible for all.*'" Ibid., no. 193 (italics and
citations omitted).

in an Angelus reflection of August 1995, he said that "the greater presence of businesswomen in executive positions in the economy is giving it a new human inspiration and removing it from the recurring temptation of dull efficiency marked only by laws of profit."[16]

This conviction that women's voices must be heard in the public sphere is strikingly similar to Hirshman's argument that "[i]f the ruling class is overwhelmingly male, the rulers will make mistakes that benefit males, whether from ignorance or from indifference." The Church agrees that women's voices add something different to the conversation about how the world should be structured. For the Church, this "something different" is crucially important to forming a healthy culture. It is intimately related to women's femininity, which is expressed for most women, but not all, in motherhood.

That is, if women *who are mothers* never rise to leadership positions in the public sphere, our families are going to continue to suffer from the mistakes the world's leaders have made on policy questions of particular importance to children and families. As the United States' former ambassador to the Holy See, Mary Ann Glendon has argued:

> [F]or the first time in history large numbers of women occupy leadership positions and almost half of these new female leaders— unlike male leaders—are childless. Will this affect our goals and values? Will it affect our programmatic agenda? You bet it will. People without children have a much weaker stake in our collective future. As our leadership group tilts toward childlessness, we can expect it to become even harder to pay for our schooling system or for measures that might prevent global warming. America's rampant individualism is about to get a whole lot worse.[17]

The Church never fails to insist on the paramount importance of the work of mothers in raising their children and caring for their families, and lauds those women who engage in that work full-time. It is crucial, however, to recognize that the Church *also* challenges the world to make it possible for women with children to work in the public sphere. Both Pope John Paul II and Pope Benedict XVI have spoken of the need to *harmonize* the roles of women as mothers and as workers, rather than eliminate one of those roles.[18] In *Laborem Exercens*, the Church challenges society to restructure the workplace to ensure that women who work are not penalized professionally for the work they do in caring for their family. And the

Church also calls for economic support for women who choose to devote themselves exclusively to the work of caring for their family—either through a family wage or other financial support.[19]

Calls to restructure the workplace to accommodate family life can also be found in papal documents such as *Familiaris Consortio*[20] and *Evangelium Vitae*.[21] The U.S. Conference of Catholic Bishops has also called for this in such documents as its 1986 pastoral letter *Economic Justice for All*[22] and the 1991 publication *Putting Children and Families First: A Challenge for Our Church, Nation, and World*.[23] Among the concrete proposals of the U.S. Conference of Catholic Bishops are social welfare and tax policies that properly value parental care; affordable, quality day care; parental leave policies; and family-friendly work options such as job sharing, flex-time, and reduced work weeks.[24]

These sorts of proposals have much in common with suggestions of an emerging school of secular feminists known as "care feminists," "dependency feminists," "cultural feminists," or "relational feminists."[25] These feminists oppose the school of feminism represented by Hirshman that counsels women to eschew "care work" and its high professional cost. The care feminists argue for a social revaluation of care work, rather than a rejection of care work by women. They also argue for changes to our social structures and workplaces to permit women to engage in care work without sacrificing entirely their careers or financial security. Their proposals include ideas such as changes to welfare and tax policies to support the currently unpaid childcare performed mostly by women,[26] paid maternity leave and job protections during maternity leave,[27] and more radical proposals to restructure the workplace to remove penalties for child care responsibilities. Such proposals include amending labor laws that now permit employers to demand overtime work without paying overtime pay; alternative work schedules and flex-time arrangements; and even thirty-hour work weeks for *all* workers.[28]

Of course, most of the world is not yet ready to adopt proposals such as these. The largely unpaid work of caring for families continues to be undervalued, and women continue to be penalized in the workplace for the work they do within the family. Indeed, the United States has especially resisted responding to this challenge, keeping company with that illustrious group of nations in the world that do not guarantee *any* paid maternity leave: Australia, Lesotho, Papua New Guinea, and Swaziland.[29]

Hirshman argues that "elite women" have a particular responsibility to stay in the workplace, because they are the ones most likely to achieve positions "where they may occasionally wield real social power." I would argue that our Church is suggesting something similar in her charge to women to make their voices heard in the public sphere. "Elite women"—those who have the financial option to work or not, and the education and access to power structures that might put them in a position to effect social change—cannot entirely ignore their responsibilities to those women who do *not* have those privileges. Women of privilege cannot entirely neglect their social responsibilities to the outside world in favor of their private vocations.

Most women in the world do not have any choice but to work outside the home, typically in jobs where they will never wield any sort of social power. So if women with "social power" do not speak up for them, who will? Who will argue for the sorts of changes to laws and to individual workplaces that would allow women *without social power* to balance *their* work and family responsibilities? Who will argue for the sorts of changes to laws and to individual workplaces that would allow *men* to more rationally balance *their* work and family responsibilities? (Recent studies are showing a generational shift in the attitudes of younger men, who are growing increasingly dissatisfied with the toll current workplace structures impose on them at the expense of their ability to father their children.)[30]

The voices of such women are important at two levels: first, at the level of individuals pushing for changes in their particular workplaces, and second, at the level of those with social influence working for changes to laws and policies to accommodate the dual vocations of others. Law professor Joan Williams has demonstrated convincingly that our contemporary workplaces are structured around a model that posits the childless man, with *no* private vocation of any type, as the "ideal" worker. [31] Workers who deviate from that model in any way are inevitably punished in the workplace. Who but women with children, women speaking from a Catholic vantage point, will push employers to properly value parenting? Who else will advocate for changes to this "ideal worker" model around which our workplaces are currently structured?

Catholic women's voices are equally important at the level of national and global policy shaping. Who but women with children, women speak-

ing from a Catholic vantage point, will continue to remind the nation and
the world, as Mary Ann Glendon reminded the United Nations, that

> three-quarters of the world's poverty population today is composed
> of women and children. In the developing world, hundreds of mil-
> lions of women and children lack adequate nutrition, sanitation,
> and basic health care. And even in affluent societies, the faces of the
> poor are predominantly those of women and children, for ... [t]here
> is a strong correlation between family breakdown and the feminiza-
> tion of poverty. The costs of rapid increases in divorce and single-
> parenthood have fallen heavily on women, and most heavily of all
> on those women who have made personal sacrifices to care for chil-
> dren and other family members.[32]

The Church insists that the feminine genius has particular access to
fundamental truths underlying the Church's social teachings. Without the
voices of women in the public sphere (especially the voices of mothers),
that unique feminine genius will not gain the hearing required to address
these sorts of social woes.

Catholic Resources for Navigating the Tensions
Between our Private and Public Vocations

If women are called to engage in public life in some way, *and* women
continue to do most of the dependent care work in the world, *and* the
world continues to resist calls to moderate social and workplace structures to better accommodate parenting obligations, women are caught in
the middle of some fairly knotty difficulties. But this particular conflict is
simply one manifestation of the basic conflict between the public and the
private vocations to which all people are called. Responding to either of
these calls takes time, and since time is a finite resource, we have to decide
where to spend our time at any given point in our lives.

One thing that we as Christians have to accept, though, is that managing these tensions is not easy. Christianity makes heavy demands on
believers. I vividly recall a striking image from the television coverage of
one of Pope John Paul II's early globe-trotting trips. After responding to
initial questions from reporters, he turned away and headed down the
aisle. But an additional question caught his attention: "How do you

respond to critics who say you are traveling too much, trying to do too much at once?" The Pope whipped around, wagged his finger sternly at the reporter, and said, "Sometimes it is necessary to do some of what is too much."

The Church does demand much of us. We should not be surprised when responding to the challenges of our dual vocations seems more than we can handle. Fortunately, the Church also offers us the means to flourish in the midst of such difficulties. It provides us resources both to navigate the difficult trade-offs required in managing our dual vocations, and to comfort us when the demands mount up. The Church does not offer us three crisp rules for success the way Hirshman does. It does, however, offer us some ways of thinking about what is at stake in each vocation that can be helpful in navigating these tensions. It offers us rich conceptions of "family," "work," and "human flourishing," conceptions that contrast sharply with the vision of Hirshman and many secular feminists.

1. Family

Clearly, Hirshman's view of the family as the biggest hindrance to woman's success in the workplace bears little relation to the Church's conception of the family, as described recently by Pope Benedict XVI: "an indispensable base for society and for peoples, as well as an irreplaceable good for children, worthy of coming into life as a fruit of love, of the parents' total and generous surrender."[33] The Church sees the family as indispensable to society, as the first and best school of the social virtues necessary to a healthy social order.[34] In sharp contrast, Hirshman sees the family as something a woman should consciously contain and manage through strategic marriage to either a young stud or an elderly sugar daddy, and by having no more than one child in order to minimize the impact on her career. There is simply no common ground between Hirshman and the Church there.

In the Church's sacramental understanding of marriage, the husband and wife receive graces to pursue the good of the other for their shared lifetimes. Each is called to assist the other as he and she carry out their individual and common public and private vocations. The creation of a family is a joint enterprise of husband and wife, each generously giving of time and resources to beget, nurture, and educate children. (Indeed, Hirshman and other secular feminists might be surprised to learn that church-going Christian men—not their secular, liberal counterparts—are more apt to view both mother and father as equally responsible for the care of their children.[35]) The energies expended on their children's formation and well-being not only bring potential benefit to both the Church and the world, they also help the husband and wife grow in virtues—e.g., industry, patience, justice, charity—that help them carry out their own public vocations more effectively.

2. Work

Hirshman's three "rules" for women who want to succeed at work are, indeed, practical and probably quite effective. If you follow Hirshman's rules, you will no doubt succeed in your "work"— if you think of work merely as something you do to make money and achieve social power.

However, that notion of work bears little relation to the Catholic Church's notion of work. *Laborem Exercens* explains, "The Church is convinced that work is a fundamental dimension of man's existence on earth."[36] The human person's activity on earth, his or her work, is part of how he or she images God. God's charge to Adam and Eve in *Genesis* to "fill the earth and subdue it" is a charge to complete the task that God began in creating the world. Pope John Paul II writes:

> In carrying out this mandate, man, every human being, reflects the very action of the Creator of the universe. . . .Each and every individual, to the proper extent and in an incalculable number of ways, takes part in the giant process whereby man "subdues the earth" through his work.[37]

Dorothy Sayers vividly captured this view of work, suggesting that a Christian attitude toward work should cause us to see it:

> . . . not as a necessary drudgery to be undergone for the purpose of making money, but as a way of life in which the nature of man should find its proper exercise and delight and so fulfill itself to the glory of God. That it should, in fact, be thought of as a creative activity undertaken for the love of the work itself; and that man, made in God's image, should make things, as God makes them, for the sake of doing well a thing that is well worth doing.[38]

If we view our "work" in this way, as a participation in the ongoing creation of the universe, the sharp distinction between the work we do in the public sphere and the work we do in the private sphere becomes blurred. When that happens, the trade-offs that are an inevitable part of the choices we have to make when we devote our limited time for one vocation over the other become easier to accept.

I am not suggesting that this vision of work always makes it easier to decide *which* vocation has priority at any one time. I am suggesting that the consequences of what we do become easier to live with. And sometimes this notion of work does, in fact, help us to prioritize. Everything we do is part of how we image God—not just what we do in caring for our families, and not just what we do for money in the workplace. So when we realize that the time we need to spend on our private vocation—such as caring for a loved one—*will* limit our advancement at work, that becomes easier to accept. *Both* of these obligations are part of our Christian vocation. Similarly, when the need to spend an evening working on testimony to a legislative committee to support women in crisis pregnancies prevents us from watching our child's soccer game, that trade-off becomes easier to accept when we appreciate that *both* obligations are part of our vocation.

Of course, sometimes the obligation that takes us away from our child's soccer game is not so noble. Sometimes it's an evening of document review in defense of a bank that has profited from arguably predatory lending practices. But when we are faced with such a conflict, viewing both our job and our family obligations as vocations is still useful. It forces us to think about *why* that particular job is the way we are fulfilling the call of our public vocation. Is it because we need this particular job to support our family financially? If so, making that choice *does* serve our private vocation, in a different way from our physical presence, but in a necessary way. Or is it because we need that job to pay for the vacation home and the SUV? Then maybe we *do* need to be troubled by this particular trade-off. Is it because this particular job gives us a platform for pro bono work or private volunteer work in support of a Catholic understanding of the stewardship of the environment? If so, perhaps the cost of that choice *may* be an appropriate cost of being a Christian in the world. Or is it rather the case that, although this particular job theoretically gives us such a platform, we are just "too busy" to ever use it? In that case, maybe the cost of that choice is not so clearly justified.

There is no question that women sacrifice professionally more than men do to care for their children as part of their private vocation. But because they do, they are actually confronted more often with the need to make the kinds of assessments I have just described. They are more attuned to the very real costs that are incurred in having to choose one set of vocational duties over another at any one time. One of the women interviewed by journalist Lisa Belkin in her article on the "opt-out revolution" suggests that the exodus of professional women from the workplace is not all about motherhood, but rather, is also very much about work:

> That is the gift biology gives women.... It provides pauses, in the form of pregnancy and childbirth, that men do not have. And as the workplace becomes more stressful and all-consuming, the exit door is more attractive. "Women get to look around every few years and say, 'Is this still what I want to be doing?'" she says. "Maybe they have higher standards for job satisfaction because there is always the option of being their child's primary caregiver. When a man gets that dissatisfied with his job, he has to stick it out."[39]

What I would like to suggest, however, is that viewing *all* of our work, our work in furthering our private and our public vocations, as part of our ongoing participation with God in the creation of the universe, should spur all of us to make such assessments from time to time. Maybe not just when we are having a baby, but periodically, all of us should stop and ask ourselves not simply "Is this still what I want to be doing?" but also "Is this still what God wants me to be doing?" Whether we are men or women, whether we are parents or not, we should all periodically reflect on the costs of excessive attention to one or the other of our vocations. The tension between the two is inevitable, and some cost will always be paid at the expense of the other. We simply need to be honest in assessing whether that cost is justifiable in light of our calling as Christians.

3. Human Flourishing

Like the Church, Hirshman does talk about human flourishing. One of the reasons she argues that staying home with children is bad for women is that:

> The family—with its repetitive, socially invisible, physical tasks—is a necessary part of life, but it allows fewer opportunities for full human flourishing than public spheres like the market or the government. This less-flourishing sphere is not the natural or moral responsibility only of women. Therefore, assigning it to women is unjust.

She also writes: "A good life for humans includes the classical standard of using one's capacities for speech and reason in a prudent way, the liberal requirement of having enough autonomy to direct one's own life, and the utilitarian test of doing more good than harm in the world."

Not only is this understanding of human flourishing dramatically at odds with the Catholic view of human flourishing, it also leads to a significant inconsistency in Hirshman's argument. Hirshman's major mistake is buying into the notion that flourishing means meeting the standards of success established by the contemporary marketplace. Her own research suggests that a central reason her "elite women" are leaving the marketplace is that they are dissatisfied with those structures. She writes:

> Half my *Times* brides quit *before* the first baby came. In interviews, at least half of them expressed a hope never to work again.... [W]hen they quit, they were already alienated from their work or at least not committed to a life of work. One, a female MBA, said she could never figure out why the men at their workplace ... were so excited about making deals. "It's only money," she mused.

Hirshman recognizes that women are rejecting current workplace environments for reasons *other* than simply the desire to be home for their children. They do *not* feel they are truly flourishing in their jobs. Yet she ignores this very important observation. Oblivious to what she's missed, she challenges women to go back to those (unfulfilling) workplaces and gives advice for how to be successful under the criteria for success that those (unfulfilling) workplaces have established.

The blindness of many secular feminists to the reality that simply being in the workplace does not guarantee human flourishing has been the subject of growing attention by the aforementioned care feminists. They are becoming increasingly critical of liberal theories of justice based on autonomy—theories like Hirshman's that posit autonomous, independent actors as the ideal around which notions of justice are constructed. In rejecting the account of the human as essentially autonomous, these feminists come closer to a Catholic understanding of the human person, and thus of human flourishing, than do many secular feminists. In the words of care feminist Robin West:

> We are not insular atoms, sufficient unto ourselves, wanting nothing but to be left alone. Rather, for substantial parts of our lives, we are dependent on the caregiving of others for our very survival, and

throughout our lives, we remain interdependent social beings. These basic social and biological facts of life, furthermore, inform not just our self-understanding, but our moral sense as well: we have moral obligations to the weak and to those dependent on us, and we know we have those moral obligations, because we know we have been, and will be, weak and dependent ourselves. We sympathize with others in crisis or in need, and we depend on their sympathetic response when we are in need ourselves. We build community because we are communal creatures who depend on it. It is, therefore, not surprising that the liberal world, justified by a false understanding of who we are, is so apparently morally barren. It is at war with out [sic] moral intuitions about the way in which we ought to live, because it is at war with the true conception of our nature that informs our moral sense.[40]

The care feminists do come closer to the Catholic notion of human flourishing in their recognition that we are communal beings. So they recognize that we cannot measure flourishing solely by how well we do for ourselves independent of our relationships with others. They stop short, however, of the more dramatic consequences the Church draws from this insight. According to the Catholic Church, our communal nature as human beings is an image of God's nature as a Trinity of divine beings in relationship with one another. As Pope John Paul II explained, we were made for communion with others because we were created in the "image and likeness" of this Triune God. Thus, we can only achieve full self-realization and full human flourishing, the Church teaches, through the sincere gift of ourselves to others.[41]

So, under a Catholic notion of human flourishing, sometimes, out of love, our own individual flourishing, as Hirshman understands it, does have to be sacrificed for others. But that *gift* we make of ourselves to others, at the expense of more interesting work or rapid career advancement, does, in the Catholic view, contribute in a very real way to our human flourishing. I suspect that many of the women that Hirshman talked to—and many of those who disagreed with her—did give up their jobs out of love, did sacrifice for the love of their spouses and their kids. But here's the trouble: when women truly realize the professional and the personal cost of their self-sacrifice, they have few resources from within Hirshman's secular feminist perspective for understanding this as anything but an affront to their personal flourishing, to their autonomy. The

Catholic Church offers women—and men—far richer resources for assessing these costs.

Understanding the costs of sacrifices made out of self-giving love as an *element* of flourishing is helpful in sorting through the tensions between our private and public vocations. It certainly ought to be helpful in accepting the cost to one's career of truly nurturing and being attentive to the relationships to which we are called—relationships with our children, parents, spouses, colleagues, neighbors, and God. But I think that it should also be applied in the other direction, too. Some of the sacrifices demanded of us, *or demanded of those with whom we have relationships*, for the sake of our public vocations, might also be justified as contributions to human flourishing. The sacrifice of the child in not having her mother watch her soccer game might be a sacrifice that contributes to *her* flourishing. The lessons about sacrifice of individual glory for the good of the soccer team that even the youngest child should be learning on the field can be given a deeper meaning when her mother explains the aspect of her public vocation that requires her attention at that time.

Unlike Hirshman, the Catholic Church does not offer us three pithy rules for resolving all of the tensions that are an inevitable part of our complex vocations as Christians. However, a truly Catholic understanding of family, of work, and of flourishing, should make it easier to not just accept, but perhaps also to embrace, the challenges posed by such tensions.

Conclusion:
Reflections on the Kinship Between
Catholic Sexual and Social Teaching

Erika Bachiochi

Among the intellectual class of Catholics in America, one tends to hear two distinctive and mutually critical voices: liberal, progressive, or "social justice" Catholics on the one hand, and conservative or "traditional" Catholics on the other.

Liberal Catholics praise the Church for her positions on war and peace, her privileged care or "preferential option" for the poor, and her strong opposition to the death penalty. They disapprove of the Church's teachings on sexuality, tend to downplay her teachings on abortion and euthanasia—and vote Democrat.

Conservative Catholics, on the other hand, adhere to and often defend the Church's sexual teachings, and are ardently and actively pro-life. They tend to disfavor the social justice teachings of the Church *as expressed by* the U.S. Conference of Catholic Bishops, view the free market much more favorably than do their liberal counterparts—and vote Republican.

Conservative Catholics deride liberal Catholics for their "cafeteria Catholicism," while liberal Catholics disdain conservatives for their apparent lack of faithfulness to the Church's central mission of promoting peace, social justice, and charity to the poor.

This analysis is hardly new. As Catholic theologian Charles Curran wrote in 1988:

> Many conservative and neo-conservative Roman Catholics have objected strenuously to the recent social teachings of the United States bishops but seem to have no problem with the official church teaching on sexual ethics. On the other hand, liberal Catholics have applauded the recent social teachings while often dissenting from the sexual teachings.[1]

While this hard and fast breakdown may be media-generated to some extent, some real theological, philosophical, and political disagreements certainly exist among the faithful within the Catholic Church in America. Putting aside the more theoretical debates about theological anthropology, political philosophy, economic theory, and social welfare policy, and even the inaptly political titles of "liberal" and "conservative" in discussions of Church teaching, one thing has become remarkably clear in undertaking this book project: on a practical level, the Church's preferential option for the poor (the supposed province of "liberals") intersects with, and even depends upon, the Church's sexual teachings (the supposed province of "conservatives").

That is, if we truly want to stand in solidarity with the poor—nonnegotiable for the Christian, whatever his or her economic theory—we have to admit that however unpopular Church teaching is on sex and marriage, it is a prerequisite for authentic social justice. In the words of University of Virginia sociologist Bradford Wilcox, "[T]he Church's commitment to the poor requires nothing less than a vigorous proclamation of the Church's ... teaching about sex and marriage."[2]

Just as many in the 1960s and 1970s believed easier access to abortion and contraception would be an untrammeled good for women, so too was it assumed that the same would cure poverty in America and the world. Sociological, biological, and medical data have now revealed that women in general have lost much as a result of the loosening of sexual mores. But leading social scientists, over the past ten to fifteen years, have reported that the biggest losers in the sexual revolution have been poor women and children. A true ethic of social justice requires Catholics to take seriously the data that have mounted over the years, revealing just how devastating straying from traditional sexual norms has been for the poor.

So what do all the data say?

Single motherhood, the leading indicator of poverty among women and children in the United States, began its steady rise during the 1960s and 1970s, at the same time Americans on the whole were throwing off traditional sexual norms.[3] Eminent social scientists such as William Julius Wilson and Charles Murray had pointed, respectively, to changes in job availability and welfare benefits to account for the surge in out-of-wedlock births in the late 1960s and after.[4] But in 1996, Nobel prize-winning economist George Akerlof, himself not a social conservative, published a study that seemed to defy the conventional wisdom of the day. Since then his ideas have gained some currency among social scientists trying to explain the "feminization of poverty" that has taken shape in the sharp rise of single motherhood. Akerlof claimed that the fault lies with greater access to contraception and abortion.[5]

His ideas were counterintuitive at the time. Most social observers thought increased availability to contraception and abortion would decrease, not increase, unwanted pregnancy and the number of children born to unwed mothers. But Akerlof wrote that by reducing the threat of pregnancy to women, the Pill and abortion empowered men, giving them the rationale they needed to persuade women to enter into sexual relationships without a promise of marriage should pregnancy occur, as had previously been the norm. According to Akerlof, women who wished to wait until marriage to engage in sexual relations or who, as in prior times, could have at least conditioned premarital sex on a man's pledge to marry, were put at a great "competitive disadvantage" vis-à-vis women willing to use contraceptives or abortion.[6]

Not only did sexual activity outside of marriage increase substantially in the 1960s and beyond as a result of contraception and abortion, but the norm of premarital chastity dissolved. This caused many young women to be socially pressured into sexual relations that did not further their prospects for marriage.[7] Since men could find women willing to engage in contraceptive sex, Akerlof reasoned, men were less likely to commit to marriage before sex. They were also more likely to shirk parental and marital responsibilities should pregnancy unexpectedly occur.[8] After all, with contraception and abortion available, children were not what the men had bargained for.

But the increase in single motherhood, and the poor outcomes that invariably accompany it, did not occur across the socio-economic spectrum.[9] Though more highly educated women saw a small rise in the number of out-of-wedlock births, the dramatic increase came to underprivileged women, most of whom had not graduated from high school. These women were ill-prepared to provide for their children on their own. There is a sad irony in this. The more highly educated women had fought to destigmatize single motherhood as part of the feminist quest for independence both from men and from what the 1970s feminists took to be the "patriarchal" institution of marriage. Yet these women were not, for the most part, the ones attempting the herculean task of raising children on their own.[10] More privileged women were simply delaying marriage and childbearing (some of them indefinitely, as described in chapter 6 in this volume), in an effort to pursue advanced education and careers. It was their poorer, less educated sisters who saw greater hope and meaning in raising children than in dreams of education and professions they could ill-afford or manage. With their men no longer willing to make the lifestyle sacrifices needed to provide for their children, and without the social stigma that had discouraged unwed motherhood in prior days, these women determined to go it alone.[11]

The increased availability of contraception and abortion permitted the more well-off to separate sex from procreation, enabling sexually active women to pursue education and careers. As illustrated in chapters 2, 3, 5, and 8, however, decoupling sex from procreation also resulted in a casualness to sex and a devaluing of motherhood that has not benefited women on the whole. Though well-educated women may theoretically approve of having a child outside of marriage, as advocated by 1970s feminism, most still regard marriage as the institution within which children should be raised.[12] For the disadvantaged, however, contraception and abortion have encouraged procreation apart from the institution of marriage altogether. This has resulted in detrimental outcomes for these single mothers and their children (as described in chapter 4).[13] Thus, it appears that while the well-to-do can absorb some of the repercussions of the libertine lifestyle, the poor do not have the resources to do the same. The free and easy way of life may look glamorous when acted out by the rich and famous but, for most, imitation yields devastating results. As Kay Hymowitz writes in her outstanding book, *Marriage and Caste in America*:

> When Americans announced that marriage before childbearing was optional, low-income women didn't merely lose a steadfast partner, a second income, or a trusted baby-sitter.... They lost a traditional arrangement ... a way of organizing their early lives that would prize education and culminate in childbearing only after job training and marriage.... Worst of all, when Americans made marriage optional, low-income women lost a culture that told them the truth about what was best for their children.[14]

While the poor no longer regard marriage as necessary for raising children, it is not because they reject the institution outright. Both poor women and educated middle-class women share a remarkably similar view of marriage, a view that has shifted substantially over the past few decades. For both the rich and the poor, marriage is no longer primarily an institution for raising children, even if the more well-off continue to bear children almost exclusively within the marital bond.[15] Marriage, for both groups, has become first and foremost about adult fulfillment. When marriage is viewed in this way, the door is then open to putting other types of arrangements on a par with marriage. This cultural transition has made more palatable, to younger Americans at least, efforts to allow homosexuals to marry.[16]

According to the women interviewed in the groundbreaking book, *Promises I Can Keep: Why Poor Women Put Motherhood Before Marriage*, marriage among underprivileged women is regarded as something of a life goal, but certainly not something for which one should delay childbearing. For these women, a car, a mortgage, some furniture, and stable jobs for both him and her would all precede marriage, if they were fortunate enough to marry at all.[17] Economic independence from the men they would marry was a prerequisite to nuptials, theoretically granting these women the power to leave their husbands (or at least threaten to do so) should the men continue their sexually and socially devious ways.[18] Indeed, among the underprivileged populations studied by urban ethnographers Kathryn Edin and Maria Kefalas in *Promises I Can Keep*, women are now far more reluctant to marry than men.[19] They simply do not trust their men to remain faithful, duly employed, and out of jail. The data on infidelity, unemployment, and incarceration show their mistrust to be well founded.[20]

Child-rearing for these women is so central to their existence, so fundamental to their self-definition, that the idea of putting it off until one is able to find a man who is marriage-worthy seems absurd—since there are so few around. It is also why the middle-class solution of contraception misses the mark. Poor, uneducated women who have babies out of wedlock do so, by and large, because they want them.[21] They find their place in the world by bearing and raising children, and they are not going to wait around for their child's father to mature enough to join them.

The irony is that a marriage centered on raising children, and all the responsibility that goes with it, is precisely what these young men may need to save them from their antisocial behavior. According to Hymowitz, "It is marriage's dedication to child-rearing, to a future that projects far beyond passing feelings ... that has the potential to discipline adult passion."[22] In the three decades following the sexual revolution, when contraceptive sex and legal abortion made sex available to men without the concomitant duties of marriage or children, crime rates, substance abuse rates, and incarcerations (especially drug-related) rose precipitously.[23] Contraceptive sex (and abortion) made sex so readily available that it deprived men of the incentive to become marriageable, and thus further deprived them of the domesticating influence of a wife and children who depended upon them.

In an article dedicated to the cavaliering ways of unmarried men, that same left-leaning, non-Catholic economist who faulted contraception and abortion for the rise in single motherhood wrote in 1998 that the religious view of marriage as a sacrament, as an institution that transforms those who wed, actually corresponds to the empirical data.[24] Married men work harder to stay employed and advance in their jobs, are less likely to commit crimes or be the victims of crimes, and have less substance abuse and better health than their unmarried counterparts.[25] Poor and working-class unmarried men who lack educational or professional challenges are especially drawn to the competition of the streets, where their masculinity can be tested, but in socially deviant ways.[26] As George Gilder writes in Men and Marriage, "The provider role of men not only gives the society the benefit of a lifetime of hard work oriented toward long-term goals. It also channels and disciplines male energies and aggressions that otherwise turn against that society."[27]

Yet the blame does not rest with wayward men alone. For them to reengage in the lives of their children and become men upon whom women can rely, they need a new pro-marriage incentive structure imposed upon them. It is up to women, especially those in poorer communities but also among the more privileged, to stop giving men sex outside the permanent commitment of marriage. It is up to women to call men home.

As George Akerlof and other social scientists have intimated by their studies (but certainly not argued expressly), the Catholic sexual ethic offers a compelling alternative. It provides an antidote to the vicious cycle devastating poor communities where female-headed households and socially deviant single men prevail. This is because, as prominent social scientist Barbara Dafoe Whitehead has recognized, Catholic teaching "connects sexuality to marriage, the family, and children."[28] According to Whitehead, the Church has been especially prophetic in this area. Expert opinion once tended to minimize the effects on children of high divorce rates and single-parent households. But that opinion has been shifting back, in recent years, toward the Church's traditional approach.[29]

The Church has always been well regarded, inside and out, for her commitment to the poor, to those who are materially and spiritually burdened. Sociologists and economists of all stripes are now beginning to see the sense in Church teaching on sex and marriage as well. One cannot expect (but can certainly pray) that the underprivileged—and privileged alike—would enter the Church in droves for guidance on how to live and love well. But would it be asking too much for *fellow Catholics* who publicly or privately balk at such Church teaching to reassess their views in light of this new data? It surely would benefit the poor for them to do so.

The Dignity of the Human Person
at the Heart of All Catholic Teaching

Dissident Catholic intellectuals have long criticized the Church for her "uncompromising rigidity" when it comes to her teachings on sex and marriage. They fault her for what they take to be an inconsistent methodological approach between such teachings (with which they disagree) and those concerning issues of social justice (with which they agree). Such Catholics argue that the Church allows diversity of opinion among her members concerning the application of Catholic principles of social justice to particular situations, but fails to tolerate differing opinions when it comes to her sexual teachings. In his 1995 book *Sexuality and Catholicism*, Thomas Fox, editor of the *National Catholic Reporter*, writes:

> While [the documents on Catholic social teaching] are founded on basic Christian principles, their reasoning moves them into carefully nuanced examinations of the time and circumstances before drawing conclusions. By contrast, sexual sins remain absolute in nature and without nuance and without regard to circumstances. Unlike the carefully reasoned social teachings, the sexual teachings come out of a theology of fixed and uncompromising law.[30]

But it is not true to say that all the absolutes are on the side of sexual morality, and all the contingent judgments on the side of social teaching. Surely Fox would agree that modern Catholic social doctrine holds that forcing someone into slavery is the type of act that is always wrong, regardless of time and circumstances. And in her sexual ethics, the Church teaches that so long as moral means are used, a married couple ought to carefully examine circumstances to determine for themselves whether it is responsible to conceive a child at a particular time. Absolute principles guide particular judgments in both areas of Church teaching.

It is, however, true to say that Catholic social teaching lends itself more readily to the exercise of prudence; indeed, that the virtue of prudence, of applying broad principles to concrete situations, is essential to make good judgments in the realm of social justice. But the institutional Church does not understand *herself* to be equipped to make those judgments about particularities in the economic and political realms. In his 1987 encyclical *Sollicitudo Rei Socialis (On Social Concern)*, Pope John Paul II wrote: "[T]he Church does not propose economic and political systems or programs, nor does she show preference for one or the other, provided that human dignity is properly respected and promoted, and provided she herself is allowed the room she needs to exercise her ministry in the world."[31]

The Church lays out fundamental principles. It is up to persons properly situated and knowledgeable about specific situations, including lay members of the Church engaged in economic and political occupations, to exercise their prudence in applying such principles. Social justice teaching is not methodologically "gray," as one theologian put it, because it is somehow more philosophically nuanced or compassionate than sexual teaching.[32] Rather, the Church's social teachings and sexual teachings simply have different objects. The object of social doctrine, the political, social, and economic order, is wildly complex, with innumerable players and a multiplicity of historical, geographical, and demographic factors. It is not conducive to specificity of teaching, nor are particular judgments in the realm of politics and economics the proper object of Church teaching. Jesus Christ did not come to build earthly kingdoms (or even democracies) but to save souls—souls that are certainly complex and personally unique, but are definitively embodied, ordered toward an end which is God, and interdependent on other embodied souls.

Difference in methodology, or level of specificity of teaching, then, is hardly grounds for claiming an inconsistency in Church teachings on social justice and sexual issues. In fact, these teachings could hardly be more consistent, or interdependent, as revealed by the data above. The internal consistency between these two sets of teachings cannot be found in how they treat their objects, since one is focused on the social order and the other on the human person. Rather, it is found in their common focus on protecting human dignity and advancing human happiness. Empirical data aside, the sexual and social teachings of the Church exhibit a striking kinship.

When the Church promotes the just distribution of human goods to the poor, and criticizes the materialism and consumerism of the rich, she is defending their shared human dignity, and promoting their longing for happiness. In like manner, when she objects to sexual relations outside the protections of the marital bond, and seeks to guard each unborn human life, she is defending human dignity and promoting human happiness.

The Church calls her people to almsgiving and other charitable acts because such behavior dignifies *both* the recipient of the good or service *and* the benefactor, the poor and the rich alike. Charity promotes the development of the virtues of humility, on the one hand, and of generosity on the other, both of which engage the human spirit and advance human happiness. Similarly, the Church calls her people to treat others as subjects worthy of respect rather than as objects to be used for pleasure or power. Treating others with respect dignifies *both* the beloved and the lover, the powerless and the powerful. In engaging persons as the human subjects they are, we develop the virtues of temperance (or self-mastery) and justice, virtues that, again, advance human happiness. This is why, for the Catholic, "charity is not a kind of welfare activity which could equally well be left to others [like some government agency], but is a part of her nature, an indispensable expression of her very being."[33] And this is why, for the Catholic, sex cannot be casual or expunged of its sacred meaning.

Catholics are called to care for the materially and spiritually poor by meeting them face-to-face, by recognizing each as a human person, another Christ, a beloved child of God. In respecting their inherent human dignity and treating them with the justice they deserve, we advance our own moral and spiritual development. Such attention to the human person, and to the growth in virtue that it entails, is quite similar to how we are to live out the Catholic sexual ethic.

Rather than seeking to escape a burdensome pregnancy or marriage by ending it, Catholics are called to humbly and prayerfully seek assistance for the underlying difficulties at issue, and to attend, in a spirit of generosity, to the other human persons concerned. Rather than suppressing the gift of female fertility with contraceptives, Catholics are called to be attentive to the woman's reproductive design, and, guided by prayer, to generously and responsibly determine family size. Rather than respond to the passionate and fleeting plays of sexual desire, Catholics are called to recognize the human person before us, in all his or her complexity and vulnerability, to cautiously and patiently discern whether he or she is the one to whom we want to commit our life. Like the call to authentic charity and justice in the social order, each of these acts demands our growth in virtue; each of these practices requires us to selflessly place the other ahead of ourselves.

The Priority of Culture

Growth in virtue through a life of generosity and self-restraint in one's personal relationships is not only a recipe for happiness, it is also the means toward economic stability and civic engagement. The habits that enable a courting man and woman to forgo immediate sexual pleasure in order to build a sure foundation for a happy marriage are the same habits that enable them to save and invest (rather than spend) their present earnings in the hope of future monetary gain. As Pope Leo XIII wrote in

Rerum Novarum: "Christian morality, when adequately and completely practiced, leads of itself to temporal prosperity...; it powerfully restrains the greed of possession and the thirst for pleasure—twin plagues, which too often make a man who is void of self-restraint miserable in the midst of abundance...."[34] Sacrificing the desires of the self for the common good of one's spouse and children, as a person must if he or she is to live the sexual teachings of the Church, also prepares that person to do the same for the wider community. As the Founders themselves taught, the American experiment in self-governance requires self-sacrifice and self-discipline—in a word, personal virtue—if our democratic republic and free-market economy are to succeed.[35]

This is why it is wrong-headed to attempt to bring about social justice in our communities, our nation, and our world by focusing solely on reforming the political and economic realms. Catholics certainly must make efforts to persuade lawmakers and fellow citizens to pass humane laws and enact just economic policies, but we must not believe our priorities lie in changing the political and economic order alone. We must not become so engrossed with shoring up our social order through political means that we fail to recognize the supreme importance of a strong and vibrant culture as the root of authentic social justice.

American political and economic systems have shown themselves to be the best in the history of the world at guaranteeing individual liberty and creating wealth, but they must be buffered by a humane and virtuous culture if they are to do so with justice and humanity. Without families, schools, and churches to teach boys and girls to become men and women of integrity, self-mastery, and self-sacrifice, democracy and capitalism will eat away at themselves. Without a culture that values the dignity of human life over the consumption of the free market, the capitalist quest for individual material gain will be that which informs, corrodes, and ultimately erodes, the culture. Rather than using our talents for the good of the whole, we begin to believe we are justified in seeking goods and pleasures for ourselves alone.

Without a vibrant culture to ennoble sexuality, marriage, and the family, our constitutional democracy's tendency to give equal hearing to all ideas, even those harmful to the person and the family, will inform, corrode, and erode society. We begin to view every way of life as commendable, whatever its harms. Rather than focus on the responsibilities we have to others, we focus on our rights, those things to which we feel entitled. When families, schools, and churches can no longer ward off the individualist, hedonistic, and relativistic influences of democratic capitalism, those cultural institutions themselves become subject to these influences. Rather than transform and strengthen the political and economic realms, the culture is transformed, and deformed, by them.

As papal biographer George Weigel has written, among John Paul II's distinctive contributions to Catholic social teaching was his articulation of this very principle. As the world's most beloved pastor and its supreme advocate for peace, John Paul II witnessed in both word and deed to the "priority of culture over politics and economics as the engine of historical change."[36] This insight of John Paul's made him a critic not so much of democratic capitalism itself, but of the deleterious influence such a system could have on society were it not tethered to a vibrant culture. He wrote in 1991:

> If economic life is absolutized, if the production and consumption of goods become the center of social life and society's only value, not subject to any other value, the reason is to be found not so much in the economic system itself as in the fact that the entire socio-cultural system, by ignoring the ethical and religious dimension, has been weakened, and ends by limiting itself to the production of goods and services alone.[37]

Changing laws and policies can only marginally protect against these systemic tendencies in democracy and capitalism. Moreover, placing too many rules and regulations on the systems themselves in an effort to restrain their ill effects simply limits their ability to do what they were designed to do: protect individual liberties, govern with stability and fairness, foster ingenuity and progress, and create wealth. Virtuous individuals, intact families, character-building schools, and faithful churches are much more capable of harnessing and directing the power of democratic capitalism for the common good.

The Centrality of Women

As the world's first teachers of self-sacrifice and compassion, women are the foremost shapers of culture. In John Paul's view, then, women stand as a vital force for guarding against the modern tendencies toward the love of self, of money, and of pleasure. Women wield this transformative power first and foremost in their own homes, by modeling, teaching, and nurturing their children in the ways of love and service. But their influence is much broader in scope. Through their professional work as well as their involvement and leadership in civic organizations, they hold the power to attest to and defend the very dignity of the human person. By their lives and the personal and professional choices they make, they can reveal to the world the way of attentive, humanizing, self-giving love. As John Paul II wrote in 1988:

> In our own time, the successes of science and technology make it possible to attain material well-being to a degree hitherto unknown. While this favors some, it pushes others to the edges of society. In this way, unilateral progress can also lead to a gradual *loss of sensitivity for man, that is, for what is essentially human.* In this sense, our time in particular *awaits the manifestation* of that "genius" which belongs to women, and which can ensure sensitivity for human beings in every circumstance: because they are human!—and because "the greatest of these is love" (cf. 1 Cor 13:13).[38]

But women can only achieve this transformative influence in society if they recognize their own dignity and value as beloved children of God. As contributors to this volume have shown, the contemporary denigration of sex, marriage, motherhood, and life itself has been a blow to women, their self-concept, their quest for happiness, and their ability to flourish in relationships. If women are to be the shapers of a strong and vibrant culture that values the sacredness of life, sex, marriage, and motherhood, they must allow themselves to be shaped by a force far greater than themselves. If they are to lead the way in a renewal of culture, they must go constantly to the true source of all healing, power, and strength: Christ himself. "Anyone who wishes to give love must also receive love as a gift ... [O]ne can become a source from which rivers of living water flow.... Yet to become such a source, one must constantly drink anew from the original source, which is Jesus Christ, from whose pierced heart flows the love of God...."[39]

Both the Church's sexual and social teachings call us to love as Christ loves. At times, this call to love generously is more than we can handle. At times, loving as Christ loves feels impossible. And this is the moment when the sexual and social teachings of the Church have taught us precisely what they are meant to teach us: *by our own strength*, following Christ *is* often impossible. But with him, reborn in Baptism, healed through frequent confession, strengthened through the grace of our vocation, and transformed in the Eucharist, we are made anew. The selfless love that Catholic sexual and social teaching demands of us is always possible when we are united, sacramentally, to the God who is love.

Notes

Introduction

1. Rodney Stark, *The Rise of Christianity: How the Obscure, Marginal Jesus Movement Became the Dominant Religious Force in the Western World in a Few Centuries* (New York: HarperOne, 1997), 95ff.

2. William D'Antonio et al., *American Catholics Today: New Realities of Their Faith and Their Church* (Lanham, MD: Rowman & Littlefield, 2007).

3. Rosemary Radford Ruether, "American Catholic Feminism" in *Reconciling Catholicism and Feminism?: Personal Reflections on Tradition and Change*, eds. Sally Barr Ebest and Ron Ebest (Notre Dame, IN: University of Notre Dame Press, 2003), 8.

4. Lisa Sowle Cahill, *Women and Sexuality* (New York: Paulist Press, 1992), 51.

5. Elizabeth A. Johnson, *Feminism and Sharing the Faith: A Catholic Dilemma* (Tulsa, OK: University of Tulsa, 1993), 6 (paraphrasing a statement of Catholic theologian Rosemary Radford Ruether).

6. Elizabeth Fox-Genovese, "Equality, Difference, and the Practical Problems of a New Feminism" in *Women in Christ: Toward a New Feminism*, ed. Michele M. Schumacher (Grand Rapids, MI: Wm. B. Eerdmans, 2003), 300.

1

Authentic Freedom and Equality in Difference

1. See Pope John Paul II, *Christifideles Laici* (Boston: Pauline Books & Media, 1989), no. 51.

2. "Universal Declaration of Human Rights," United Nations, Articles 1–2, www. un.org/events/humanrights/udhr60/hrphotos/declaration _eng.pdf.

3. Jeffner Allen, "Motherhood: The Annihilation of Women" in *Mothering: Essays in Feminist Theory*, ed. Joyce Trebilcot (Totowa, NJ: Rowman & Allanheld, 1983), 316.

4. Margaret L. Andersen, *Thinking About Women: Sociological Perspectives on Sex and Gender*, 3rd ed. (New York: Macmillan, 1993), 339.

5. Martha Farrell Erickson and Enola G. Aird, *The Motherhood Study: Fresh Insights on Mothers' Attitudes and Concerns* (New York: Institute for American Values, 2005).

6. John Paul II, *Familiaris Consortio* (Washington, DC: USCCB Publishing, 1982), no. 23.

7. I argue for this claim at greater length in "Natural Kinds, Persons, and Abortion," *National Catholic Bioethics Quarterly* 8, no. 2 (Summer 2008): 265–73.

8. Karol Wojtyla, *Love and Responsibility* (San Francisco: Ignatius Press, 1981), 41. In this formulation, inspired by Immanuel Kant, the moral law rules out certain actions and attitudes toward persons. Wojtyla prefers to state the law in its positive form: "A person is an entity of a sort to which the only proper and adequate way to relate is love." It's not obvious that the two statements are equivalent, however. While the positive formulation entails the negative one, it does not seem that the reverse is true.

9. Andersen, *Thinking About Women*, 339. Andersen cites Eleanor Leacock, "Women's Status in Egalitarian Society," *Current Anthropology* 19, no. 2 (June 1978): 247–75.

10. See references at notes 13, 14, and 15 below.

11. Steven E. Rhoads, *Taking Sex Differences Seriously* (San Francisco: Encounter Books, 2004).

12. *Mommy Wars: Stay-at-Home and Career Moms Face Off on Their Choices, Their Lives, Their Families*, ed. Leslie Morgan Steiner (New York: Random House, 2006); see also Sylvia Ann Hewlitt, *Creating a Life: Professional Women and the Quest for Children* (New York: Miramax, 2002).

13. Rhoads' discussion of brain research is on pp. 27–28 of *Sex Differences*, where he cites the work of Anne Moir and David Jessel, *Brain Sex: The Real Difference Between Men and Women* (New York: Delta, 1989) and Marguerite Holloway, "Profile: Vive la Difference: Doreen Kimura Plumbs Male and Female Brains," *Scientific American*, October 1990.

14. Nikhil Swaminathan, "Girl Talk: Are Women Really Better at Language?" *Scientific American*, March 2008, www.sciam.com/article.cfm?id=are-women-really-better-with-language.

15. Larry Cahill, "His Brain, Her Brain," *Scientific American*, May 2005, www.sciam.com/article.cfm?id=his-brain-her-brain.

16. Ibid. Cahill reports, "Women with schizophrenia have a decreased OAR [orbitofrontal-to-amygdala ratio] relative to their healthy peers, as might be expected. But

men, oddly, have an increased OAR relative to healthy men. These findings remain puzzling, but, at the least, they imply that schizophrenia is a somewhat different disease in men and women and that treatment of the disorder might need to be tailored to the sex of the patient."

17. Prudence Allen discusses the differences in historical theories of complementarity in "Man-Woman Complementarity: The Catholic Inspiration," *Logos* 9, no. 3 (Summer 2006). She writes that fractional complementarity posits that man and woman each possess a fraction of the human person's attributes (e.g., woman is intuitive while man is rational). This view of complementarity often casts gender differences in a way we would today view as stereotypical, and implies that woman (and man) are incomplete without the other. Integral complementarity, on the other hand, views gender differences at the level of the spirit (rather than with regard to particular attributes). This view of complementarity, espoused by Dietrich von Hildebrand, Edith Stein, and Pope John Paul II, holds that man and woman are each whole persons in themselves and so together make up much more than a sum of their individual parts.

18. Drucilla Cornell, "Fatherhood and Its Discontents: Men, Patriarchy, and Freedom" in *Lost Fathers: The Politics of Fatherlessness in America*, ed. Cynthia R. Daniels (New York: Macmillan, 2000). There are many excellent recent books on the importance of fathers. Among these are David Popenoe, *Life Without Father: Compelling New Evidence That Fatherhood and Marriage Are Indispensable for the Good of Children and Society* (New York: Free Press, 1996), and David Blankenhorn, *Fatherless America: Confronting Our Most Urgent Social Problem* (New York: Basic Books, 1995).

19. Rhoads, *Sex Differences*, 80.

20. John Paul II, *Evangelium Vitae* (Boston: Pauline Books & Media, 1995), no. 99, quoting Pope John Paul II, *Mulieris Dignitatem* (Boston: Pauline Books & Media, 1988), no. 18.

21. Ibid.

22. Moral education in the public schools reinforces the kind of relativism this view tends to produce, so that even to make a moral judgment is condemned as a kind of intolerance. Many parents and educators lament that the moral code in our schools has been reduced to two rules: embrace diversity (vis-à-vis gender, race, ethnicity, and sexual preferences) and protect the environment. The goal of building character in children, or even the more utilitarian goal of preparing them to be good citizens, no longer appears on the agenda.

23. *Planned Parenthood of Southeastern Pennsylvania v. Casey*, 505 U.S. 833 (1992), 851.

24. *Mulieris Dignitatem*, no. 10.

25. Rhoads, *Sex Differences*, 35–36. He cites especially Janice M. Steil, *Marital Equality: Its Relationship to the Well-Being of Husbands and Wives* (Thousand Oaks, CA: Sage Publications, 1997).

26. Sara Ruddick, *Maternal Thinking: Toward a Politics of Peace* (Boston: Beacon Press, 1989), 217.

27. See Carol Gilligan, *In a Different Voice: Psychological Theory and Women's Development* (Cambridge, MA: Harvard University Press, 1993).

2

The Uniqueness of Woman:
Church Teaching on Abortion

1. Fifty-one percent of white Catholics and 52 percent of the general population believe that abortion should be legal in most cases. Catholics who attend church weekly are far more opposed to legal abortion than those who do not (36 percent versus 60 percent). "A Portrait of American Catholics on the Eve of Pope Benedict's Visit to the U.S.," *The Pew Forum on Religion in Public Life Publications*, http://pewforum. org/docs/?DocID=295#social.

2. See generally Uta Ranke-Heinemann, *Eunuchs for the Kingdom of Heaven: Women, Sexuality, and the Catholic Church* (Garden City, NY: Doubleday, 1990); also see chapter 3 of this volume.

3. See, for instance, George Weigel, "Were They at the Same Meeting?" *National Review Online*, February 18, 2009 (regarding Speaker of the House Nancy Pelosi's private audience with Pope Benedict XVI in February 2009), http://article.nationalreview.com/?q=NTQyMDRiMDc1ODQzZjY5MDU4YzBhYWQwZjA5OTZlMWQ=.

4. "Cardinals, Bishops, and Congressmen Slam Pelosi on Abortion," Lifesite news. com, August 26, 2008, http://www.lifesitenews.com/ldn/2008/aug/ 08082601. html.

5. See generally, "When Does Human Life Begin: A Scientific Perspective," *The Westchester Institute for Ethics and the Human Person*, White Paper, vol. 1, no. 1 (October 2008).

6. Robert P. George and Christopher Tollefsen, *Embryo: A Defense of Human Life* (New York: Doubleday, 2008), 50–51.

7. Ibid., 61–143.

8. Ibid., 79–81.

9. Patrick Lee and Robert P. George, "Fundamentalists? We? Bad Science, Worse Philosophy, and McCarthyite Tactics in the Human-Embryo Debate," *National Review Online*, October 3, 2006, http://article.nationalreview.com/?q=OTNiYWM2ZjJi YWVlN2IyMzFjOWYwMDZmMTc4MzU2MGU=.

10. See U.S. Constitution, Article I, Section 2.

11. See George and Tollefsen, *Embryo*, 112–43.

12. Naomi Wolf, "Rethinking Pro-Choice Rhetoric: Our Bodies, Our Souls," *The New Republic*, October 16, 1995.

13. Camille Paglia, "Fresh Blood for the Vampire," *Salon.com*, September 10, 2008, http://www.salon.com/news/opinion/camille_paglia/2008/09/10/palin/index. html.

14. Frances Kissling, "Is There Life After Roe? How to Think About the Fetus," *Conscience*, Winter 2004–5.

15. Small portions of this chapter appeared in Erika Bachiochi, "How Abortion Hurts Women: The Hard Proof," *Crisis*, June 2005; used here with permission.

16. See Erika Bachiochi, "The Easy Road to Heaven: Love, Sex, and the Cross," *Crisis*, December 2006.

17. Erika Bachiochi, "Coming of Age in a Culture of Choice" in *The Cost of "Choice": Women Evaluate the Impact of Abortion*, ed. Erika Bachiochi (San Francisco: Encounter Books, 2004), 22.

18. Ibid., 22–32.

19. See the Feminists for Life Web site for several pro-life statements by early American feminists: http://feministsforlife.com/history/index.htm.

20. Serrin Foster, "The Feminist Case Against Abortion" in *The Cost of "Choice,"* ed. Bachiochi, 33–38.

21. Ibid., 35.

22. Ibid.

23. "Abortion and the Early Feminists," BBC Home, http://www.bbc.co.uk/ethics/abortion/mother/early.shtml.

24. *Planned Parenthood of Southeastern Pennsylvania v. Casey,* 505 U.S. 833 (1992), 856.

25. Ibid.; see also *Gonzalez v. Carhart,* 550 U.S. 124 (2007) (Ruth Bader Ginsberg, dissenting).

26. See William Blackstone, *Commentaries on the Laws of England*, ed. Thomas M. Cooley (Chicago: Callaghan and Company, 1884), 441–42.

27. "Election Poll Finds Work and Family Issues—Amid Economic Worries—Are a Frequent Daily Concern for Majority of America's Voting Parents," *Reuters*, November 13, 2008.

28. Brian C. Robertson, *Day Care Deception: What the Child Care Establishment Isn't Telling Us* (San Francisco: Encounter Books, 2003), 111.

29. Ibid., 42–91.

30. Ibid., 128–31.

31. Erickson and Aird, "The Motherhood Study," 30. (The Motherhood Study surveyed more than 2,000 demographically diverse U.S. mothers 18 and older with at least one child under the age of 18.)

32. Ibid. (with 41 percent of mothers currently working full-time).

33. Ibid. (33 percent wanted to work part-time; 30 percent wished to work for pay from home).

34. See, for example, Brian C. Robertson, *Forced Labor: What's Wrong with Balancing Work and Family* (Dallas, TX: Spence Publishing, 2000), 117–18.

35. See conclusion in this volume for further discussion. —Ed.

36. Paglia, "Fresh Blood for the Vampire."

37. *Beal v. Doe,* 432 U.S. 438 (1977), 463 (Harry Blackmun, dissenting).

38. Ibid.

39. See Paul Erich, *The Population Bomb* (New York: Ballantine Books, 1971), but compare to Maria Sophia Aguirre and Cecilia Hadley, "The Ideology of Population Assistance," *The Family in America*, 15:2 (2001), 2; Julian Simon, *The Ultimate Resource 2* (Princeton, NJ: Princeton University Press, 1996); and John Paul II, *Evangelium Vitae*, 16.

40. Pope Benedict XVI, "Fighting Poverty to Build Peace," message for the celebration of the World Day of Peace (January 1, 2009), no. 3.

41. Phillip Longman, *The Empty Cradle: How Falling Birthrates Threaten World Prosperity and What to Do About It* (New York: Basic Books, 2004), 61–67.

42. The risks included here are those that have amassed a good number of scientifically significant studies. Some studies have also shown a correlation between induced abortion and ectopic pregnancy, and abortion and infertility; more research must be conducted to determine whether such an association is scientifically significant.

43. See Elizabeth M. Shadigian, "Reviewing the Evidence, Breaking the Silence: Long-Term Physical and Psychological Health Consequences of Induced Abortion" in *The Cost of "Choice"*, ed. Bachiochi, 63–71; and J. M. Thorp, K. E. Hartmann, E. M. Shadigian, "Long-Term Physical and Psychological Health Consequences of Induced Abortion: A Review of the Evidence," *Obstetrical and Gynecological Survey* 58, no. 1 (January 2003): 75.

44. Thorp et al., "Consequences of Induced Abortion," 70.

45. About.com, "Placenta Previa," http://adam.about.com/encyclopedia/infectiousdiseases/Placenta-previa.htm.

46. Bryan C. Calhoun et al., "Cost Consequences of Induced Abortion as an Attributable Risk," *Journal of Reproductive Medicine* 52, no. 10 (October 2007): 929–37.

47. Committee on Understanding Premature Birth and Assuring Healthy Outcomes, *Preterm Birth: Causes, Consequences, and Prevention*, ed. Richard E. Behrman (National Academies Press, 2007).

48. Ibid., 935

49. Thorp et al., "Consequences of Induced Abortion," 75.

50. Quoted in ibid.

51. Gabriel J. Escobar, Benjamin Littenberg, and Diana B. Petitti, "Outcome Among Surviving Very Low Birth-Weight Infants; a Meta-analysis," *Archives of Disease in Childhood* 66, no.2 (February 1991): 204–11.

52. Barbara Luke, H. Bigger, S. Leurgas, and D. Sietsema, "The Cost of Prematurity: A Case-control Study of Twins vs. Singletons," *American Journal of Public Health* 86, no. 6 (June 1996): 809–14.

53. Shadigian, "Reviewing the Evidence," 63–64.

54. Ibid. According to Thorp, "This loss of protection will be in proportion to the length of time that elapses before they experience their first delivery," Thorp et al., "Consequences of Induced Abortion," 77.

55. Janet R. Daling et al., "Risk of Breast Cancer Among Young Women: Relationship to Induced Abortion," *Journal of the National Cancer Institute* 86, no. 21 (November 2, 1994): 1584 (finding that teenagers with a family history of breast cancer who have abortions before their eighteenth birthday have an *incalculably* high risk of developing breast cancer—because of this early loss of the first full-term pregnancy's protective effect. *All twelve* women in this study, conducted by a publicly pro-choice researcher, were diagnosed with breast cancer by the age of forty-five.

56. Angela Lanfranchi, "The Abortion-Breast Cancer Link: The Studies and the Science," in *The Cost of "Choice,"* ed. Bachiochi, 72–86. Through abortion, the breast physiology shows, a woman artificially terminates her pregnancy at a time when her breast cells have been exposed to high levels of potentially cancer-initiating estrogen but before her breast cells have matured into cancer-resistant cells (as they ultimately do in a full-term pregnancy).

57. Jesse R. Cougle, David C. Reardon, and Priscilla K. Coleman. "Generalized Anxiety Following Unintended Pregnancies Resolved Through Childbirth and Abortion: A Cohort Study of the 1995 National Survey of Family Growth," *Journal of Anxiety Disorders* 19, no. 1 (2005): 137–42.

58. David Fergusson et al., "Abortion in Young Women and Subsequent Mental Health," *Journal of Child Psychology and Psychiatry* 47, no. 1 (January 2006): 16–24. (Of some note, this particular study was conducted by a self-proclaimed pro-choice scientist who expected to find women were not so adversely affected by abortion.)

59. D. C. Reardon and P. G. Ney, "Abortion and Subsequent Substance Abuse," *American Journal of Drug and Alcohol Abuse*, 26, no. 1 (February 2000): 60–75.

60. M. Gissler et al., "Suicides After Pregnancy in Finland, 1987–1994: Register Linkage Study," *British Medical Journal* 313 (December 7, 1996): 1431–34; D. C. Reardon et al., "Deaths Associated with Pregnancy Outcome: A Record Linkage Study of Low Income Women," *Southern Medical Journal* 95, no. 8 (August 2002): 834.

61. M. Paul et al., *A Clinician's Guide to Medical and Surgical Abortion* (New York: Churchill Livingstone, 1999), 20–21; see also Royal College of Obstetricians and Gynecologists (UK), *The Care of Women Requesting Induced Abortion: Evidence-Based Clinical Guidelines* (London: Royal College of Obstetricians and Gynecologists, 2000) (concluding that the immediate physical complication rate of induced abortion, including infection and damage to reproductive organs, was at least 11 percent).

62. The reasons for undercounting are many. First, there are no mandatory reporting of abortion complications (including death), see H. Atrash et al., "The Relation between Induced Abortion and Ectopic Pregnancy," *Obstetrics and Gynecolology* 89, no. 4 (April 1997): 512–18. Further, physicians or coroners often report the death as due to hemorrhage or some other secondary cause, rather than reporting the abortion connection. D. C. Reardon et al., "Deaths Associated with Abortion Compared with Childbirth—A Review of New and Old Data and the Medical and Legal Implications," *Journal of Contemporary Health Law & Policy* 20, no. 2 (Spring 2004): 279, 289–91. See also footnote ii on page 47.

63. Center for Disease Control, Morbidity and Mortality weekly report, *Abortion Surveillance — United States*, 1989–present.

64. H. W. Lawson et al., "Abortion Mortality, United States, 1972 through 1987," *American Journal of Obstetrics & Gynecology* 171, no. 5 (November 1994): 1365–72.

65. Michael F. Greene, "Fatal Infections Associated with Mifepristone-Induced Abortion," *New England Journal of Medicine* 353, no. 22 (December 1, 2005): 2317–18.

66. See amicus brief of the American Center for Law and Justice in Support of Petitioner, *Gonzales v. Planned Parenthood* (no. 05-1382), 2–3.

67. Ibid. See also, Mika Gissler et al., "Pregnancy-associated deaths in Finland 1987–1994—definition problems and benefits of record linkage," *Acta obstetricia et gynecologica Scandinavica* 76, no. 7 (August 1997): 651 (finding that, adjusting for age, women who abort were 3.5 times more likely to die within a year than women who gave birth); see also, M. Gissler et al., "Pregnancy-Associated Mortality After Birth, Spontaneous Abortion, or Induced Abortion in Finland, 1987–2000," *American Journal of Obstetrics & Gynecology* 190, no. 2 (February 2004): 422–27; D. C. Reardon et al.,

"Deaths Associated With Pregnancy Outcome: A Linkage Based Study of Low Income Women," *Southern Medical Journal* 95, no. 8 (August 2002): 834–41 (findings based on women after adjusting for age).

68. Bernard Nathanson, *Aborting America: A Doctor's Personal Report on the Agonizing Issue of Abortion* (New York: Doubleday, 1979), 193.

69. Paige Cunningham and Clarke Forsythe, "Is Abortion the 'First Right' for Women?" in *Abortion, Medicine and the Law*, 4th ed., eds. J. Douglas Butler and David F. Walbert (New York: Facts On Files 1992), 127 (citing figures from the Centers for Disease Control).

70. Ibid.

71. Warren M. Hern, *Abortion Practice* (Philadelphia: Lippincott, 1984), 101.

72. Aida Torres and J. D. Forrest, "Why Do Women Have Abortions?" *Family Planning Perspectives* 20, no. 4 (July/August 1988): 170.

73. "Survey of Attitudes toward Elective Abortions," *American College of Obstetricians and Gynecologists*, 1985; "National Survey of Obstetricians/Gynecologists on Contraception and Unplanned Pregnancy: Attitudes and Practices with Regard to Abortion," *Kaiser Family Foundation*, 1995.

74. See generally Denise Burke, "Abortion Clinic Regulation: Combating the True 'Back-Alley'" in *The Cost of "Choice,"* ed. Bachiochi, 122–32.

75. George Akerlof, Janet L. Yellen, and Michael L. Katz, "An Analysis of Out-of-Wedlock Childbearing in the United States," *The Quarterly Journal of Economics* 111, no. 2 (May 1996): 277–317. See also Rhoads, *Sex Differences*. For further discussion of Akerlof, see the Conclusion to this volume.

76. Daniel Callahan, "An Ethical Challenge to Prochoice Advocates: Abortion and the Pluralistic Proposition," *Commonweal* 17, no. 20 (November 23, 1990): 684.

77. Catherine MacKinnon, *Feminism Unmodified: Discourses on Life and Law* (Cambridge, MA: Harvard University Press, 1987), 99.

78. *Planned Parenthood v. Casey*, 893; for resources for men who suffer from abortion see generally, Vincent M. Rue, *Forgotten Fathers: Men and Abortion* (Lewiston, NY: Life Cycle Books, 1997), pamphlet.

79. Frederica Mathewes-Green, *Real Choices: Listening to Women; Looking for Alternatives to Abortion* (Ben Lomond, CA: Conciliar Press, 1997), appendix D; V. M. Rue et. al., "Induced Abortion and Traumatic Stress: A Preliminary Comparison of American and Russian Women," *Medical Science Monitor* 10, no. 10: SR5–16 (October 2004); see also *Evangelium Vitae*, no. 59.

80. I am indebted to Joseph De Cook, MD, for this formulation.

81. See, e.g., "Abortion in the United States," http://en.wikipedia.org/wiki/Abortion_in_the_United_States.

82. Prudence dictates that pro-life advocates work incrementally to achieve a culture of life. Advocates and lawmakers alike must seek to protect those unborn lives they can, even if, at a particular time, the political landscape does not allow for full protection of the unborn. It would be far better to pass a law prohibiting (or restricting) some abortions than to pass no law at all. See generally Clarke D. Forsythe, *Politics for the Greatest Good: The Case for Prudence in the Public Square* (Downers Grove, IL: InterVarsity Press, 2009).

83. Sandra Mahkom, "Pregnancy and Sexual Assault," *The Psychological Aspects of Abortion*, eds. D. Mall and W. F. Watts (Washington, DC: University Publications of America, 1979), 53–72 (finding that victims of rape who aborted their children feel victimized twice and angry about the abortion).

84. Ibid. (finding that 75 to 85 percent of rape victims chose against abortion).

85. See John Paul II, *Letter to Women*, 5.

86. Dianne N. Irving, MA, PhD, "Abortion: Correct Application of Natural Law Theory," *Linacre Quarterly* (publication of the Catholic Medical Association) 67, no. 1 (February 2000): 45–55.

87. Caroline Mansfield, Suellen Hopfer, and Theresa M. Marteau, "Termination Rates After Prenatal Diagnosis of Down Syndrome, Spina Bifida, Anencephaly, and Turner and Klinefelter Syndromes: A Systematic Literature Review," *Prenatal Diagnosis* 19, no. 9 (September 1999): 808–12.

88. See Elizabeth Schiltz, "Living in the Shadow of Mönchberg: Prenatal Testing and Genetic Abortion" in *The Cost of "Choice,"* 39–49; see also Melinda Tankard Reist, *Defiant Birth: Women Who Resist Medical Eugenics* (North Melbourne, Vic.: Spinifex Press, 2006).

89. See B. Calhoun et al., "Perinatal Hospice: Comprehensive Care for the Family of the Fetus with a Lethal Condition," *Journal of Reproductive Medicine* 48, no. 5 (May 2003): 343–48; N. Hoeldtke and B. Calhoun, "Perinatal Hospice," *American Journal of Obstetrics & Gynecology* 185, no. 3 (September 2001): 525–29.

90. Michael Alison Chandler, "Leap of Love: Adoptions of Children with Down Syndrome Are on the Increase," *Washington Post*, November 9, 2008, C01 (reporting that 200 families are on a waiting list to adopt a child with Down Syndrome in the United States).

91. B. D. Blumberg, et al., "The Psychological Sequelae of Abortion Performed for Genetic Indication," *American Journal of Obstetrics & Gynecology* 122, no. 7 (August 1, 1975): 799–808 (reporting that depression after genetic abortion was much higher than depression after elective abortion).

92. See, e.g., Alice von Hildebrand, *The Privilege of Being a Woman* (Ypsilanti, MI: Ave Maria, Sapientia Press, 2004), 86; see also *Evangelium Vitae*, no. 99.

93. See Richard Stith, "Abortion as Betrayal of Natural Dependents," presented at The Family: Searching for Fairest Love Conference, Notre Dame Center for Ethics and Culture, November 8, 2008.

94. *Evangelium Vitae*, no. 19.

95. The Archdiocese of Milwaukee founded Project Rachel in 1984 as a resource for both women and men seeking to resolve abortion loss. Now present in 144 dioceses in the United States and in several other English-speaking countries, Project Rachel is on the Web at http://www.hopeafterabortion.com/index.cfm.

96. Mary Ann Glendon, *Rights Talk: The Impoverishment of Political Discourse* (New York: Free Press, 1991), 65; see also Glendon, *Abortion and Divorce in Western Law: American Failures, European Challenges* (Cambridge, MA: Harvard University Press, 1987), 10–62.

97. Ann Crittenden, *The Price of Motherhood: Why the Most Important Job in the World Is Still the Least Valued* (New York: Metropolitan Books, 2001).

3

The Fullness of Sexuality:
Church Teaching on Premarital Sex

1. Pope John Paul II explores the "nuptial analogy" between marriage and Christ's union with the Church in his celebrated theology of the body. See footnote 66 in chapter 5 for more on this work. —Ed.

2. *Catechism of the Catholic Church* (hereafter cited as *CCC*), 2nd ed. (Washington, DC: United States Conference of Catholic Bishops, 2006), no. 2348.

3. Ibid., 2349.

4. Ranke-Heinemann, *Eunuchs for the Kingdom of Heaven*, 119.

5. Ibid., 120.

6. Ibid., 120–21.

7. Ibid., 121.

8. Ibid., 122.

9. Ibid., 124.

10. Rosemary Radford Ruether, *Sexism and God-talk: Toward a Feminist Theology* (Boston: Beacon Press, 1983), 80.

11. Ibid., 74.

12. Ibid., 96.

13. Mary Daly, *The Church and the Second Sex* (Boston: Beacon Press, 1985), 54.

14. Ibid., 54–55.

15. Simone de Beauvoir, *The Second Sex* (New York: Vintage Books, 1974), 418.

16. Ibid., 763.

17. See Rhoads, *Sex Differences*, 96–97.

18. For a broad philosophical and historical perspective on the views of the saints and doctors of the Church concerning women, see Prudence Allen, *The Concept of Women: The Aristotelian Revolution 750 BC–AD 1250* (Grand Rapids, MI: Wm. B. Eerdmans, 1997). Allen hypothesizes that the better the male saint/Church doctor knew women, the more likely he was to hold a view of sex complementarity (or equality) rather than sex polarity (inequality). Also ibid., 269. This hypothesis certainly holds true with regard to Pope John Paul II and the theory of sex complementarity he espoused in *Mulieris Dignitatem* and other documents. The Pope is known to have had many women as close friends in his formative years and as a young priest and bishop. —Ed.

19. STI and STD are used interchangeably in this chapter. Strictly speaking, sexually transmitted infections are only referred to as diseases when they cause symptoms; it is, however, quite common to refer to such symptomless infections as STDs, or to use the terms interchangeably. In this chapter, the author has used whichever term the reference upon which she is relying used. —Ed.

20. Miriam Grossman, *Unprotected: A Campus Psychiatrist Reveals How Political Correctness in Her Profession Endangers Every Student*, 2nd ed. (New York: Sentinel, 2007), 27.

21. National Institute of Allergy and Infectious Diseases, "Topical Microbicides: Preventing Sexually Transmitted Diseases," National Institutes of Health, Publication No. 03-5316 (June 2003): 2, http://www3.niaid.nih.gov/topics/topicalmicrobicides/PDF/topicalMicrobicides.pdf.

22. Ibid.

23. See chapter 6 in this volume for further discussion of the connection between sexually transmitted diseases and infertility. —Ed.

24. National Institute of Allergy and Infectious Diseases, "Women's Health in the U.S.: Research on Health Issues Affecting Women," National Institutes of Health, Publication No. 04-4697 (February 2004): 17, http://www3.niaid.nih.gov/topics/womensHealth/PDF/womenshealth.pdf.

25. National Institute of Allergy and Infectious Diseases, "Workshop Summary: Scientific Evidence on Condom Effectiveness for Sexually Transmitted Disease (STD) Prevention," National Institutes of Health (2001): i–ii, http://www3.niaid.nih.gov/about/organization/dmid/PDF/condomReport.pdf.

26. K. K. Holmes, R. Levine, and M. Weaver, "Effectiveness of Condoms in Preventing Sexually Transmitted Infections," *Bulletin of the World Health Organization* 82, no. 6 (June 2004): 454–61.

27. National Institute of Allergy and Infectious Diseases, "Women's Health in the U.S.: Research on Health Issues Affecting Women," 20. http://www.niaid.nih.gov/publications/womenshealth/womenshealth.pdf.

28. The 2004 study did find two studies finding an association between condom use and higher clearance rates of cervical HPV infection in women; because HPV is concentrated in semen, decreasing the load of HPV to the cervix or penis makes it easier for the immune system to clear it.

29. Miriam Grossman, *Unprotected*, 14.

30. Ibid., 15.

31. Ibid., 15–16.

32. Centers for Disease Control and Prevention, "1 in 4 Americans has an STD," http://www.cdcnpin.org/stdawareness/STD04.html.

33. Centers for Disease Control and Prevention, "Genital HPV Infection—CDC Fact Sheet," http://www.cdc.gov/std/HPV/STDFact-HPV.htm.

34. Ibid.

35. National Institute of Allergy and Infectious Diseases, "Human Papillomavirus and Genital Warts," http://www3.niaid.nih.gov/topics/genitalWarts/understanding/complications.htm.

36. Centers for Disease Control and Prevention, "Common Questions about HPV and Cervical Cancer," http://www.cdc.gov/std/HPV/common-questions.htm.

37. Meg Meeker, *Strong Fathers, Strong Daughters: 10 Secrets Every Father Should Know* (New York: Ballantine Books, 2006), 102.

38. Ibid.

39. Ibid., 103.

40. Ibid., 107–108.

41. Lydia A. Shrier, Sion Kim Harris, and William R. Beardslee, "Temporal Associations Between Depressive Symptoms and Self-reported Sexually Transmitted

Disease Among Adolescents," Archives of Pediatrics and Adolescent Medicine 156, no. 6 (June 2002): 599–606, http://archpedi.ama-assn.org/cgi/content/full/156/6/599.

42. Miriam Grossman, *Unprotected*, 4; Robert Rector, Kirk Johnson, and Lauren Noyes, "Sexually Active Teenagers Are More Likely to Be Depressed and to Attempt Suicide," the Heritage Foundation Center for Data Analysis Report no. 03–04 (2003), http://www.heritage.org/Research/Abstinence/cda0304.cfm.

43. Miriam Grossman, *Unprotected*, 4.

44. Meeker, *Strong Fathers*, 87.

45. Rhoads, *Sex Differences*, 198.

46. Ibid.

47. Miriam Grossman, *Unprotected*, 7.

48. de Beauvoir, *The Second Sex*, 763.

49. Robert Rector and Kirk A. Johnson, "Teenage Sexual Abstinence and Academic Achievement," (conference paper, Abstinence Clearinghouse Conference, August 2005), http://www.heritage.org/research/abstinence/whitepaper10272005-1.cfm.

50. Ibid.; http://www.familyfacts.org/findingdetail.cfm?finding=8904.

51. Ibid.; http://www.familyfacts.org/findingdetail.cfm?finding=8903.

52. Renata Forste and Koray Tanfer, "Sexual Exclusivity Among Dating, Cohabiting, and Married Women," *Journal of Marriage and Family* 58, no. 1 (1996): 33–47, http://www.familyfacts.org/findingdetail.cfm?finding=6693.

53. Jay Teachman, "Premarital Sex, Premarital Cohabitation, and the Risk of Subsequent Marital Dissolution Among Women," *Journal of Marriage and Family* 65, no. 2 (May 2003): 444–55. Summarized at http://www.familyfacts.org/findingdetail.cfm?finding=8905.

54. Susan Brown and Alan Booth, "Cohabitation versus Marriage: A Comparison of Relationship Quality," *Journal of Marriage and Family* 58, no. 3 (August 1996): 668–78, http://www.familyfacts.org/findingdetail.cfm?finding=5050; Steven L. Nock, "A Comparison of Marriages and Cohabiting Relationships," *Journal of Family Issues* 16, no. 1 (1995): 53–76, http://www.familyfacts.org/findingdetail.cfm? finding =5006.

55. Scott F. Christopher and Susan Sprecher, "Sexuality in Marriage, Dating, and Other Relationships: A Decade Review," *Journal of Marriage and Family* 62, no. 4 (2000): 999–1017, http://www.familyfacts.org/findingdetail.cfm?finding=5637.

56. F. Carolyn Graglia, *Domestic Tranquility: A Brief Against Feminism* (Dallas, TX: Spence Publishing Company, 1998), 7.

57. Benedict XVI, *Deus Caritas Est* (*God Is Love*) (Boston: Pauline Books & Media, 2006), no. 4.

58. Ibid.

59. Ibid.

60. Ibid.

61. Laura Sessions Stepp, *Unhooked: How Young Women Pursue Sex, Delay Love, and Lose at Both* (New York: Riverhead Books, 2007), 35.

4

The Liberation of Lifelong Love:
Church Teaching on Marriage

1. *CCC*, no. 2201; "The Lord Jesus insisted on the original intention of the Creator who willed that marriage be indissoluble." *CCC*, no. 2382.

2. *CCC*, no. 2383.

3. *CCC*, nos. 2384–85; The difference between an annulment and a civil divorce is that an annulment is a statement that no real marriage ever existed. A civil divorce dissolves a valid marriage. [For a marriage to be considered an indissoluble, sacramental bond recognized by the Church, each party must have given full and free consent at the time of the nuptial ceremony. If the tribunal determines no such consent was present, then a Declaration of Nullity will be granted. See William Sanders, "Explaining an Annulment," Catholic Education Resource Center, http://catholic-education.org/articles/religion/re0381.html —Ed.]

4. *CCC*, nos. 2380–81. "Adultery is an injustice. He who commits adultery fails in his commitment." See also, *CCC*, no. 1756.

5. "Fornication ... is gravely contrary to the dignity of persons and of human sexuality which is naturally ordered to the good of spouses and the generation and education of children." *CCC*, no. 2353.

6. *CCC*, nos. 2390–91.

7. I have written a book arguing that the family cannot properly be compared with the individualism of the market. The original subtitle of the book, *Love and Economics: Why the Laissez-Faire Family Doesn't Work* (Dallas, TX: Spence Publishing, 2001), suggests this argument. The paperback edition of the book has a new subtitle, *Love and Economics: It Takes a Family to Raise a Village* (San Marcos, CA: Ruth Institute Books, 2008).

8. For a summary of the best-known feminist authors, see Patrick Fagan, Robert Rector, and Lauren Noyes, "Why Congress Should Ignore Radical Feminist Opposition to Marriage," *Heritage Foundation Backgrounder*, no. 1662 (June 16, 2003), http://www.heritage.org/Research/Family/bg1662.cfm#pgfld-1033814.

9. Betty Friedan, *The Feminine Mystique* (New York: W. W. Norton, 1997).

10. Kate Millett, *Sexual Politics* (New York: Avon Books, 1969), 34–35.

11. Germaine Greer, *The Female Eunuch* (New York: McGraw-Hill, 1971), 317.

12. Barbara Ehrenreich, "Will Women Still Need Men?" *Time Magazine* (February 21, 2000), http://www.time.com/time/printout/0,8816,996170,00.html.

13. See chapter 1 in this volume for further discussion. —Ed.

14. Frederick Engels, *The Origin of the Family, Private Property, and the State*, edited with an introduction by Eleanor Burke Leacock (New York: International Publishers, 1972), 128–29.

15. Ibid., 137–38 (emphasis in original). The term "bourgeois" refers to the middle or merchant classes, while "proletariat" refers to the class of people working in factories.

16. Betty Friedan, author of *The Feminine Mystique*, had been a committed leftist since her student days at Smith. She wrote for radical publications, including the journal of one of the most radicalized labor unions. See Daniel Horowitz, *Betty Friedan and the Making of The Feminine Mystique: The American Left, the Cold War, and Modern Feminism* (Amherst: University of Massachusetts Press, 2000).

17. See, for instance, Linda R. Hirshman, *Get to Work ... And Get a Life, Before It's Too Late* (New York: Viking Adult, 2006). Hirshman's leftist sympathies are especially evident in the first edition of this book, which had a subtitle of "A Manifesto for the Women of the World," and was a small red volume reminiscent of Chairman Mao's *Little Red Book*.

18. See, for instance, Ellen Willis, "Radical Feminism and Feminist Radicalism," *Social Text* (Spring-Summer, 1984), 91–118.

19. For useful summaries, see Maggie Gallagher and Joshua Baker, "Do Moms and Dads Matter?: Evidence from the Social Sciences on Family Structure and the Best Interests of the Child," *Margins* (University of Maryland School of Law Journal) 4 (2004): 161–80; Kristen Anderson Moore, Susan M. Jekielek, and Carol Emig, "Marriage from a Child's Perspective: How Does Family Structure Affect Children and What Can We Do About It?" *Child Trends Research Brief* (June 2002); Jennifer Roback Morse, *Smart Sex: Finding Life-long Love in a Hook-up World* (Dallas, TX: Spence Publishing, 2005); Linda Waite and Maggie Gallagher, *The Case for Marriage: Why Married People Are Happier, Healthier, and Better Off Financially* (New York: Doubleday, 2000); and Steven Nock et al., *Why Marriage Matters: Twenty-One Conclusions from the Social Sciences* (New York: Institute for American Values, 2002).

20. Nancy Vaden-Kiernan et al., "Household Family Structure and Children's Aggressive Behavior: A Longitudinal Study of Urban Elementary School Children," *Journal of Abnormal Child Psychology* 23, no. 5 (October 3, 1995): 553–68.

21. Cynthia C. Harper and Sara S. McLanahan, "Father Absence and Youth Incarceration," *Journal of Research on Adolescence* 14, no. 3 (September 2004) 369–97.

22. Sarah Hall, "Schizophrenia Much More Likely in Children of Single Parents," *Guardian* (UK), November 2, 2006.

23. Gunilla Ringback Weitoft et al., "Mortality, Severe Morbidity, and Injury in Children Living with Single Parents in Sweden: A Population-Based Study," *The Lancet* 361, no. 9354 (January 25, 2003): 289–95.

24. Paul R. Amato, "The Impact of Family Formation Change on the Cognitive, Social, and Emotional Well-being of the Next Generation," *The Future of Children* 15, no. 2 (Fall 2005): 89, cited in David Blankenhorn, *The Future of Marriage* (New York: Encounter Books, 2007), 243–44.

25. Matthew Bramlett and William Mosher, "First Marriage Dissolution, Divorce, and Remarriage: United States," *Advance Data from Vital and Health Statistics* 323 (May 31, 2001), National Center for Health Statistics. Compare figures 1 and 2 with figures 7 and 8.

26. Waite and Gallagher, *The Case for Marriage*, 67.

27. Ibid., 70.

28. Ibid., 131.

29. Ibid., 132.

30. Ibid., 128.

31. Paul R. Amato and Fernando Rivera, "Parental Involvement and Children's Behavior Problems," *Journal of Marriage and Family* 61, no. 2 (May 1999): 375–84.

32. Elizabeth C. Cooksey and Michelle M. Fondell, "Spending Time with His Kids: Effects of Family Structure on Fathers' and Children's Lives," *Journal of Marriage and Family* 58, no. 3 (August 1996): 693–707.

33. Amato and Rivera, "Parental Involvement"; Cooksey and Fondell, "Spending Time with His Kids."

34. Amato and Rivera, "Parental Involvement."

35. Robert Whelan, *Broken Homes and Battered Children: A Study of the Relationship Between Child Abuse and Family Type* (London: Family Education Trust, 1994); Martin Daly and Margo Wilson, "Discriminative Parental Solicitude: A Biological Perspective," *Journal of Marriage and Family* 42, no. 2 (May 1980): 277–88; and Nico Trocme, Debra McPhee, and Kwok Kwan Tam, "Child Abuse and Neglect in Ontario: Incidence and Characteristics," *Child Welfare* 74, no. 3 (May–June 1995): 563–87.

36. Paul Amato and Alan Booth, *A Generation at Risk: Growing Up in an Era of Family Upheaval* (Cambridge, MA: Harvard University Press, 1997).

37. Paul R. Amato and Bryndl Hohmann-Marriott, "Comparison of High and Low Distress Marriages that End in Divorce," *Journal of Marriage and Family* 69, no. 3 (August 2007): 621–38.

38. No-fault divorce laws allow either husband or wife to request a divorce without a showing of wrongdoing on the part of either party. The first no-fault divorce law in the U.S. went into effect in 1970 in California. By the mid-1980s, almost all states had adopted no-fault divorce. —Ed.

39. Margaret Brinig and Douglas W. Allen, "These Boots Are Made for Walking: Why Wives File for Divorce," *American Law and Economics Review* 2, no. 1 (2000); and Paul R. Amato and Stacy J. Rogers, "A Longitudinal Study of Marital Problems and Subsequent Divorce," *Journal of Marriage and Family* 59, no. 3 (August 1997): 612–24. Amato and Hohmann-Marriott in "Comparison of High and Low Distress Marriages" define about half of the marriages in their sample as being "high distress," but indicate that only 43 percent of the "high distress" couples were violent. This amounts to about 21 percent of all couples in their sample being violent.

40. David Popenoe and Barbara Dafoe Whitehead, *Should We Live Together? What Young Adults Need to Know about Cohabitation Before Marriage: A Comprehensive Review of Recent Research* (Rutgers, NJ: The National Marriage Project, 2002).

41. See, e.g., this short summary, "Multiple Partner Fertility," Fragile Families Research Brief 8 (June 2002): http://www.aecf.org/upload/publicationfiles/multiple%20partner.pdf. In the *Fragile Families and Child Well-Being Study*, about one-fifth of married men have children with more than one woman. One-third of cohabiting fathers, more than two-fifths of visiting fathers, and more than three-fifths of noninvolved fathers exhibit multiple partner fertility.

42. See "Multiple Partner Fertility," Fragile Families Research Brief. The Fragile Families Public Use Data are drawn from a nationally representative sample from twenty cities with populations over 200,000. See the introduction to the Fragile Families Public Use Data, prepared by the Bendheim-Thoman Center for Research on

Child Wellbeing at Princeton University in August 2008, for more details on the sample. The introduction is available at http://www.fragilefamilies.princeton.edu/documentation/core/4waves_ff_public.pdf.

43. "Births: Final Data for 2005," National Vital Statistics Report 56, no. 6, Centers for Disease Control (December 2007), Table 20, http://www.cdc.gov/nchs/data/nvsr/nvsr56/nvsr56_06.pdf.

44. Haishan Fu et al., "Contraceptive Failure Rates: New Estimates from the 1995 National Survey of Family Growth," *Family Planning Perspectives* 31, no. 2 (March-April 1999): Table 2.

45. See Jan E. Stets, "Cohabiting and Marital Aggression: The Role of Social Isolation," *Journal of Marriage and Family* 53, no. 3 (August 1991): and 669–80; Nicky Ali Jackson, "Observational Experiences of Intrapersonal Conflict and Teenage Victimization: A Comparative Study among Spouses and Cohabitors," *Journal of Family Violence* 11, no. 3 (1996): 191–203. See also the references in Popenoe and Whitehead, *Should We Live Together?*

46. Judith Treas and Deirdre Giesen, "Sexual Infidelity among Married and Cohabiting Americans," *Journal of Marriage and Family* 62, 1 (February 2000): 48–60; and Renate Forste and Koray Tanfer, "Sexual Exclusivity among Dating, Cohabiting, and Married Women," *Journal of Marriage and Family* 58, no. 1 (February 1996): 33–47.

47. Susan L. Brown, "The Effects of Union Type on Psychological Well-being: Depression among Cohabitors versus Marrieds," *Journal of Health and Social Behavior* 41, no. 3 (2000): 241–55.

48. Lynne Casper and Susan Bianchi, *Continuity and Change in the American Family* (Thousand Oaks, CA: Sage Publications, 2002).

49. William S. Comanor, "Child Support Payments: A Review of Current Policies," in *The Law and Economics of Child Support Payments*, ed. William S. Comanor (Northampton, MA: Edward Elgar, 2004), 3–8, especially figures 1.3 and 1.4.

50. Wendy Manning and Daniel Lichter, "Parental Cohabitation and Children's Economic Well-being," *Journal of Marriage and Family* 58, no. 4 (November 1996): 998–1010.

51. Amato and Rivera, "Parental Involvement," 375–84.

52. Ronald L. Simons et al., "Explaining the Higher Incidence of Adjustment Problems Among Children of Divorce," *Journal of Marriage and Family* 61, no. 4 (November 1999): 1020–33.

53. Whelan, *Broken Homes*; Daly and Wilson, "Discriminative Parental Solicitude," 277–88; Trocme et al., "Child Abuse and Neglect in Ontario," 563–87.

54. Patricia G. Schnitzer and Bernard G. Ewigman, "Child Deaths Resulting from Inflicted Injuries: Household Risk Factors and Perpetrator Characteristics," *Pediatrics* 116, no. 5 (November 2005): 687–93.

55. Julie E. Artis, "Maternal Cohabitation and Child Well-being among Kindergarten Children," *Journal of Marriage and Family* 69, no. 1 (February 2007): 222–36. To be fair, some of the significance of cohabiting per se diminishes when controls are added for maternal depression, supportive parenting practices, length of the parents' union, and number of residences. But children in cohabiting unions face worse pros-

pects in each of these dimensions, so sorting out the factors statistically doesn't much help the child.

56. Bruce Ellis et al., "Does Father Absence Place Daughters at Special Risk for Early Sexual Activity and Teenage Pregnancy?" *Child Development* 74, no. 3 (May–June 2003): 801–21.

57. Bruce Ellis, "Timing of Pubertal Maturation in Girls: An Integrated Life History Approach," *Psychological Bulletin* 130, no. 6 (November 2004): 920–58.

58. Ellis, "Father Absence," 801–21. See also the references in Nock, *Why Marriage Matters*.

59. Harper, "Father Absence," 369–97; Chris Couglin and Samuel Vuchinich, "Family Experience in Preadolescence and the Development of Male Delinquency," *Journal of Marriage and Family* 58, no. 2 (May 1996): 491–501; see also the references in Nock, *Why Marriage Matters*.

60. Steven L. Nock, *Marriage in Men's Lives* (New York: Oxford University Press, 1998).

61. Waite, *The Case for Marriage*, 47–51; Nock, *Why Marriage Matters*.

62. Augustine J. Kposowa, "Marital Status and Suicide in the National Longitudinal Mortality Study," *Journal of Epidemiology and Community Health* 54, no. 4 (April 2000): 254–61; Waite, *The Case for Marriage*, 52; Nock, *Why Marriage Matters*.

63. Waite, *The Case for Marriage*, 78–90; Nock, *Why Marriage Matters*.

64. Jay Zagorsky, "Marriage and Divorce's Impact on Wealth," *Journal of Sociology* 41, no. 4 (2005): 406–24; see also the references in Nock, *Why Marriage Matters*.

65. Nock, *Marriage in Men's Lives*, 75–83.

66. Data on this point are usefully summarized in Warren Farrell, *Why Men Earn More: The Startling Truth About the Pay Gap and What Women Can Do About It* (New York: American Management Association, 2005).

67. See chapter 6 in this volume for further discussion of infertility and assisted reproductive technology, and their effects on women. —Ed.

68. Steven Nock and Brad Wilcox, "What's Love Got to Do With It?" *Social Forces* 84, no. 3 (March 2006). A summary of results from the study is available online at http://www.happiestwives.org.

69. John Paul II, *Man and Woman He Created Them: A Theology of the Body*, trans. Michael Waldstein (Boston: Pauline Books & Media, 2006).

70. *CCC*, no. 2360.

71. As John Paul puts it, male and female are "two reciprocally completing ways of being a body and at the same time of being human—as two complementary dimensions of self-knowledge and self-determination ... being male or female is 'constitutive for the person' (not only 'an attribute of the person.')." *Man and Woman He Created Them*, 166; see also Jennifer Ferrara "Ordaining Women: Two Views," *First Things*, April 2003.

72. John Paul II, *Man and Woman He Created Them*, 163 (emphasis in original).

73. Michael Waldstein makes this point in a particularly dramatic fashion: "The scientific rationalism spearheaded by Descartes is above all an attack on the body." Introduction, *Man and Woman He Created Them*, 95.

74. Patrick Lee and Robert P. George, "Dualistic Delusions," *First Things*, February 2005.

75. See *CCC*, nos. 2201–07.

76. *CCC*, no. 2203.

77. *CCC*, no. 2207.

78. *CCC*, no. 2202; see also *Rerum Novarum* (1891) which holds that the family is prior to the state and that the state has obligations to the family.

79. *Goodrich v. Department of Public Health,* 798 N.E. 2nd 941, 954 (Mass. 2003).

5

The Gift of Female Fertility:
Church Teaching on Contraception

1. Resolution 15 of the 1930 Lambeth Conference, http://www.lambethconference.org/resolutions/1930/1930-15.cfm.

2. "Fortieth Anniversary of *Humanae Vitae*," New England Cable Network, July 25, 2008, http://www.necn.com/Boston/World/-40th-anniversary-of-Humanae-Vitae/1217037152.html.

3. See, e.g., Mark M. Gray, Paul M. Perl, and Tricia C. Bruce, *Marriage in the Catholic Church: A Survey of U.S. Catholics* (Center for Applied Research in the Apostolate, Georgetown University, October 2007), 1. Dissenting theologians and their followers often express alarm at the popularity among the young of the theology of the body proclaimed by Pope John Paul II; e.g., David Cloutier, "Heaven Is a Place on Earth?: Analyzing the Popularity of Pope John Paul II's Theology of the Body," in *Sexuality and the U.S. Catholic Church: Crisis and Renewal*, the Boston College Church in the 21st Century Center series, eds. Lisa Sowle Cahill, John Garvey, and T. Frank Kennedy (New York: Herder & Herder, 2006), 18–31. Befuddlement at the young would be expected of dissenting thinkers.

4. Luke Timothy Johnson, "A Disembodied 'Theology of the Body': John Paul II on Love, Sex, and Pleasure," *Commonweal* (January 26, 2001): 16.

5. Charles E. Curran, *The Moral Theology of Pope John Paul II*, Moral Traditions Series, ed. James F. Keenan (Washington, DC: Georgetown University Press, 2005), 116.

6. Johnson, "Disembodied," 15.

7. Rosemary Radford Ruether, "Sex in the Catholic Tradition," in *The Good News of the Body: Sexual Theology and Feminism*, ed. Lisa Isherwood (New York: New York University Press, 2000), 51.

8. See, for instance, Gallup poll, "U.S. Catholics Would Support Changes," CNN.com, April 3, 2005, http://www.cnn.com/2005/US/04/03/pope.poll/index.html.

9. The best presentation of this history is in Janet E. Smith, *Humanae Vitae: A Generation Later* (Washington, DC: The Catholic University of America Press, 1993), 1–35.

10. For primary source materials and other references to the history given here, see Angela Franks, *Margaret Sanger's Eugenic Legacy: The Control of Female Fertility* (Jefferson, NC: McFarland, 2005).

11. Emma Goldman was one of the pioneering leftist eugenic birth controllers who also promoted unrestricted sexual freedom. See ibid., 27–28.

12. Margaret Sanger, *Woman and the New Race* (New York: Blue Ribbon Books, 1920), 1, italics mine.

13. Woman has "chained herself to her place in society and the family through the maternal functions of her nature, and only chains thus strong could have bound her to her lot as a brood animal for the masculine civilizations of the world." Ibid., 2.

14. "Nor have famine and plague been as much 'acts of God' as acts of too prolific mothers. They, also, as all students know, have their basic causes in over-population." Ibid., 3–4.

15. Ibid.

16. Ibid., 5–6.

17. "By her failure to withhold the multitudes of children who have made inevitable the most flagrant of our social evils, she incurred a debt to society. Regardless of her own wrongs, regardless of her lack of opportunity and regardless of all other considerations, *she* must pay that debt." Ibid., 6.

18. "She must not think to pay this debt in any superficial way. She cannot pay it with palliatives—with child-labor laws, prohibition, regulation of prostitution and agitation against war." Ibid.

19. See, for instance, "The Declaration of Sentiments," Seneca Falls Convention, 1848, reprinted in *The Modern History Sourcebook*, http://www.fordham.edu/halsall/mod/senecafalls.html.

20. Linda Gordon, "Voluntary Motherhood: The Beginning of Feminist Birth Control Ideas in the United States," in *Women and Health in America: Historical Readings*, 2nd ed., ed. Judith Walzer Leavitt (Madison: University of Wisconsin Press, 1999), 254.

21. Quoted in Catholics for Contraception, "A Matter of Conscience: Catholics on Contraception," pamphlet, http://www.catholicsforchoice.org/topics/prevention/documents/1998amatterofconsciece.pdf.

22. Charles J. Chaput, "Of Human Life: A Pastoral Letter to the People of God of Northern Colorado on the Truth and Meaning of Married Love," EWTN.com, July 22, 1998, http://www.ewtn.com/library/bishops/chaputhv.htm.

23. Germaine Greer, *The Whole Woman* (New York: Alfred A. Knopf, 1999), 47–48.

24. When the eugenic scapegoating of the "unfit" became widely unpopular after World War II, eugenicist neo-Malthusians such as Sanger simply shifted their focus to the "quantity" side of the "quality, not quantity" equation. Explicit eugenics was out; eugenics as population control was in. See my *Margaret Sanger's Eugenic Legacy* for a detailed history of the shift from eugenic rhetoric to population-control agitation (although the latter was always the driving factor in the neo-Malthusian equation). The link between eugenics and population control may seem startling, but it is generally recognized by historians of eugenics. See, for example, feminist and Marxist historian Linda Gordon: "The eugenics people slid into the population control move-

ment gracefully, naturally, imperceptibly … there was nothing to separate the two movements because there was no tension between their two sorts of goals." ("The Politics of Population: Birth Control and the Eugenics Movement," *Radical America* 8, no. 4 (1974): 85). Less politically charged works on the same connection are Daniel J. Kevles, *In the Name of Eugenics: Genetics and the Uses of Human Heredity*, 2nd ed. (Cambridge, MA: Harvard University Press, 1995), and Edwin Black, *War Against the Weak: Eugenics and America's Campaign to Create a Master Race* (New York: Basic Books, 2003).

25. Margaret Sanger, "The Eugenic Value of Birth Control Propaganda," *Birth Control Review* (October 1921): 5.

26. Buck v. Bell, 274 U.S. 200 (1927).

27. Jonas B. Robitscher, ed., *Eugenic Sterilization* (Springfield, IL: Charles C. Thomas, 1973), 118–19.

28. Warren M. Hern, "Is Pregnancy Really Normal?" *Family Planning Perspectives* 3, no. 1 (January 1971): 5–9; "Is Human Culture Carcinogenic for Uncontrolled Population Growth and Ecological Destruction?" *Bioscience* 43, no. 11 (December 1993): 768–73.

29. Betsy Hartmann, *Reproductive Rights and Wrongs: The Global Politics of Population Control* (Boston: South End Press, 1995), 280; and Asoka Bandarage, *Women, Population and Global Crisis: A Political-Economic Analysis* (London: Zed, 1997), 87. For more on American research efforts in this regard, see the Population Research Institute, "A 'Stick' in Time Saves Nine," *PRI Weekly Briefing*, March 2, 2001, http://www.pop.org/20010302487/a-aquotstickaquot-in-time-saves-nine.

30. "Final Report Concerning Voluntary Surgical Contraception during the Years 1990–2000," Subcommittee Investigation of Persons and Institutions Involved in Voluntary Surgical Contraception, June 2002, http://pop.org/main.cfm?EID=589.

31. Quoted in Hartmann, *Reproductive Rights and Wrongs*, 243–44.

32. John Paul II, *Humanae Vitae (Of Human Life)* (San Francisco: Ignatius Books, 2002), no. 17; Janet Smith's incomparable translation, *Humanae Vitae: A Challenge to Love*, can be acquired at http://www.omsoul.com/catalog/humanae-vitae-a-challenge-to-love-p144.html.

33. J. Bryan Hehir, "The Church and the Population Year: Notes on a Strategy," *Theological Studies* 35, no. 1 (March 1974): 71–82.

34. David Hollenbach, *The Right to Procreate and Its Social Limitations: A Systematic Study of Value Conflict in Roman Catholic Ethics*, PhD dissertation, Yale University (1975), 442. He summarizes his argument on pp. 427–44.

35. Ibid., 426, no. 2.

36. Daniel C. Maguire, *Sacred Choices: The Right to Contraception and Abortion in Ten World Religions*, Sacred Energies Series (Minneapolis: Fortress Press, 2001), 150.

37. On the false assumptions concerning population control and the promotion of contraception for the developing world, see the Web site of the Population Research Institute (www.pop.org); Stephen W. Mosher, *Population Control: Real Costs, Illusory Benefits* (New York: Transaction Books, 2008); and Jacqueline Kasun, *The War Against Population: The Economics and Ideology of World Population Control*, 2nd ed. (San Francisco: Ignatius, 1999).

38. Mary Eberstadt, "The Vindication of *Humanae Vitae*," *First Things*, August/September 2008.

39. United Nations World Prospects Report (2004 revision), http://www.un.org/esa/population/publications/WPP2004/WPP2004_Volume3.htm.

40. Cited in Lara V. Marks, *Sexual Chemistry: A History of the Contraceptive Pill* (New Haven, CN: Yale University Press, 2001), 132; emphasis mine.

41. Cited in Smith, *Humanae Vitae*, 25; emphasis mine.

42. Christine Montone, "The Perfect Fit for Our Healthy Lifestyle," *Natural Family Planning Blessed Our Marriage: 19 True Stories*, ed. Fletcher Doyle (Cincinnati, OH: Servant Books, 2006), 28.

43. Claudia Panzer et al., "Impact of Oral Contraceptives on Sex Hormone-Binding Globulin and Androgen Levels: A Retrospective Study in Women with Sexual Dysfunction," *Journal of Sexual Medicine* 3, no. 1 (January 2006): 104–13.

44. See *Margaret Sanger's Eugenic Legacy* for a detailed history of the disregard of human dignity evinced by researchers in the development of various methods of contraception. For contemporary feminist objections to hormonal contraception, see www.ourbodiesourselves.org, the former Boston Women's Health Book Collective, which produced the many volumes of the *Our Bodies, Ourselves* series.

45. Jean-Patrice Baillargeon et al., "Association between the Current Use of Low-Dose Oral Contraceptives and Cardiovascular Arterial Disease: A Meta-Analysis," *Journal of Clinical Endocrinology and Metabolism* 90, no. 7 (July 2005): 3863–70.

46. Jane Green et al., "Cervical Cancer and Hormonal Contraceptives: Collaborative Reanalysis of Individual Data for 16,573 Women with Cervical Cancer and 35,509 Women without Cervical Cancer from 24 Epidemiological Studies," *The Lancet* 370, no. 9599 (November 10, 2007): 1609–21.

47. One of the more controversial claims about the dangers of hormonal contraception has been that oral contraceptives are correlated to an increased risk of breast cancer, especially in younger women who have not yet carried a pregnancy to term. The cells in the breast are immature until the hormones of a woman's first full-term pregnancy help to mature them. Mature breast cells are less susceptible to becoming cancerous. See Jose Russo, Irma Russo, and Lee K. Tay, "Differentiation of the Mammary Gland and Susceptibility to Carcinogenesis," *Breast Cancer Research and Treatment* 2, no. 1 (1982): 5–73, cited in Chris Kahlenborn, *Breast Cancer: Its Link to Abortion and the Birth Control Pill* (Dayton, OH: One More Soul, 2000), 5–6. The use of powerful hormones in the young can make the immature cells more prone to becoming cancerous later. As one medical text explains: "Several studies have suggested that the use of oral contraceptives in the early teen years may increase the risk of subsequent breast cancer," C. M. Haskell, *Cancer Treatment*, 4th ed. (Philadelphia: W. B. Saunders, 1995), 327. A recent study shows a 44 percent increased risk in developing breast cancer when oral contraceptives are taken before the first full-term pregnancy, and the risk rises to 52 percent if the Pill is taken for more than four years. See Kahlenborn et al., "Oral Contraceptive Use as a Risk Factor for Premenopausal Breast Cancer: A Meta-analysis," *Mayo Clinic Proceedings* 81, no. 10 (October 2006): 1290–1302; and Salynn Boyles, "The Pill May Raise Breast Cancer Risk," WebMD. com, October 31, 2006, http://www.webmd.com/sex/birth-control/news/ 20061031/pill-

may-raise-breast-cancer-risk. See also Kahlenborn, *Breast Cancer*, 36, in which he notes that studies that do not show a link between breast cancer and the Pill generally do not isolate the population that has used oral contraceptives before the first full-term pregnancy. The risk for breast cancer in women taking the Pill *after* the maturation of breast cells seems to be reduced. A meta-analysis (or overview of the most significant research papers on a subject) focusing on the risk of the Pill to women using it for more than four years before their first full-term pregnancy, set the risk even higher, at a 72 percent increased risk of developing breast cancer. See Isabelle Romieu et al., "Oral Contraceptives and Breast Cancer: Review and Meta-analysis," *Cancer* 66, no. 11 (December 1, 1990): 2253–63, cited in Kahlenborn, *Breast Cancer*, 9.

48. Michel Foucault, *History of Sexuality*, vol. 1, An Introduction (New York: Vintage Books, 1990), 157.

49. Eberstadt, "Vindication of *Humanae Vitae*."

50. *Humanae Vitae*, no. 17, in Janet Smith, *Why* Humanae Vitae *Was Right* (San Fransisco: Ignatius Books, 1993), appendix.

51. Mohandas Gandhi, *Gandhi's Health Guide* (Berkeley: The Crossing Press, 2000), 161.

52. Robert T. Michael, presentation at Emory University, March 2003, quoted in *Natural Family Planning Blessed Our Marriage*, xii; see also Robert T. Michael, "Why Did U.S. Divorce Rates Double in a Decade?" *Research in Population Economics* 6 (1988): 367–99.

53. George A. Akerlof, Janet L. Yellen, and Michael L. Katz, "An Analysis of Out-of-Wedlock Childbearing in the United States," *Quarterly Journal of Economics* 111, no. 2 (May 1996): 277–317, 281. According to Akerlof, with the coming of contraception, women and girls lost bargaining power to pressure a man to be chaste with them until marriage, or to marry them if premarital intercourse resulted in a pregnancy. After contraception, a man could easily obtain sexual pleasure elsewhere without having to make such commitments. [See the conclusion of this volume for further discussion of Akerlof's findings. —Ed.]

54. Andrew P. Sirotnak and Richard D. Krugman, "Child Abuse and Neglect," in *Current Pediatric Diagnosis and Treatment*, 16th ed., ed. William W. Hay et al. (New York: McGraw-Hill Professional, 2004), 215; Child Welfare Information Gateway, FAQs, http://www.childwelfare.gov/can/faq.cfm.

55. "Bush Administration Tries to Redefine Contraception as Abortion," Speaker of the House Nancy Pelosi's blog ("The Gavel"), July 16, 2008, http://speaker.house.gov/blog/?p=1441.

56. Peter Arcidiacono et al., "Habit Persistence and Teen Sex: Could Increased Contraception Have Unintended Consequences for Teen Pregnancies?" (October 3, 2005), http://www.econ.duke.edu/~psarcidi/addicted13.pdf.

57. W. Bradford Wilcox, "The Facts of Life and Marriage: Social Science and the Vindication of Christian Moral Teaching," *Touchstone* 18, no. 1 (January/February 2005).

58. *Humanae Vitae*, no. 17.

59. Ibid., no. 10.

60. "Natural Family Planning Method as Effective as Contraceptive Pill, New Research Finds," *ScienceDaily*, February 21, 2001, http://www.sciencedaily.com/releases/2007/02/070221065200.htm; "Infertility," Naprotechnology.com, http://www.naprotechnology.com/infertility.htm. [See chapter 6 in this volume for further discussion of the use of NFP to achieve pregnancy. —Ed.]

61. See chapter 4 in this volume for further discussion of the true nature of marriage. —Ed.

62. See *CCC*, 2nd ed., nos. 1750–54; John Paul II, *Veritatis Splendor* (Boston: Pauline Books & Media, 1993), nos. 71–83.

63. I owe thanks to my husband, J. David Franks, for his insights on these topics.

64. *Humanae Vitae*, no. 12.

65. Here we can see that even if the "serious reason" for avoiding pregnancy is manifestly grave—for example, the life of the mother would be endangered by pregnancy—we cannot resort to permanent sterilization (such as tubal ligation). A permanent "solution" is certainly an understandable temptation in this circumstance, in which one would not be tempted by contraception precisely given the rates of contraceptive failure. But mutilating oneself (an intrinsically evil act), as in sterilization, of itself *cannot* lead to human happiness. Strictly adhered to, NFP is the moral resolution to this extreme case, the way that will lead to happiness. (And given the gravity of the situation, a man would not be tempted to fudge the method.)

66. See Waldstein, "Introduction," *Man and Woman He Created Them*, 32; *Humanae Vitae*, no. 21. Waldstein's is the definitive English translation of the audience talks in which Pope John Paul II lays out his groundbreaking theology of the body. A wonderful introduction is provided by Mary Healy in *Men and Women Are from Eden: A Study Guide to John Paul II's Theology of the Body* (Cincinnati, OH: St. Anthony Messenger Press, 2005).

67. See, e.g., Mercedes Arzú Wilson, "The Practice of Natural Family Planning versus the Use of Artificial Birth Control: Family, Sexual, and Moral Issues," *Catholic Social Science Review* 7 (November 2002) (showing a 0.2 percent divorce rate among NFP couples). Couple to Couple League's own studies of NFP couples indicate a divorce rate of up to 4 percent; see "Marital Duration and Natural Family Planning," http://web.archive.org/web/20070818184432/http://ccli.org/nfp/marriage/maritalduration.php.

68. Thomas Aquinas, *Summa Theologiae*, I–II, q. 73, a. 5, trans. Fathers of the English Dominican Province (Westminster, MD: Christian Classics, 1981).

69. Michael Waldstein, "Introduction," *Man and Woman He Created Them*, 108–17, and Benedict XVI, *Deus Caritas Est* (Boston: Pauline Books & Media, 2006), nos. 3–8.

70. Fletcher Doyle, "Better Late than Never," in *Natural Family Planning Blessed Our Marriage*, 53.

71. John Paul II, in *Man and Woman He Created Them*, nos. 128–31: 644–55.

72. Ibid., no. 131:4.

73. I am grateful to my husband, J. David Franks, for this formulation.

74. *Gaudium et Spes* (*Pastoral Constitution on the Church in the Modern World*) (Boston: Pauline Books & Media, 1966), no. 24.

6

The Church's Best Kept Secret:
Church Teaching on Infertility Treatment

1. A. B. Jose-Miller et al., "Infertility," *American Family Physician* 75, no. 6 (March 15, 2007): 849.

2. A. Chandra et al., *Fertility, Family Planning, and Reproductive Health of U.S. Women: Data from the 2002 National Survey of Family Growth.* National Center for Health Statistics. Vital Health Stat 23 (25), 2005, http://www.cdc.gov/nchs/data/series/sr_23/sr23_025.pdf.

3. National Women's Health Information Center, U.S. Department of Health and Human Services, "Infertility: Frequently Asked Questions," May 2006, http://www.womenshealth.gov/faq/infertility.cfm.

4. RESOLVE: The National Infertility Association, "Infertility Diagnosis," http://www.resolve.org/site/PageServer?pagename=lrn_wii_id.

5. Louis De Paolo, "Polycystic Ovary Syndrome: Frequently Asked Questions," *Office of Woman's Health, U.S. Department of Health and Human Services,* http://www.4woman.gov/faq/polycystic-ovary-syndrome.cfm#b.

6. M. Ulukus and A. Arici, "Immunology of Endometriosis," *Minerva Ginecologica* 57, no. 3 (June 2005): 237–48.

7. Serder E. Bulun, "Endometriosis," *The New England Journal of Medicine* 360, 3 (January 15, 2009): 268–79.

8. Mory Nouriani, "Endometriosis: Frequently Asked Questions," Office of Woman's Health, U.S. Department of Health and Human Services, http://www.4woman.gov/faq/endometriosis.cfm#a.

9. *American Society for Reproductive Medicine*, "Endometriosis and Infertility: Can Surgery Help?" (patient fact sheet), http://www.asrm.org/Patients/FactSheets/endometriosis_infertility.pdf.

10. C. Augood, K. Duckitt, and A. A. Templeton, "Smoking and Female Infertility: A Systematic Review and Meta-analysis," *Human Reproduction* 13, no. 12 (December 1998): 1532–39.

11. J. Willem van der Steeg et al., "Obesity Affects Spontaneous Pregnancy Chances in Subfertile, Ovulatory Women," *Human Reproduction* 23, no. 2 (February 2008): 324–28, *Advance Access* (December 11, 2007), http://humrep.oxfordjournals.org/cgi/reprint/dem371v1.

12. Centers for Disease Control and Prevention, "Sexually Transmitted Disease Surveillance, 2007: National Overview," http://www.cdc.gov/STD/stats07/natoverview.htm.

13. S. D. Hillis and J. N. Wasserheit, "Screening for Chlamydia—A Key to the Prevention of Pelvic Inflammatory Disease," *New England Journal of Medicine* 334, no. 21 (May 23, 1996): 1399–1401.

14. Centers for Disease Control and Prevention, "Genital HPV Infection—CDC Fact Sheet," http://www.cdc.gov/STD/HPV/STDFact-HPV.htm#common.

15. John C. Jarrett and Deidra T. Rausch, *The Fertility Guide: A Couples' Handbook for When You Want to Have a Baby (More than Anything Else)* (Santa Fe, NM: Health Press, 1998), 86.

16. Thomas W. Hilgers, T*he Scientific Foundations of the Ovulation Method* (Omaha, NE: Pope Paul VI Institute Press, 1995), 27. Long-term consequences of exposure to these drugs include increased invasive cervical cancer; see D. B. Thomas et al., "Invasive Squamous-Cell Cervical Carcinoma and Combined Oral Contraceptives: Results from a Multinational Study," *International Journal of Cancer* 53, no. 2 (September 9, 1993): 228–36. On increased risk of breast cancer, see Chris Kahlenborn, *Breast Cancer: Its Link to Abortion and the Birth Control Pill* (Dayton: One More Soul, 2000), 33–37.

17. Brenda Wilson, "For Prospective Moms, Biology and Culture Clash," National Public Radio (May 8, 2008), http://www.npr.org/templates/story/story.php?storyId =90227229 (quoting Marcelle Cedars, director of reproductive endocrinology at the University of California, San Francisco).

18. "Age and Fertility: A Guide for Patients," Patient Education Series, American Society for Reproductive Medicine, http://www.asrm.org/Patients/patientbook-lets/agefertility.pdf.

19. Joyce A. Martin et al., "Births: Final Data for 2005," Centers for Disease Control and Prevention, National Vital Statistics Reports 56, no. 6 (December 5, 2007), http://www.cdc.gov/nchs/data/nvsr/nvsr56/nvsr56_06.pdf.

20. National Women's Health Information Center, "Infertility: Frequently Asked Questions."

21. Brenda Wilson, "For Prospective Moms"; see Protect Your Fertility, a Web site of the American Society for Reproductive Medicine, "Where Can I Find Out More About the PSAs?" http://www.protectyourfertility.org/psas.html.

22. Jennifer Roback Morse, "The Social Effects of Contraception," prepared for the Human Fertility Conference, Catholic University, August 11, 2006.

23. Jose-Miller et al., "Infertility," 850.

24. Ibid. (This percentage varies by cause of infertility, age of patient, history of prior fertility, and length of infertility.)

25. Ibid., 856, no. 41; Z. Pandian, S. Bhattacharya, L. Vale, and A. Templeton, "In Vitro Fertilisation for Unexplained Subfertility," *Cochrane Database of Systematic Reviews* 2005, Issue 2, art. no.: CD003357. DOI: 10.1002/14651858.CD003357.pub2.

26. Stephanie Saul, "Birth of Octuplets Puts Focus on Fertility Clinics," *New York Times*, February 11, 2009.

27. Ibid.

28. Between 2000 and 2004, the number of live-born infants conceived through ART increased from 35,025 to 49,458. V. C. Wright et al., *Assisted Reproductive Technology Surveillance—United States, 2000*, Morbidity and Mortality Weekly Report 52, no. SS-9 (August 29, 2003); Morbidity and Mortality Weekly Report 56, no. SS-06 (June 8, 2007).

29. Helen Alvare, "The Case for Regulating Collaborative Reproduction: A Children's Rights Perspective," *Harvard Journal on Legislation* 40, no. 1 (Winter 2003), 32.

30. "Reproduction and Responsibility: The Regulation of New Biotechnologies," President's Council on Bioethics, Washington, DC, March 2004, http://bioethics. gov/reports/reproductionandresponsibility/index.html.

31. Alvare, "The Case for Regulating," 4, 25; Marsha Garrison, "Law Making for Baby Making: An Interpretive Approach to the Determination of Legal Parenting," *Harvard Law Review* 113, no. 4 (February 2000): 835; Weldon E. Havins and James J. Dalessio, "Ever-Widening Gap Between the Science of Artificial Reproductive Technology and the Laws which Govern that Technology," *DePaul Law Review* 48, no. 4 (Summer 1999): 825; Lori B. Andrews and Nanette Elster, "Regulating Reproductive Technologies," *Journal of Legal Medicine* 21, no. 1 (March 2000): 35, 38, 45; Alexander N. Hecht, "Wild Wild West: Inadequate Regulation of Assisted Reproductive Technology," *Houston Journal of Health Law and Policy* 1 (2001): 227; and "Human Cloning and Human Dignity: An Ethical Inquiry," President's Council on Bioethics, Washington, DC, July 2002, http://www.bioethics.gov/reports/cloningreport/ pcbe_cloning_report.pdf.

32. Joanna Perlman, "Is This Any Way to Have a Baby?" *O, The Oprah Magazine*, February 1, 2004, 190.

33. Ibid.; see also, Hecht, "Wild Wild West," 227.

34. Intrauterine insemination (IUI) is the first ART procedure recommended when conventional treatments have failed. IUI is a procedure that harvests sperm, usually through masturbation. The sperm are "washed" and then drawn into a syringe attached to a small catheter to be deposited through the woman's cervix into her uterus. The success rates of IUI are low, so many women are fast-tracked to IVF. See M. Kdous et al., "Intrauterine Insemination with Conjoint Semen. How to Increase the Success Rate?" *Tunisia Medical* 85, no. 9 (September 2007): 781–87; and Sarah E. Richards, "Skipping Baby Steps," Slate.com (November 20, 2007), http://www.slate. com/id/2178377/fr/flyout.

35. Two rarely performed ART procedures are gamete intrafallopian tube transfer (GIFT) and zygote intrafallopian tube transfer (ZIFT). GIFT involves injecting harvested gametes, sperm, and egg(s), into the fallopian tube in the hope that fertilization will occur there and the zygote(s) will proceed to the uterus for implantation. ZIFT is similar but involves passing the zygote(s), conceived in vitro, into the fallopian tube. In 2001, GIFT and ZIFT procedures each accounted for less than 1 percent of all ART. Centers for Disease Control and Prevention, 2001 *Assisted Reproductive Technology Success Rates, National Summary, and Fertility Clinic Reports* (2003), 37, 71.

36. For some IVF procedures, fertilization involves a specialized technique known as intracytoplasmic sperm injection (ICSI). In ICSI, a single sperm is injected directly into the woman's egg. Often the sperm for this procedure are obtained via a needle placed directly into the testicle. ICSI was initially used when the man suffered from a low sperm count, but is now frequently used when that is not the case. See Centers for Disease Control and Prevention, "Assisted Reproductive Technology Report" Section 2 (2006), Figure 29, http://www.cdc.gov/ART/ART2006/sect2_fig27-41. htm#f29.

37. President's Council on Bioethics, "Reproduction and Responsibility," March 2004.

38. See chapter 2 for a discussion of the moral status of the embryo, and further on in the present chapter for a discussion of the morality of ART procedures. —Ed.

39. Lori B. Andrews, *The Clone Age: Adventures in the New World of Reproductive Technology* (New York: Henry Holt, 1999), 33; see R. Edwards and P. C. Steptoe, "Current Status of In-Vitro Fertilisation and Implantation of Human Embryos," *Lancet* 2, 8362 (December 1983): 1265–69; and K. Gould, "Ovum Recovery and In Vitro Fertilization in the Chimpanzee," *Fertility and Sterility* 40, 3 (September 1983): 378–83.

40. Alvare, "The Case for Regulating," 21; Saul, "Birth of Octuplets": "The total number of embryos transferred per cycle varies, usually according to the age of the recipient. For women under 35, the average number of never-frozen embryos transplanted per transfer procedure was 2.8. For women 35 to 37, 38 to 40, and 41 to 42, the average numbers of never-frozen embryos transplanted per transfer procedure were, respectively, 3.1, 3.4, and 3.7."; "Reproduction and Responsibility," President's Council on Bioethics, March 2004, citing Centers for Disease Control and Prevention, *2001 Assisted Reproductive Technology Success Rates*, 71.

41. President's Council on Bioethics, "Reproduction and Responsibility."

42. Jean-Noel Hugues, "Ovarian Stimulation for Assisted Reproductive Technologies," in *Current Practices and Controversies in Assisted Reproduction: Report of a WHO Meeting on Medical, Ethical and Social Aspects of Assisted Reproduction*, eds. Effy Vayena et al. (Geneva: World Health Organization, 2002), 102–25.

43. A. Delvigne et al., "Systematic Review of Data Concerning Etiopathology of Ovarian Hyperstimulation Syndrome," *International Journal of Fertility and Women's Medicine* 47, no. 5 (September–October 2002): 211–26 (reporting 0.5 to 5 percent).

44. Open Letter from Suzanne Parisian, January 31, 2005, http://www.geneticsandsociety.org/article.php?id=181.

45. K. Lazar, "Wonder Drug for Men Alleged to Cause Harm in Women," *Boston Herald*, August 22, 1999.

46. Perlman, "Is This Any Way to Have a Baby?", 200.

47. M. Hansen et al., "The Risk of Major Birth Defects after Intracytoplasmic Sperm Injection and In Vitro Fertilization," *New England Journal of Medicine* 346, 10 (March 7, 2002): 725–30; see also M. Bonduelle et al., "Neonatal Data on a Cohort of 2,889 Infants Born After ISCI (1991–1999) and of 2,995 Infants Born After IVF (1983–1999)," *Human Reproduction* 17, no. 3 (March 2002): 761; T. Bergh et al., "Deliveries and Children Born after In-Vitro Fertilisation in Sweden 1982–1985," *Lancet* 354, 9190 (1999): 1579–85.

48. A. Moll et al., "Incidence of Retinoblastoma in Children Born after In-Vitro Fertilisation," *Lancet* 361, no. 9354 (January 25, 2003): 309–10; R. Mestel, "Some Studies See Ills for In Vitro Children: Evidence of Increases in Eye Cancer and Mental Retardation Needs to Be Verified," *Los Angeles Times*, January 24, 2003, A1.

49. Centers for Disease Control and Prevention, 2001 Assisted Reproductive Technology Success Rates.

50. American Society for Reproductive Medicine, Patient Information Series, "Multiple Pregnancy and Birth: Twins, Triplets, and Higher Order Multiples," 2004, http://www.asrm.org/Patients/patientbooklets/multiples.pdf; see also references in President's Council on Bioethics, "Reproduction and Responsibility," March 2004.

51. American Society for Reproductive Medicine, "Multiple Pregnancy and Birth."

52. Ibid.

53. Ibid.

54. F. Helmerhorst et al., "Perinatal Outcome of Singletons and Twins after Assisted Conception: A Systematic Review of Controlled Studies," *British Medical Journal* 328 (2004): 261; L. Schieve et al., "Low and Very Low Birth Weight in Infants Conceived with Use of Assisted Reproductive Technology," *The New England Journal of Medicine* 346, no. 10 (March 7, 2002): 731–37.

55. Mark I. Evans, "Selective Reduction for Multifetal Pregnancy: Early Options Revisited," *Journal of Reproductive Medicine* 42 (December 1997): 771–73.

56. Andrews, *The Clone Age,* 58; President's Council on Bioethics, "Reproduction and Responsibility."

57. M. Evans et al., "Efficacy of Transabdominal Multifetal Pregnancy Reduction: Collaborative Experience Among the World's Largest Centers," *Obstetrics and Gynecology* 82, no. 2 (July 1993): 61.

58. New York State Task Force on Life and the Law, *Assisted Reproductive Technologies: Analysis and Recommendations for Public Policy,* 1998, 71.

59. See *Iatrogenic Multiple Pregnancy: Clinical Implications,* eds. Isaac Blickstein and Louis G. Keith (New York: Parthenon, 2000); Meredith O'Brien, "Selective Reduction: A Painful Choice," Babyzone.com, http://www.babyzone.com/preconception/infertility/tests_and_treatments/article/selective-reduction; and Andrews, *The Clone Age,* 58.

60. A. D. Domar, P. C. Zuttermeister, and R. Friedman, "The Psychological Impact of Infertility: A Comparison with Patients with Other Medical Conditions," *Journal of Psychosomatic Obstetrics and Gynecology,* 14 suppl. (1993): 45–52.

61. Perlman, "Is This Any Way to Have a Baby?", 190.

62. Anthony Dyson, *The Ethics of IVF* (London: Mowbray, 1995), 46–49; Deborah Lynn Steinberg, "The Depersonalization of Women Through the Administration of 'In Vitro Fertilisation'" in *The New Reproductive Technologies,* eds. Maureen McNeil, Ian Varcoe, and Steven Yearley (London: Macmillan, 1990).

63. Stephen F. Torraco, "Pope John Paul II's Eleventh Encyclical: *The Gospel of Life,*" *Catholic International* 6, no. 6 (June 1995): 253, referencing Leon Kass, *Toward a More Natural Science: Biology and Human Affairs* (New York: The Free Press, 1985).

64. Congregation for the Doctrine of the Faith, *Dignitas Personae: Instruction on Certain Bioethical Questions* (Boston: Pauline Books & Media, 2008), no. 4.

65. The morally reprehensible use of "spare" IVF embryos in embryonic destructive research and therapeutic (or reproductive) cloning is beyond the scope of this essay. See generally the Congregation for the Doctrine of the Faith, *Donum Vitae: Instruction on Respect for Human Life in Its Origin and on the Dignity of Procreation* (February 22, 1987) (Boston: Pauline Books & Media, 2003).

66. The Pontifical Academy for Life, *Final Communique on "The Dignity of Human Procreation and Reproductive Technologies: Anthropological and Ethical Aspects"* (February, 2004), http://www.vatican.va/roman_curia/pontifical_academies/acdlife/documents/rc_pont-acd_life_doc_20040316_x-gen-assembly-final_en.html.

67. See generally Karen Peterson-Iyer, *Designer Children: Reconciling Technology, Feminism, and Christian Faith* (Cleveland, OH: Pilgrim Press, 2004).

68. John Paul II, *Puebla: A Pilgrimage of Faith* (Boston: Pauline Books & Media, 1979), 86.

69. Christopher West, "Sex, Contraception, and the Meaning of Life," Catholic.net http://www.catholic.net/index.php?id=620&option=dedestaca#.

70. I am indebted to John M. Haas for this formulation.

71. "Responding to Luke Timothy Johnson's Critique of John Paul II's Theology of the Body: What Luke Timothy Johnson Leaves Out," Theology of the Body.net, http://www.theologyofthebody.net/index.php?option=com_content&task=view&id=27&Itemid=48&limit=1&limitstart=2, paraphrasing John Paul II, *Love and Responsibility*, 233.

72. *Donum Vitae*, Introduction, sec. 3.

73. Pontifical Academy for Life, "The Dignity of Human Procreation," (2004).

74. *Donum Vitae*, II, sec. 4b (quoting John Paul II, Discourse to Those Taking Part in the 35th General Assembly of the World Medical Association, October 29, 1983).

75. *Donum Vitae*, II, sec. 8.

76. Pope Paul VI Institute for the Study of Human Reproduction, http://www.naprotechnology.com.

77. "Endometriosis," American College of Obstetricians and Gynecologists patient education pamphlet, http://www.acog.org/publications/patient_education/bp013.cfm.

78. Substantial evidence also indicates that endometriosis shares many similarities with autoimmune diseases. Many investigators now are looking at immunomodulators and inflammatory modulators as possible treatments for endometriosis. Thomas W. Hilgers, *The Medical and Surgical Practice of NaProTECHNOLOGY* (Omaha, NE: Pope Paul VI Institute Press, 2004), 500.

79. See note 34 for a description of intrauterine insemination (IUI).

80. Estradiol levels at the time of ovulation should be between 200 and 325 ng/ml (see Hilgers, *NaProTECHNOLOGY*, 287); similarly, most doctors are satisfied that progesterone is made at all, but NPT doctors want to see the progesterone plateau between 10 and 22 ng/ml.

81. Though the drugs are not yet FDA-approved for these purposes, NPT doctors have achieved good success in increasing cervical fluid through their use, and they pose no harm whatsoever to the patient.

82. J. B. Stanford, T. A. Parnell, and P. C. Boyle, "Outcomes from Treatment of Infertility with Natural Procreative Technology in an Irish General Practice," *Journal of the American Board of Family Medicine* 21, no. 5 (2008): 375–84.

83. Ibid., 379. Though the crude live birth rate was 25.5 percent, the adjusted rate of 52.8 is comparable to the "optimistic" or Kaplan-Meier method in some IVF studies. See, e.g., B. A. Malizia, M. R. Hacker, and Alan Penzias, "Cumulative Live-Birth Rates after In Vitro Fertilization," *New England Journal of Medicine* 360, no. 3 (2009): 236–43.

84. Stanford et al., "Outcomes from Treatment of Fertility," 379.

85. Ibid., 380.

86. Ibid., 377.

87. Hilgers, *NaProTECHNOLOGY*, 680. IVF success rates in cohorts with multiple attempts at the procedure range from 32 percent (see G. Nargund et al., "Cumulative Conception and Live Birth Rates in Natural (Unstimulated) IVF Cycles," *Human Reproduction* 16 (2001): 259–62), to 72 percent after six IVF cycles (see Malizia et al., "Cumulative Live-Birth Rates," 236–43). No scientific study has compared IVF and NPT success rates, and many factors indicate accurate comparison requires rigorous epidemiological method. We will not attempt such a comparison here. However, it is fair to say that the risk to women and children is substantially reduced through the use of NPT (e.g., NPT has yielded lower rates of miscarriage, multiple pregnancies, and prematurity, among others).

88. Paul A. Carpentier, "NaProTechnology Treatment of Infertility in New England," unpublished presentation at the annual meeting of the International Institute for Restorative Reproductive Medicine, Witchita, Kansas, July 18, 2007.

89. Centers of Disease Control and Prevention, *2001 Assisted Reproductive Technology Success Rates*, as adapted in Hilgers, *NaProTECHNOLOGY*, 484.

90. Toni Weschler, *Taking Charge of Your Fertility* (New York: Harper Collins, 2006), Professional Praise Page.

91. Ibid., 296.

7

Embodied Ecclesiology:
Church Teaching on the Priesthood

1. My arguments rely on the basic trustworthiness of Scripture and tradition.

2. John Paul II, *Ordinatio Sacerdotalis* (*On Reserving Priestly Ordination to Men Alone*) (Boston: Pauline Books & Media, May 22, 1994).

3. Catholic teaching distinguishes the "ministerial" priesthood of bishops and priests from the "common" priesthood of the faithful. (See Second Vatican Council, *Lumen Gentium* [*Dogmatic Constitution on the Church*] [Boston: Pauline Books & Media, 1964], no. 10). This essay will use "priesthood" for the "ministerial" priesthood. It will not consider whether women should be candidates for the diaconate.

4. Betty Friedan, *The Feminine Mystique* (New York: W. W. Norton, 1997).

5. See Second Vatican Council, *Gaudium et Spes*, no. 29: "True, all men [*homines*] are not alike from the point of view of varying physical power and the diversity of intellectual and moral resources. Nevertheless, with respect to the fundamental rights of the person, every type of discrimination, whether social or cultural, whether based on sex, race, color, social condition, language or religion, is to be overcome and eradicated as contrary to God's intent."

6. Some of the reasons advanced in the past depended heavily on unacceptable assumptions about women's nature, inferior status, and subordinate social roles.

7. Haye van der Meer, *Women Priests in the Catholic Church? A Theological-Historical Investigation*, trans. Arlene Swidler and Leonard Swidler (Philadelphia: Temple University Press, 1973). Most of the historical arguments that sought to explain the all-male priesthood were based on biblical texts from Genesis and Saint Paul, interpreted to show that women are subordinate in the "order of creation," that they do not share the fullness of the "image of God," that like Eve they are easily deceived by the devil, that they are "helpmeets" as compared to males, the normative human beings. Historical and cultural conditioning is evident in the theory that assimilates the man to "spirit" or soul and the woman to "body," and faulty biological speculation in the opinion that a woman is a "defective male." Some of the "authorities" quoted wrote of women elsewhere in disparaging terms. In 1989 van der Meer retracted his thesis.

8. Manfred Hauke challenges van der Meer's findings and addresses the larger issues he had left to one side in *Women in the Priesthood? A Systematic Analysis in the Light of the Order of Creation and Redemption* (San Francisco: Ignatius, 1988).

9. Sacred Congregation for the Doctrine of the Faith, *Inter Insigniores* (*Declaration on the Question of the Admission of Women to the Ministerial Priesthood*) (Boston: Pauline Books & Media, 1976).

10. The practice of admitting only men to priestly and episcopal orders has been challenged in the past, and innovations have always been noted and condemned.

11. This includes some theological arguments based on the "Pauline ban." The development of doctrine in Catholic social teaching regarding the dignity of women and their equal rights, as persons, with men is traced in chapter 2 of Sara Butler, *The Catholic Priesthood and Women* (Chicago: Hillenbrand, 2006).

12. This distinction is found in *Inter Insigniores*, no. 5, but its importance has been widely overlooked.

13. I shall say more later in the chapter about the theological arguments proposed in *Inter Insigniores*.

14. See John Paul II, *Mulieris Dignitatem* (*On the Dignity and Vocation of Women*), chapter 5. The Pope appeals to Jesus' example as the norm for interpreting the teaching of Saint Paul.

15. Some argue, in fact, that Jesus established a "discipleship of equals" in which women participated, but that the apostolic Church betrayed his intention by capitulating to cultural expectations.

16. At the very least, it is impossible to claim with certainty that in this choice Jesus was guided by expediency. *Inter Insigniores* does not present this traditional and contemporary New Testament evidence as if it were sufficient on its own to resolve questions not asked at the time. The will of Christ is discerned in the living tradition of the Church, that is, in the concrete historical experience of the Christian community.

17. See Congregation for the Doctrine of the Faith, *Letter to the Bishops of the Catholic Church on the Collaboration of Men and Women in the Church and in the World* (2004), no. 13, http://www.vatican.va/roman_curia/congregations/cfaith/documents/rc_con_cfaith_doc_20040731_collaboration_en.html.

18. See, e.g., Mary Daly, *Beyond God the Father: Toward a Philosophy of Women's Liberation* (Boston: Beacon Press, 1973); Rosemary Radford Ruether, "Sex in the Catholic

Tradition," in *The Good News of the Body: Sexual Theology and Feminism*, ed. Lisa Isherwood (New York: New York University Press, 2000); and Sandra M. Schneiders, *Beyond Patching: Faith and Feminism in the Catholic Church* (Mahwah, NJ: Paulist Press, 2004).

19. See *CCC*, nos. 748–810, 857–879, 1536ff.

20. *Lumen Gentium*, no. 32; see Galatians 3:28.

21. See *Code of Canon Law*, canons 204, 208–23.

22. Canon 208.

23. See canon 207 §1. Canon 207 §2 notes that some persons, drawn from both the laity and the clergy, profess the evangelical counsels and are consecrated to God by a new and special title.

24. See canons §§224–231.

25. Canon §204.

26. The 1983 *Code of Canon Law* remedied the discriminatory inequities based on sex among the baptized found in the 1917 code. The fact that only males are eligible to be instituted in the ministries of lector and acolyte (canon 230 §1) is widely regarded as an exception; the exception is based on "venerable tradition" that situates these ministries on the path to Holy Orders.

27. Bishops are said to be the "successors of the apostles" and to share in the "fullness of the priesthood," whereas priests are regarded as the "coworkers" of the bishop. See *CCC*, nos. 1554, 1562. Some dimensions of the vocation of the Twelve, such as being the witnesses of Jesus' resurrection from the dead, are not and cannot be handed on to others.

28. See Luke 20:29–30. Scholars point out that calling the Twelve "apostles" is probably a convention that arose after the fact, during the apostolic period. Saint Luke is the evangelist who regularly adopts this usage.

29. *Ordinatio Sacerdotalis*, no. 2; John Paul II cites Mt 10:1, 7–8 and 28:16–20; Mk 3:13–16 and 16:14–15.

30. The *CCC*, no. 1548, explains the meaning of the theological term "to act in the person of Christ": "In the ecclesial service of the ordained minister, it is Christ himself who is present to his Church as Head of his Body, Shepherd of his flock, high priest of the redemptive sacrifice, Teacher of Truth."

31. *Lumen Gentium*, no. 32.

32. See ibid., no. 10.

33. See, eg., *Mulieris Dignitatem*, no. 27.

34. According to *Inter Insigniores*, no. 6, "The greatest in the Kingdom of Heaven are not the ministers but the saints."

35. The Second Vatican Council was the first ecumenical council to address the vocation of the laity in a sustained way. See *Apostolicam Actuositatem* (*Decree on the Apostolate of the Laity*) (Boston: Pauline Books & Media, 1965) and *Lumen Gentium*, ch. 4.

36. *Apostolicam Actuositatem*, no. 10.

37. *Lumen Gentium*, no. 31. This is thoroughly developed in Pope John Paul II's Post-Synodal Apostolic Exhortation *Christifideles Laici* (*On the Dignity and Vocation of the Lay Faithful*), 1988.

38. See the Congregation for the Doctrine of the Faith, *Letter to the Bishops of the Catholic Church on the Collaboration of Men and Women in the Church and in the World* (2004); this topic is addressed in chapter 3, with attention to the complementarity of masculine and feminine contributions.

39. Canon 663 §1.

40. I have discussed this in *The Catholic Priesthood and Women*, chapters 1 and 3.

41. *CCC*, §1131.

42. For an effort to reach ecumenical consensus statement on the ordained ministry, see *Baptism, Eucharist, and Ministry*, Faith and Order Paper No. 111 (Geneva: World Council of Churches, 1982).

43. It has become apparent that the question of whether the Church is free to change her long-standing (and unbroken) tradition of conferring priestly ordination only on men is logically intertwined with several of the controversies that marked the Reformation—those concerning the ordained ministry and also the constitution of the Church.

44. According to Catholic doctrine, it was by Jesus' command at the Last Supper, "Do this in memory of me," (Lk 22:19) that he instituted the sacrament of Holy Orders.

45. See Guy Mansini, "On Affirming a Dominical Intention of a Male Priesthood," *The Thomist* 61, no. 2 (April 1997): 301–16. The Church's belief is not based on a historical reconstruction of these events, but arises from her confidence that the practice of the apostles faithfully carried forward the Lord's design.

46. For an example of attempts to resolve contemporary questions on the basis of scholarly reconstructions of Christian origins, see Robert J. Egan, "Why Not? Scripture, History, and Women's Ordination," *Commonweal* 135, no. 7 (April 11, 2008): 17–27. My reply appears July 18, 2008.

47. See *Ordinatio Sacerdotalis*, no. 4. This is not the place to defend Christ's foundation of the Church and institution of the Christian priesthood, but it should be evident that divergence of doctrine on these matters has direct implications for determining whether women should be ordained.

48. *Inter Insigniores*, no. 5.

49. See Aquinas, *In IV Sent.*, dist. 25, q. 2, a. 1 ad 4; see also *Summa Theologiae* III, q. 83, a. 1 ad 3.

50. The indelible mark or "character" imprinted on the priest's soul is invisible. He himself, as a man, participates in the constitution of the visible sign.

51. See *CCC*, no. 1142. Saint Ignatius of Antioch (A.D. 110) regards the bishop as the sign of God the Father.

52. *Ordinatio Sacerdotalis*, no. 2.

53. *Inter Insigniores* has a footnote to Saint Bonaventure; his contribution is explained well by Hauke in *Women in the Priesthood?*, but it should be noted that Bonaventure's other arguments contain judgments about women that have since been abandoned. Many scholars find the same reasoning implicit in the *Summa Theologiae* of Saint Thomas, for example, in III, q. 83, a. 1 ad 3.

54. See Sara Butler, "The Priest as Sacrament of Christ the Bridegroom," *Worship* 66 (November 1992): 498–517.

55. See Jn 3:27–29; Mk 2:19–20.

56. See also 2 Cor 11:2 and Rev 19:7, 9. This sketch only begins to suggest the symbolic connection between the maleness of Christ and the divine economy of salvation, but it shows that drawing on the symbolism of sexual difference need not imply relationships of superiority and inferiority that legitimate male domination.

57. *Mulieris Dignitatem*, no. 26.

58. *Inter Insigniores*, no. 5.

59. Some critics charge that nuptial symbolism makes too much of what is simply a metaphor. The image of the Church as Bride is, of course, a metaphor, a biblical metaphor. The "Bride" in this case is a "corporate personality," in keeping with a long tradition of regarding the Church as feminine. The Church is to accept Christ's gift of self in the Eucharist and to reciprocate with her own gift of self.

60. The Catholic Church rejects the idea that the equalization of rights requires the identical treatment of women and men.

8

Dueling Vocations: Managing the Tensions Between Our Private and Public Callings

1. A version of this chapter was presented at a program sponsored by Fordham University School of Law's Institute on Religion, Law, and Lawyer's Work. I am indebted to Amy Uelmen, director of the institute, for her support, friendship, and insightful comments.

2. Lisa Belkin, "The Opt-Out Revolution," *The New York Times*, October 26, 2003.

3. Although she did not originate the term "mommy track," it was coined in response to the work of Felice M. Schwartz, first in an article entitled, "Management Women and the New Facts of Life," *Harvard Business Review* 1 (January–February 1989): 65–76, and later in the book *Breaking with Tradition: Women, Management, and the New Facts of Life* (New York: Warner, 1992).

4. Linda Hirshman, "Homeward Bound," *The American Prospect* (Nov. 21, 2005). In response to the debate surrounding *The American Prospect* article, Hirshman wrote *Get to Work . . . And Get a Life Before It's Too Late* (New York: Viking Adult, 2006).

5. For more statistics on the percentages of women (particularly women with children) staying in academia long enough to rise to tenured status, see Elizabeth R. Schiltz, "Motherhood and the Mission: What Catholic Law Schools Could Learn from Harvard about Women," *Catholic University Law Review* 56 (Winter 2007): 405, 416–24.

6. See, e.g., Katherine Franke, "Theorizing Yes: An Essay on Feminism, Law, and Desire," *Columbia Law Review* 101 (2001): 181; Mary Ann Case, "How High the Apple Pie? A Few Troubling Questions about Where, Why, and How the Burden of Care for Children Should Be Shifted," *Chicago-Kent Law Review* 76, 3 (2001): 1753; and Vickie Schultz, "Life's Work," *Columbia Law Review* 100 (2000): 1881.

7. Franke, "Theorizing Yes," 185.

8. In addition, the Church's commitment to the gender theory of complementarity, under which men and women are acknowledged to be fundamentally different while being fundamentally equal, suggests that she would not necessarily insist that men and women share equally in all aspects of child raising. This topic is too complex to fully explore in this chapter; however, I recommend the writings of Prudence Allen, such as "Integral Sex Complementarity and the Theology of Communion," *Communio* 17 (1990): 523, 534–35; "A Woman and a Man as Prime Analogical Beings," *American Catholic Philosophical Quarterly* 66 (1992): 465, 477; "Can Feminism Be a Humanism?" in *Women in Christ: Toward a New Feminism*, ed. Michelle M. Schumacher (Grand Rapids, MI: Wm. B. Eerdmans, 2004), 251, 284; "Man-Woman Complementarity: The Catholic Inspiration," *Logos* 9 (2006): 87; and "Analogy, Law and the Workplace: Complementarity, Conscience, and the Common Good," *University of St. Thomas Law Journal* 3 (2007): 350.

9. For a more detailed discussion of the evolution of the Church's teachings on the respective roles of women and men in the workplace and family, see Schiltz, "Motherhood and the Mission," 428–29 and 435–36; see also Claire E. Wolfteich, *Navigating New Terrains: Work and Women's Spiritual Lives* (Mahwah, NJ: Paulist Press, 2000), 8, 29–31, 64–66, and 181–82.

10. John Paul II, *Mulieris Dignitatem*.

11. John Paul II, *Centesimus Annus (On the Hundredth Anniversary of Rerum Novarum)* (Boston: Pauline Books & Media, 1991), no. 11.

12. Pontifical Council for Peace and Justice, *Compendium of the Social Doctrine of the Church* (Washington, DC: United States Conference of Catholic Bishops, 2005).

13. Pope John Paul II, *Letter of Pope John Paul to Women* (Boston: Pauline Books & Media, 1995), no. 2.

14. Ibid., no. 4.

15. Ibid., no. 9.

16. John Paul II, "Equal Opportunity in the World of Work," (Angelus Reflection, August 20, 1995) in *John Paul II on the Genius of Women* (Washington, DC: United States Conference of Catholic Bishops, 1997), 32.

17. Sylvia Ann Hewlett, *Creating a Life: Professional Women and the Quest for Children* (New York: Talk Miramax Books, 2002), 158–59.

18. John Paul II, *Familiaris Consortio*, 23; Congregation for the Doctrine of the Faith, *Collaboration of Men and Women*, no. 13.

19. John Paul II, *Laborem Exercens (On Human Work)* (Boston: Pauline Books & Media, 1981), no. 19.

20. John Paul II, *Familiaris Consortio*, no. 23.

21. John Paul II, *Evangelium Vitae* (1992), no. 90.

22. National Conference of Catholic Bishops, *Economic Justice for All: Pastoral Letter on Catholic Social Teaching and the U.S. Economy* (1986), 101–2.

23. U.S. Catholic Conference, *Putting Children and Families First: A Challenge for Our Church, Nation, and World* (1991), 10–11.

24. *Economic Justice for All*, 82–83, 101–2. See also *Putting Children and Families First*, 10–11.

25. See, e.g., Robin L. West, *Re-Imagining Justice: Progressive Interpretations of Formal Equality, Rights and the Rule of Law* (Burlington, VT: Ashgate, 2003); Eva Feder Kittay, *Love's Labor: Essays on Women, Equality, and Dependency* (London: Taylor & Francis, 1998); Martha Albertson Fineman, *The Autonomy Myth: A Theory of Dependency* (New York: New Press, 2004). I have written more extensively about this school of feminism in Schiltz, "Motherhood and the Mission"; Elizabeth R. Schiltz, "Should Bearing the Child Mean Bearing All the Cost?" *Logos* 10, no. 3 (Summer 2007): 15; and Elizabeth R. Schiltz, "West, MacIntyre, and Wojtyla: Pope John Paul II's Contribution to the Development of a Dependency-Based Theory of Justice," *Journal of Catholic Legal Studies* 45, no. 2 (2006): 369.

26. Mary Becker, "Care and Feminists," *Wisconsin Women's Law Journal* 17 (2002) 59–60, 105, 108–9; and Ann Crittenden, *The Price of Motherhood: Why the Most Important Job in the World Is Still the Least Valued* (New York: Metropolitan Books, 2001), 186, 201, 665–66.

27. See Crittenden, *The Price of Motherhood*, 259, and Joan C. Williams, *Unbending Gender: Why Family and Work Conflict and What to Do About It* (Oxford: Oxford University Press, 1999), 112.

28. Becker, "Care and Feminists," 81; Crittenden, *The Price of Motherhood*, 260–61; Williams, *Unbending Gender*, 92, 111.

29. Jody Heymann et al., The Project on Global Working Families, *The Work, Family, and Equity Index: Where Does the United States Stand Globally?* (2004), 23 http://www.hsph.harvard.edu/globalworkingfamilies/images/report.pdf.

30. Joan C. Williams, "The Politics of Time in the Legal Profession," *University of St. Thomas Law Journal* 4 (Spring 2007): 379, 395–96.

31. Ibid., 381–82; see generally, Williams, *Unbending Gender*.

32. Mary Ann Glendon, *Address to the Economic and Social Council Commission on the Status of Women* (March 7, 2005).

33. "There's No Place Like Home, Says Benedict XVI," *ZENIT*, January 19, 2009, http://zenit.org/article-24839?l=english.

34. *Familiaris Consortio*, no. 42.

35. See W. Bradford Wilcox, *Soft Patriarchs and New Men: How Christianity Shapes Fathers and Husbands* (Chicago: University of Chicago Press, 2000).

36. *Laborem Exercens*, no. 4.

37. Ibid.

38. Dorothy L. Sayers, "Why Work?" in *Creed or Chaos?* (London: Methuen, 1947), 47.

39. Belkin, "The Opt-Out Revolution."

40. West, *Re-Imagining Justice*, 81.

41. *Mulieris Dignitatem*, no. 7.

Conclusion

Reflections on the Kinship Between
Catholic Sexual and Social Teaching

1. Charles Curran, "Catholic Social and Sexual Teaching: a Methodological Comparison," in *Theology Today* 44, no. 4 (January 1988): 425–26.

2. W. Bradford Wilcox, "The Facts of Life & Marriage," *Touchstone* (January-February, 2005). I am indebted to Professor Wilcox for many of the insights (and references) used in this section.

3. George Akerlof, Janet L. Yellen, and Michael L. Katz, "An Analysis of Out-of-Wedlock Childbearing in the United States," *The Quarterly Journal of Economics*, 111, no. 2 (May 1996), 278.

4. See, for instance, William Julius Wilson, *The Truly Disadvantaged: The Inner City, the Underclass, and Public Policy* (Chicago: University of Chicago Press, 1987); and Charles A. Murray, *Losing Ground: American Social Policy 1950–1980* (New York: Basic Books, 1984).

5. Akerlof, 278.

6. Ibid., 291ff. and 307.

7. Ibid., 307.

8. Ibid., 297, 307; Sara McLanahan, "Diverging Destinies: How Children are Faring under the Second Demographic Transition," *Demography* 41, no. 4 (November 2004), 617.

9. McLanahan, "Diverging Destinies," 612; Kay Hymowitz, *Marriage and Caste in America: Separate and Unequal Families in a Post-Marital Age* (Chicago: Ivan R. Dee, 2006), 4, 18–20.

10. McLanahan, "Diverging Destinies," 617.

11. Ibid.

12. Hymowitz, *Marriage and Caste*, 28, 70.

13. "Children raised outside of intact marriages are significantly more likely than other children [to be poor,] to use drugs, to drop out of school [or otherwise have lower educational attainment], to commit crimes, to suffer from depression[,] emotional distress [and physical illness], to be neglected or abused, to be sexually active early, to commit or consider suicide and, later in life, to bear children outside of marriage or get divorced themselves." Center for Marriage and Families, "What Is America's Most Serious Social Problem?" Fact Sheet No. 1 (February 2006), http://www.americanvalues.org/pdfs/factsheet1.pdf; see also, McLanahan, "Diverging Destinies," 620–21; see also chapter 4 in this volume.

14. Hymowitz, *Marriage and Caste*, 29–30.

15. Ibid., 42; Kathryn Edin and Maria Kefalas, *Promises I Can Keep: Why Poor Women Put Motherhood before Marriage* (Berkeley: University of California Press, 2005), 136.

16. Hymowitz, *Marriage and Caste*, 41, 46.

17. Edin and Kefalas, *Promises I Can Keep*, 111; McLanahan, "Diverging Destinies," 619.

18. Edin and Kefalas, *Promises I Can Keep*, 112.

19. Ibid., 126.

20. Hymowitz, *Marriage and Caste*, 103; George Akerlof, "Men Without Children," *Economic Journal* 108 (1998).

21. Hymowitz, *Marriage and Caste*, 65; Edin and Kefalas, *Promises I Can Keep*, 31ff.

22. Hymowitz, *Marriage and Caste*, 46.

23. Akerlof, "Men Without Children," 287.

24. Ibid., 291.

25. Ibid., 298.

26. Ibid., 289.

27. George F. Gilder, *Men and Marriage* (Gretna, LA: Pelican, 1986), 153.

28. Barbara Dafoe Whitehead, "Connecting Sexuality, Marriage, Family, and Children," in *American Catholics, American Culture: Tradition and Resistance*, ed. Margaret O'Brien Steinfels (Lanham, MD: Sheed & Ward, 2004), 41.

29. Ibid.

30. Thomas C. Fox, *Sexuality and Catholicism* (New York: George Braziller, 1995), 126.

31. John Paul II, *Sollicitudo Rei Socialis (On Social Concern)* (Boston: Pauline Books & Media, 1987), 41.

32. Curran, "Catholic Social and Sexual Teaching," 439.

33. Benedict XVI, *Deus Caritas Est*, no. 25.

34. Leo XIII, *Rerum Novarum (Of New Things)* (1891), 28.

35. See Gordon S. Wood, *The Creation of the American Republic: 1776–1787* (Chapel Hill: University of North Carolina Press, 1998), 68ff.; see also Alexis de Tocqueville, *Democracy in America* (Chicago: University of Chicago Press, 2002).

36. George Weigel, "John Paul II and the Priority of Culture," *First Things* (February 1998).

37. John Paul II, *Centesimus Annus*, no. 39.

38. John Paul II, *Mulieris Dignitatem*, 30 (emphasis in original).

39. Benedict XVI, *Deus Caritas Est*, 7.

About the Authors

ERIKA BACHIOCHI holds a JD from Boston University School of Law (2002) and an MA in theology from Boston College (1999), where she was a Bradley Fellow at the Institute for the Study of Religion and Politics. She obtained her undergraduate degree magna cum laude at Middlebury College (1997), where she majored in political science, minored in sociology (and took enough credits to fulfill a minor in women's studies). In 2004, Ms. Bachiochi published *The Cost of "Choice": Women Evaluate the Impact of Abortion* (Encounter Books), for which she served as the editor. She lectures at colleges, universities, and law schools on feminism, the family, abortion, and the Church, and keynotes various conferences and retreats for Catholic women, including the First Annual Boston Catholic Women's Conference in 2006. She lives outside Boston with her husband, Dan, and their five young children.

SISTER SARA BUTLER, MSBT, STL, PhD, holds her doctorate in systematic theology from Fordham University, her STL from the University of St. Mary of the Lake, and her MA in religious education from the Catholic University of America. Sister Butler is a member of the Missionary Servants of the Most

Blessed Trinity and professor of dogmatic theology at Saint Joseph's Seminary in the Archdiocese of New York, and currently serves as a consultant to the U.S. Bishops' Committee on Doctrine. A long-standing member of the Anglican-Roman Catholic International Commission, she was appointed by Pope John Paul II to a five-year term on the International Theological Commission, a group of thirty theologians that advises the Congregation for the Doctrine of the Faith. The author of numerous scholarly articles, she recently published *The Catholic Priesthood and Women: A Guide to the Teaching of the Church* (Hillenbrand, 2007).

DR. PAUL CARPENTIER, MD, CFCMC (Certified Fertility*Care* Medical Consultant) graduated magna cum laude from Assumption College and St. Louis University School of Medicine with honors in ethics and high-risk obstetrics. He is board certified in family practice medicine and by the American Academy of Fertility*Care* Professionals. Dr. Carpentier is a graduate of the Natural Family Planning Medical Consultant Program of the Pope Paul VI Institute for the Study of Human Reproduction in Omaha, Nebraska, and is a part-time faculty member for that institute. He practices obstetrics at Heywood Hospital in Gardner, Massachusetts. He and his wife have four children.

KATIE ELROD obtained her BA (1992) and her MA (1994) in philosophy from Boston College, where she was a Lonergan Fellow. She has been a humanities teacher and administrator at independent schools for more than ten years, and has taught in the Perspectives program at Boston College. Ms. Elrod has spoken on natural fertility treatment in the Archdiocese of Boston with Dr. Paul Carpentier, with whom she writes in this volume. She and her husband, Kevin, live outside Boston with their son, T.J.

ANGELA FRANKS, PhD, holds a doctorate in systematic theology from Boston College (2006), an MA in philosophy from Catholic University of

America (1997), and an undergraduate degree summa cum laude from the University of Dallas (1995). An author and speaker, Dr. Franks is the author of *Margaret Sanger's Eugenic Legacy: The Control of Female Fertility* (McFarland, 2005), a scholarly work and feminist indictment of the eugenic foundations of the American birth-control movement. She was recently appointed by the bishops of Massachusetts to serve with her husband, David, as the coordinator for the Massachusetts Catholic Conference Marriage Initiative, The Future Depends on Love, a statewide effort to educate the public about the Church's teaching on marriage, human sexuality, and the meaning of man and woman. She is also associate director, with her husband, of the Master of Arts in Ministry program at St. John's Seminary. Dr. Franks teaches part-time at the postgraduate level for several Catholic institutions, speaks at universities and conferences across the country, and, with her husband, home-schools their four young children. They reside in Boston.

LAURA L. GARCIA, PhD, graduated summa cum laude from Westmont College and obtained her doctorate in philosophy from the University of Notre Dame. She has taught philosophy at St. Mary's College, Notre Dame; the University of St. Thomas (Saint Paul, Minnesota); the Catholic University of America; Georgetown; and Rutgers, the State University of New Jersey; and is currently a member of the philosophy department at Boston College. Dr. Garcia publishes widely on the nature of the human person and on various topics in the philosophy of religion. Recent publications include an essay, "Preserving Persons" in *The Contribution of John Paul II to Catholic Bioethics* (Springer, 2005) and "Toward a Personalist Feminism" in *Teaching, Faith, and Service: The Foundation of Freedom Conference, June 2–4, 2005* (University of Portland, 2006). Dr. Garcia is a founding member and past officer of both Women Affirming Life and University Faculty for Life, and speaks to college and other audiences on life issues, the meaning of sexuality, and the vocation of the family. She and her husband, Jorge, have four children.

CASSANDRA HOUGH holds a Bachelor of Arts degree from Princeton University, where she founded the Anscombe Society, a student organization that seeks to uphold the institution of marriage, the special role of the family, and chastity on Princeton's campus. In 2007, Ms. Hough received the Spirit of

Princeton award for her work's contribution to the university, as well as the William E. Simon Fellowship for Noble Purpose. After graduating in 2007, she founded the Love and Fidelity Network to equip students with arguments, resources, and direction to effectively and articulately defend marriage, family, and sexual integrity at their own universities. Ms. Hough is a former contributor to the blog Modestly Yours.net, and regularly speaks to college students and parents about the "hookup culture," its harms, and its healthier and more loving alternatives. She and her work have been featured by numerous publications and shows, including the *New York Times*, the Associated Press, *Teen Vogue*, the *Glenn Beck Program, CatholicTV, EWTN*, and Bill Bennett's *Morning in America*. Ms. Hough is a native of Massachusetts and currently lives in New Jersey with her husband.

JENNIFER ROBACK MORSE, PhD, is the founder and president of the Ruth Institute, a nonprofit educational institute promoting lifelong married love to the young. She received her PhD in economics from the University of Rochester in 1980 and spent a postdoctoral year at the University of Chicago in 1979–80. She taught economics at Yale University and George Mason University for fifteen years, and was the John M. Olin visiting scholar at the Cornell Law School in the fall of 1993. Dr. Morse's scholarly articles have appeared in the *Journal of Political Economy*; the *Journal of Economic History*; *Publius: The Journal of Federalism*; the *University of Chicago Law Review*; the *Harvard Journal of Law and Public Policy; Social Philosophy and Policy*; and the *Notre Dame Journal of Law, Ethics & Public Policy*. From 1997 to 2005, she served as a Research Fellow for Stanford University's Hoover Institution. She is the author of *Love and Economics: It Takes a Family to Raise a Village* (Ruth Institute), and *Smart Sex: Finding Life-Long Love in a Hook-Up World* (Spence). She and her husband have an adopted son and a birth daughter, and until 2006, they were foster parents for San Diego County, California.

ELIZABETH R. SCHILTZ holds a JD from Columbia University School of Law (1985) and a BA magna cum laude from Yale University (1982). After practicing corporate law for nine years, she taught part-time for five years at the Notre Dame Law School. In 2001, she became one of the founding members of the University of St. Thomas School of Law, where she teaches contracts, sales, credit and payment devices, banking law, and consumer law, and where she was elected teacher of the year by the graduating class of 2007. In addition to her scholarship on banking law, Professor Schiltz speaks widely on Catholic feminism and life issues such as eugenic abortion and stem cell research, and has published on these topics in *Business Week, America, Our Sunday Visitor,* the *Human Life Review, Catholic University Law Review, The Journal of Catholic Legal Studies,* and *Logos.* She blogs at mirrorof justice.blogs. com, a blog dedicated to the development of Catholic legal theory. Professor Schiltz lives in Minneapolis with her husband, U.S. District Court Judge Patrick J. Schiltz, and their four children.

Index

BOOKS & MEDIA

The Daughters of St. Paul operate book and media centers at the following addresses. Visit, call or write the one nearest you today, or find us on the World Wide Web, www.pauline.org.

CALIFORNIA
3908 Sepulveda Blvd, Culver City, CA 90230 — 310-397-8676
935 Brewster Avenue, Redwood City, CA 94063 — 650-369-4230
5945 Balboa Avenue, San Diego, CA 92111 — 858-565-9181

FLORIDA
145 S.W. 107th Avenue, Miami, FL 33174 — 305-559-6715

HAWAII
1143 Bishop Street, Honolulu, HI 96813 — 808-521-2731
Neighbor Islands call: — 866-521-2731

ILLINOIS
172 North Michigan Avenue, Chicago, IL 60601 — 312-346-4228

LOUISIANA
4403 Veterans Memorial Blvd, Metairie, LA 70006 — 504-887-7631

MASSACHUSETTS
885 Providence Hwy, Dedham, MA 02026 — 781-326-5385

MISSOURI
9804 Watson Road, St. Louis, MO 63126 — 314-965-3512

NEW YORK
64 W. 38th Street, New York, NY 10018 — 212-754-1110

PENNSYLVANIA
Philadelphia—relocating — 215-676-9494

SOUTH CAROLINA
243 King Street, Charleston, SC 29401 — 843-577-0175

VIRGINIA
1025 King Street, Alexandria, VA 22314 — 703-549-3806

CANADA
3022 Dufferin Street, Toronto, ON M6B 3T5 — 416-781-9131

¡También somos su fuente para libros, videos y música en español!